D1333350

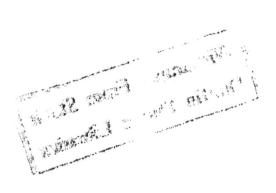

DUBLIN

A Celebration

From the 1st to the 21st Century

DEDICATION

To my wife Josephine who helped beyond earthly recompense with every facet of this production and to my children Anne Marie, Pádraig and Brendan for their encouragement, practical help and understanding during yet another invasion of book writing into our family life.

PAT LIDDY

Pat Liddy was born in 1944 and grew up in Phibsborough on Dublin's northside. This district is situated inside the boundary line created by the Royal Canal and thus Pat is qualified to claim citizenship of the area known as the Inner City.

The earlier part of his professional life was spent in Aer Lingus, Ireland's national airline, but since 1994 he has dedicated himself full-time to his main pursuits; drawing, writing and exploring historic places. His preferred subject has been his own native city in its buildings, its unique scenery and its people.

*Pat has held several successful one-man exhibitions both in Dublin and in Europe and during the 1980s his weekly illustrated series **Dublin Today** in **The Irish Times**, attained wide critical acclaim and immense popularity.*

His other publications to date are:

Dublin Today (1984)

Dublin be Proud (1987)

Dublin Stolen from Time (1990)

Temple Bar Dublin (1992)

Fifty Years a-Growin' (1995)

Walking Dublin (1998)

Secret Dublin (due 2001)

DUBLIN

A Celebration

From the 1st to the 21st Century

By

Pat Liddy

With over 1,000 illustrations & photographs

many from the Author's own hand.

Dublin Corporation
Bardas Átha Cliath

First published 2000 by Dublin Corporation
Cumberland House, Fenian Street, Dublin 2, Ireland
Tel. +353 1 661 9000 Fax. +353 1 676 1628
e-mail: dublin.city.libs@iol.ie
Website: dublin-info.com

Paperbound ISBN 0 946841 50 0
Casebound ISBN 0 946841 51 9
Special Edition ISBN 0 946841 52 7
Limited Edition ISBN 0 946841 53 5

A catalogue record for this book is available from the British Library.

Published in association with Hamilton Osborne King.
Supported by The National Millennium Committee and a distinguished
group of sponsors.

Co-ordination and Distribution by David O'Neill and Brian Scanlon.
Design, typesetting, layout and print origination by
20-20 Vision Design Ltd., Dublin.
Scanning, picture re-touching and film making by Masterphoto, Dublin.
Index compiled by Gráinne Farren.
Printed by Euroscreen Ltd., Dublin.
Printed on hannoArt matt 130gsm supplied by McNaughton Paper Ireland Ltd.
Bound by Library Bindings.
Special and limited editions bound by Antiquarian Bookcrafts, Marlay Park, Dublin.

CONTENTS

PREFACE

I HAVE BEEN *writing about and drawing aspects of my native city, Dublin, for the best part of three decades. At the outset, I was motivated by the need to draw attention to the rich heritage of Dublin that lay beneath the grime and neglect of generations and also by the urgent necessity to respond to the destruction of large parts of the historic core of Dublin that was being inflicted by those who either cared little about or were ignorant of what they were doing. Since those days of shameful and wanton destruction, carried out during the 1960s, '70s and into the early '80s in the name of so-called progress, there has occurred what amounts to a revolution in attitude towards our inheritance. Helped by the unprecedented economic boom of the late '90s, Dublin's fortunes were turned around before it became too late. The city that is now emerging is more focused about the preservation and enhancement of its unique repository of period buildings and their associated history while at the same time it is learning not to be shy in embracing quality new architecture in appropriate settings.*

This book would not have been possible without the support, financial or otherwise, of a large group of sponsors. Many of these sponsors have themselves been involved in the development of the city but I am not, nor have I been asked to be, an apologist for their work. Indeed, some of them may have made mistakes with their own designs but the purpose of this tome is not to condemn or criticise but to celebrate good achievements. A number of modern buildings, although much superior to the efforts of the 1970s and '80s, cannot claim to be great architecture but what is important is the effect that they have had in revitalising and enhancing an area previously in decay. Indeed, several developers have shown a degree of faith and courage in being the first to tackle districts that had been run-down for generations. This alone deserves recognition.

The next decade will see the city itself growing more in density than in size and the population of the Greater Dublin Area will likely double to around two million by 2015 or thereabouts. Run-down public housing areas will be revitalised, the derelict Docklands areas will be rebuilt on a grand scale and new transport solutions will include a Port Tunnel, extended motorways, additional River Liffey bridges, several urban light rail lines and a metro system. True, Dublin also has its painful share of the growing social problems experienced by many large cities all over the world including drug abuse, crime, discrimination and homelessness. However, there is now a firmer foundation from which to begin to solve these and other problems and it is up to each and everyone who claims citizenship of our great city to realise that this very greatness is hollow unless all its citizens are equally cherished. Taking everything into consideration this is a very significant and exciting period in Dublin's history so I simply could not refuse to indulge myself by writing **Dublin a Celebration***.*

Pat Liddy
September 2000

ACKNOWLEDGEMENTS

I want to place on record my thanks to the following staff of Dublin Corporation: John Fitzgerald, Dublin City Manager, whose vision coincided with mine and led to the genesis of this book; Deirdre Ellis-King and Margaret Hayes, Dublin City Public Libraries, for their guidance and support throughout; Deirdre Ní Raghallaigh and Declan McCullough, Press and Information Office; Máire Kennedy, Dublin and Irish Collections Library; Mary Clarke and Brid Leahy, City Archives; Jim Barrett, City Architect; Daire O'Rourke, City Archaeologist; Vincent Norton, Development Department; Gerry Barry, Anne Marie Harris, Jimmy O'Doherty and Pat Coughlan, Parks Department; Michael Phillips, City Engineer; Susan Roundtree, Conservationist; Brian Callagy, Electricity and Public Lighting Department; Eamonn Elliott, Ballymun Regeneration Ltd.; Paul Maloney, Eileen Carey and their colleagues of the Intergrated Area offices and many staff too numerous to mention in various other sections and departments.

There are many others in public and private organisations whom I also wish to acknowledge for the help they gave me: My thanks also to all the sponsors, who are mentioned elsewhere in this book. In a special way I would like to thank Paul McNeive, Róisín McCarron, Triona Buckley, Aisling O'Beirne and Ronan O'Driscoll of Hamilton Osborne King; Joanne Geary, Dublin Docklands Development Authority, Gerry Weir of Aer Rianta, John Brophy of Citibank and Barry O' Kelly, Bank of Ireland.

The following individuals have also earned my deep gratitude; Brian Scanlon for his support, encouragement and inspiring many of the ideas contained within this volume; Bill Maxwell who generously helped with sales and marketing; Helen Litton and Gráinne Farren who patiently trawled through the text, proof-reading and indexing; Brian Fortune for his professional advice; Cormac Scollard, Diarmuid Scollard and David Park, 20-20 Vision Design Ltd, for their hard work, patience and sound creative ideas in putting this volume together page by page; Conor Arrigan, Aisling O'Connor, Barry Delves, Darren Nolan, Tony Williams and Jack Honan and all the production staff in Masterphoto; Paul Carey and all involved in printing this book at Euroscreen Ltd.; David O'Neill, David O'Neill & Associates, Publishers Agents and Des Breen, Antiquarian Bookcrafts.

Finally, I would like to remember Comdt Peter Young of the Irish Army Archives who sadly passed away shortly after extending his usual courtesy and kindness to me.

TO OUR SPONSORS

The publication of this book would not have been remotely possible without the kind support from the following sponsors;

ASSOCIATE PUBLISHING SPONSOR
Hamilton Osborne King

FOUNDATION SPONSORS
Aer Rianta
Flynn Property Partnership and Paddy Kelly
National Millennium Committee

PRINCIPAL SPONSORS
Allied Irish Banks
Capel Developments
CIE Group Property Division
Citibank
Euroscreen
Hollybrook Construction
Irish Life
Masterphoto
Treasury Holdings
20-20 Vision Design

PROJECT SPONSORS
Carlton Group
Cosgrave Property Group
Dublin Docklands Development Authority
Gaelic Athletic Association
Green Property
Guinness Ireland Group
McGarrell Reilly/Alcove Properties
P J McGrath
Shelbourne Developments

PUBLICATION SUPPORT SPONSORS
Anon
Alanis
Peter Barrow Photography
G & T Crampton
Dublin Port Company
Dúchas The Heritage Service
Dunloe Ewart
Eastern Regional Health Authority
Educational Building Society
FLS Aerospace
G E Capital Woodchester Bank
Institute of Education
John Paul Construction
National Gallery of Ireland
O'Callaghan Hotels
Thomas Read Holdings
Royal College of Surgeons in Ireland
John Sisk & Son
David Slattery
Temple Bar Properties
Trinity College Dublin
P J Walls
Woodgreen Builders

Hamilton Osborne King
32 Molesworth Street,
Dublin 2.
Telelphone: 618 1300.
www.hok.ie.

September 2000

Dear Reader

It is our great pleasure to sponsor this publication by Pat Liddy, celebrating Dublin's history into the new millennium.

This firm's foundations in Dublin reach back to 1935 and it is, therefore, no surprise that over the intervening years we have had extensive involvement with many of the city's best known properties, sometimes disposing of them, other times acting in their development and on several occasions organising sales involving the State and other Public Bodies.

Our return to No.20 Dawson Street, beside the Mansion House, in June this year for our new HOK Residential Headquarters has brought us almost full circle after 50 years to where the two founding firms (Hamilton & Hamilton and Osborne King & Megran) started out respectively in Nos. 17 and 64 Dawson Street. It is our pleasure to return to this historic and famous Dublin Street.

I hope that you enjoy and treasure this wonderful record of Dublin.

Yours truly,

Aidan O'Hogan
Managing Director

An tArdmhéara Ró-Onórach
Seanóir Muiris Ó hEachthighearn

The Right Honourable The Lord Mayor
Alderman Maurice Ahern

September 2000

A NUCLEAR-FREE CITY

Dear Reader,

There is no better time than the turn of the century to reminisce on times gone by and look forward to the opportunities which the new millennium presents. "Dublin - A Celebration", commissioned to mark the turn of the new century, takes us on a journey of Dublin, from the past through to the present and on to the future. Pat Liddy, through his latest book, will help the reader appreciate the jewel that is our "Fair City".

Through his books such as "Dublin Be Proud" and "Dublin – Stolen from Time", Pat Liddy has chronicled the evolution of Dublin. "Dublin – A Celebration" is an invaluable record of the development of the City and will be used as a reference book for historians, as an information source for tourists and Dubliners alike or as a fine gift for anybody interested in Dublin. Writers such as Pat provide a great service to the City by cataloguing the ever-changing face of our capital city and Dublin Corporation is proud to be involved with Pat in the publication of this book.

As we enter this new millennium, Dublin is changing for the better. The many regeneration projects for which Dublin Corporation is responsible, such as the renewal of O'Connell Street and the redevelopment of the Liberties/Coombe area, are contributing to the economic, cultural and social profile of Dublin. Much of the City's historical built environment has been preserved and these buildings are complimented by dynamic new structures in areas where dereliction was once the norm.

A stroll around the streets, squares and quaysides is a most pleasant way to view the remarkable rejuvenation of the city. Amble from the relaxed ambience of Smithfield to the hustle and bustle of the revamped Henry Street. The improvements will continue throughout this century. The Liffey Boardwalk, the regeneration of Ballymun and other projects will change the face of Dublin. From its famous shopping streets to its impressive buildings, Dublin has a lot to offer the many tourists who flock to our capital throughout the year. Our fine parks provide ideal places to relax from the stresses of modern-day living.

I hope that, with the on-going construction and upgrading of the City, Dublin Corporation can continue to provide Pat Liddy with high quality subject matter by furthering the conservation and rejuvenation of one of the world's *Great Cities.*

Alderman Maurice Ahern,
Lord Mayor of Dublin

Teach an Ardmhéara, Baile Átha Cliath, Éire, Telefón: 676 1845 & 671 2402. Feacs: 679 6573. ríomhphost: lordmayor@dublincorp.ie

Mansion House, Dublin 2, Ireland. Telephone: 676 1845 & 671 2402. Fax: 679 6573. e-mail: lordmayor@dublincorp.ie

Part One
EBLANA* ARISE!

In Nature's cycle I rise through rocks and crusts of peat,

and issue forth to a barren height of stately hills.

Gathering strength I descend, uncoiling I make for sea,

past the haven of enfolding estuary.

My ancestral waters first encountered

a skimming bark of least intrusion.

They called them Vikings, they call me Anna Livia.

* An ancient word for Dublin taken from the Greek 2nd century map of Ireland drawn by Greek astronomer and geographer Ptolemy of Alexandria. Eblana is a Latin word which was transliterated from the original Greek when the map was republished in Rome in 1490.

Chapter One

Ancestral Footprints

Above: Knockmaree Cist, a Neolithic burial mound, was discovered in 1838 close by St Mary's Hospital in the Phoenix Park. Six human remains, accompanied by food vessels, were found in the tumulus. A vivid reconstruction of the chamber is on display at the Ashtown Castle Visitor Centre, in the Phoenix Park.

Above: The Newgrange megalithic tomb was built about 3200 BC by Neolithic farmers and demonstrates their incredible skills in art, architecture, engineering and astronomy.

BEFORE PREHISTORIC people travelled to Ireland, the island itself did some of its own travelling. During the Devonian period of some 400 million years ago the country was part of the vast landmass of Euramerica, which was then positioned below the equator, partly submerged in tropical waters. Limestone, so much a feature of the rock beds in and around Dublin, would form over the next 100 million years beneath the shallow seas that covered the land. Gradually the continent drifted northwards and split into its constituent parts of America and Europe. Cataclysmic convulsions forced up mountain ranges in such places as Dublin and Wicklow and created massifs whose original heights may have easily challenged today's European Alps. Erosion has since reduced these immense peaks to the modest hills that presently form the southern boundary of Dublin.

If warmth was a feature during the birth of Ireland, severe cold would now be the sculptor of the landscape. Close to a million years ago the first of the Great Ice Ages arrived and little relief would be had from the crushing weight of mountainous ice sheets until about 12000 BC when the ice began to finally retreat. After a couple of millennia Ireland was again free from its frigid bondage. However, the resultant rise in the sea levels from the melting ice caused Ireland to lose its land link with Britain and all travel to the former from abroad would now have to be by boat. This inconvenience did not deter resolute sailors of coracles and other small craft from venturing across the Irish Sea and probing this relatively empty land for its possibilities and opportunities.

Mesolithic or Middle-Stone Age hunters may have fanned out around the present-day Dublin region as far back as 7000 BC. They based their livelihood on foraging and hunting around coasts, rivers and lakes and made no effort to form settled communities or to cut down the dense forests for farming. Cooking leftovers from fishermen, dated to around 5000 BC, have been found on Dalkey Island. Neolithic settlers arrived a millennium later and a farming economy of sorts developed, although these latest immigrants tended to settle in upland areas where there was better drainage and the forests were thinner. They evolved into a fairly complex society, a fact amply demonstrated by the remains of huge burial chambers situated along the Boyne Valley some 40km (25 miles) north of Dublin. The passage grave at Newgrange (3200 BC) shows a sophisticated people who could organise a labour-intensive project and build a massive structure that still stands intact today. Remarkably, it was constructed hundreds of years before the Great Pyramids of Egypt. Newgrange had a major surprise in store for University College Cork archaeologist, Professor Michael J. O'Kelly. In 1963 he discovered that the tomb was specially orientated so that at dawn on each midwinter day (21st December) the sun shone directly through an aperture in the roof and lit the burial chamber. The arrangement was calculated with such accuracy that 5,200 years later the phenomenon is annually repeated without fail (subject to a cloudless sky, of course!).

Left: Before the wheel was introduced into Ireland goods were most conveniently transported by boat. This example is a Bronze Age boat (c.2500BC) which was fashioned from a hollowed-out oak tree using a primitive adze implement. It was recovered from Lurgan Bog in County Galway and is now on display in the National Museum, Kildare Street.

These remarkable people were in turn followed and superseded by the better-equipped Bronze Age invaders of 4,500 years ago. Rudimentary farming became better organised and the lowlands were now exploited with the availability of metal tools. As part of their general migration from central Europe, the Celts arrived around 500 BC and introduced the Iron Age into Ireland. Their weaponry and warfare skills assured their gradual dominance over the indigenous population. The Celtic period is perhaps best remembered for the establishment of a new order and culture which was to last for two thousand years in some parts of the country before the English conquest finally obliterated it. Their language, Gaelic, is still spoken today. The Celts are especially renowned for the production of beautiful metal objects both for practical and decorative uses. They also built a number of national roads through the forests and over the bogs to link their main centres. These slighe (ways or roads) converged at a ford on the River Liffey called Áth Cliath and it may be assumed that a small village grew up around this river crossing, becoming the precursor of Dublin itself (Baile Átha Cliath, the Town of the Hurdle Ford, is the Irish name for Dublin).

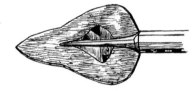

Above: Bronze spearhead and a bronze shield (c.700BC). Both are held in the collections of the National Museum, Kildare Street.

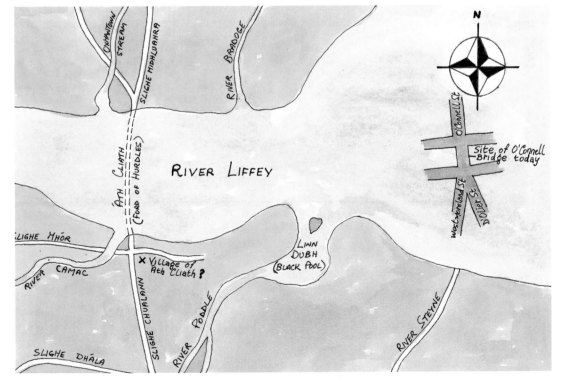

Left: The Dublin region in c.100BC had a very different topography compared with today. The River Liffey was about five times its current width and it widened into a broad estuary before it reached present-day Capel Street. The Ford of Hurdles (Áth Cliath) was at the junction of four ancient highways; Slí Mhór (to Galway), Slí Dhála (to Limerick), Slí Chualann (connected Tara to Wicklow) and Slí Midhluachra (linked Derry to Waterford).

Right: The Round Tower of Swords Abbey in North County Dublin is the only remnant of the monastery first founded by St Columba in the 6th century. The 14th century square tower belonged to the now-vanished medieval abbey. After the Battle of Clontarf in 1014, the bodies of King Brian Boru and his son, Morrough, rested overnight in the abbey.

Above: Father Mathew Bridge stands downriver from the ancient ford of Áth Cliath. Dublin's first bridge was built here around the 10th century and was later replaced by several subsequent versions. The present stone structure dates from 1818 and is named after the 19th century temperance crusader and Capuchin monk, Theobald Mathew (1790-1856.)

Above: The Brazen Head Inn, Dublin's oldest pub, stands close to Father Mathew Bridge. Dating from the 1600s it was most likely preceded by earlier taverns as its location was next to the junction of four ancient national routes.

Right: This replica Viking Ship, named 'Dyflin', was constructed in 1988 by the community of East Wall, in Dublin's north inner city.

Christianity was introduced to Ireland in the 5th century and spread rapidly throughout the country. The church left by St Patrick, his colleagues and successors grew strong, rich and internationally influential. Christian scholarship combined with Celtic art forms and together the two disciplines produced some of the world's greatest treasures in gold, silver, bronze and book illustration. Monasteries flourished and several were founded in the Dublin area. One such abbey was located at Dubh Linn (the Black Pool) just south of present-day Dublin Castle, a place that has since given the city its modern name. The reputation of these monasteries spread far and wide and sizeable communities grew up around them. Students were attracted to their schools not only from Ireland but also from Saxon Britain. The recent discovery of a Saxon house foundation off Essex Street West may attest to the presence of a Saxon nobleman's student son and his retinue.

The Saxons were not the only foreigners attracted to Ireland by the affluent monasteries. A marauding race of adventurers had heard of the more temporal treasures held in abundance in the religious houses. Besides, one of their main commercial activities, slave trading, would be well catered for by the copious supply of young people living in and around the learned institutions. From the 8th century, Ireland was to be raided with increasing frequency by the most daring and successful seafarers the world had ever seen: the Vikings.

Initially the Vikings satisfied themselves with hit-and-run raids along the coastal and river hinterlands of Ireland but in 837 a large fleet of Norwegian longboats, carrying around 3,000 people, sailed up the River Liffey and established a settlement. In 841 they built a longphort (a stockaded harbour) but at this point they had no intention of building a town as such. In any case the Norse were a rural people with little experience of urban living. Their relationships with the local chieftains were equivocal at best and often degenerated into outright conflict. The Norse suffered a major defeat in 902 and the survivors departed in their longboats but started immediately to plan for their vengeful return. A huge armada of Danish and Norwegian boats reappeared in 917 and this time, under their king, Sitric ll, they were determined to stay. Adjacent to today's Wood Quay they raised earthen ramparts surmounted by a palisade of wattle fencing. Local labour and techniques were employed to build the houses which consisted of traditional post and wattle walls and roofs of thatch. As space was severely limited inside the crude walls strict laws were laid down to govern plot sizes and boundaries. These regulations formed the first planning directives of the fledgling town of Dublin (called Dyflin by the Norse).

Over the next 250 years the Vikings built up their Dublin power base but not without regular and serious challenges from the native Irish. Despite the political and military instability of Dublin it became one of the most prominent trading centres in the Viking world. Agricultural exports, slave trading, craft work and shipbuilding represented the bulk of the outgoing commerce while imports included metals, certain foodstuffs, clothing, alcohol and fineries from Europe and the Middle East.

Top left: Ireland's Eye and Dalkey Island (top right) are positioned along the shores of Dublin Bay. The former lies off Howth Harbour and the latter is just southeast of Dun Laoghaire Harbour. The Vikings were initially attracted to the islands not so much to plunder their insignificant religious foundations but to use them as strategic bases. The "Eye" in Ireland's Eye is derived from the Norse word "Ey", meaning island.

Above: This modern representation of the Steyne Stone (sculpted by Cliodna Cusson in 1986) stands at the junction of Pearse Street and Townsend Street. It replaces the original stone reputed to have been planted by the Vikings in 837 and which stood here for almost 900 years before mysteriously disappearing.

Left: The sculptural wall by Grace Weir (1996), is a relief evoking the Vikings by the representation of their boats, their artefacts and their supreme celestial navigational skills. The wall is part of Dublin's Viking Adventure Centre on Essex Street West, Temple Bar.

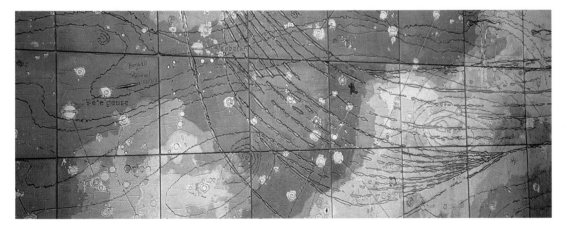

Above: A view of the early Viking town of Dyflin (the word was derived from the Gaelic, Dubh Linn, meaning the Black Pool). It was a closely packed settlement where houses were built in the traditional Irish style using wattle and daub walls and roofs of thatch. Initially earthen embankments surrounded the settlement but these were replaced with stone walls by the 12th century.

Right & above: Fishamble Street was first laid down by the Vikings in Temple Bar's West End around the 10th century as a through passageway to connect the river to the main market centre around High Street. It derived its name from the fish shambles or stalls which lined the street. In the 17th and 18th centuries it was an extremely fashionable street. It was here, in Neal's Musick Hall (above), on Tuesday 13th April, 1742, over 700 men (without their swords) and women (without their hoops) were crammed tightly in to hear the world's first performance of George Frederick Handel's new oratorio "Messiah". Now restored, number 19 Fishamble Street, an 1830s house next door to the former site of the Musick Hall, is appropriately the new headquarters for the Contemporary Music Centre.

The Vikings had little desire to conquer the whole of Ireland but they still played a pivotal role in the volatile politics of the time. Straddled as Dublin was between the various county and provincial kingships, its inhabitants and fleet proved themselves useful in a mercenary role to the competing local factions. A concerted effort by the Irish would easily have dislodged the Fionn Galls (the fair-headed strangers, as they were called by the Irish) but they provided some very useful military and trading services, albeit to the highest bidder. Also, it made practical sense from a commercial point of view to court their undisputed mastery of the shipping routes. However, this delicate balance of opportunistic politics and fragile alliances was soon to take a radical new direction with the arrival of major new players in the field: the Anglo-Normans.

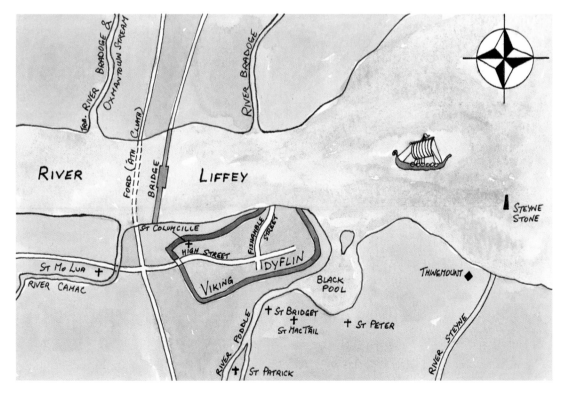

Top & above: The modern traders of Moore Street and their earlier counterparts as represented by the mythical Molly Malone (above) on Grafton Street (sculptor: Jeanne Rynhart, 1988) are direct inheritors of the traditions first handed down to Dubliners by the Vikings. Norse Dublin was internationally famous as a centre for craftwork, slave trading and shipbuilding and these items were widely exported along with staple agricultural goods.

Left: More than a thousand years have passed since the period outlined by the map on page 11. Several Christian monasteries have been established and they co-exist along with the fledgling Viking town. The Liffey channel has been narrowed and extended but is still much wider than today's river.

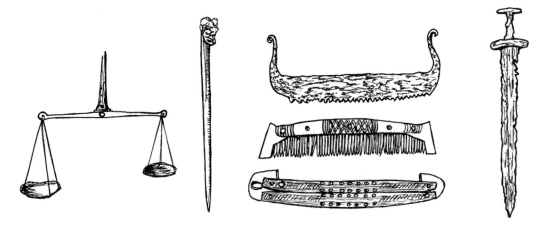

Time Watch

BC

C. 400,000,000: *Ireland part of the Euramerica land mass situated south of the equator.*

C. 1,000,000: *Ireland's Great Ice Age begins.*

C. 25000: *Cave drawings flourish in Spain and France.*

C. 12000: *Last Ice Age begins to retreat.*

C. 8000: *Arrival of prehistoric peoples to Ireland.*

C. 5000: *Mesolithic hunters roam around Dublin.*

C. 3000: *Wheel invented in Near East. Small but sophisticated settlements exist around Dublin.*

2551: *Egypt's Great Pyramid of Giza begun.*

C. 2000: *Bronze Age settlers arrive to Dublin.*

753: *Rome founded.*

C. 500: *Celts arrive in Ireland and introduce the Iron Age.*

44: *Death of Julius Caesar. Celtic civilisation reaches a high point in Ireland.*

AD

450: *St Patrick reputedly visits Dublin.*

841: *Vikings establish a permanent harbour at Dublin.*

1014: *Battle of Clontarf.*

1028: *Foundation of Christ Church Cathedral.*

1066: *The Normans conquer England.*

1169: *The Anglo-Normans land at Wexford.*

Above: Examples of some of the many thousands of Viking artefacts retrieved during various archaeological excavations. They include a 12th century scales, a polished bone pin, a small iron saw shaped like a Viking boat, a comb and its case and a 12th century iron sword (pictures are not to scale).

Photo: courtesy of Dublin Tourism.

Above left: An internal view of Dublin's Viking Adventure (architects: Gilroy McMahon), an exhibition centre dealing with the city's Viking history. The centre was built in and around the former church of Saints Michael and John. This in turn was the earlier site of the Smock Alley Theatre.

Above right: The patterns laid into the footpath on Winetavern Street are the actual-scale foundation outlines of a Viking house, its outhouses, paths and boundaries based on excavations carried out at Wood Quay and Fishamble Street in 1980/81.

Right: The boat sculpture (sculptor: Betty Newman-Maguire, 1988) on Essex Quay represents the beached skeleton of a Viking ship showing that its occupants had come to stay.

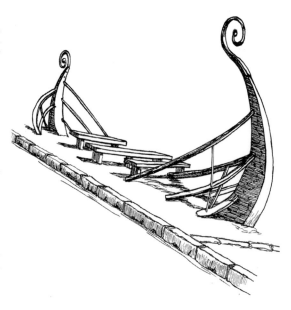

Chapter Two
Castles, Cathedrals and Consternations

Above: The Norman leader, Richard de Clare (Strongbow), was buried in Christ Church Cathedral in 1176. The present tomb replaced the original one which was destroyed when the roof above it collapsed in 1562.

THE ARRIVAL of the Anglo-Normans in 1169 was a watershed moment in Irish history but at the time it seemed relatively unimportant. The first incursion was less an invasion and more of a reconnaissance-strength landing, to use a modern term. Their ultimate success was due as much to the disunity of the Irish kings as to superior Norman weaponry and horsemanship.

Dermot Mac Murrough had been deposed as King of Leinster by an alliance of other noble families in a fight for the High Kingship of Ireland. He sought help from King Henry II of England to regain his lost kingdom and the latter, displaying little interest at the time (he had earlier declined to conquer Ireland at the behest of the Pope!), referred him to the Norman lords of Wales. They were more enthusiastic and the first contingent landed at Bannow Bay, Co. Wexford in 1169 and captured Ferns, Mac Murrough's former regal seat and restored him to power. Mac Murrough's erstwhile adversaries decided to leave him in peace and the Anglo-Normans, for their part, conquered vast tracts of land which they consolidated by first erecting small but effective garrison posts (mottes and baileys) and later by building large castles such as those at Dublin, Trim and Carrickfergus.

The most famous of the Anglo-Norman knights was Richard FitzGilbert de Clare, more popularly known as Strongbow. Upon the capture of Waterford he married Aoife, the daughter of Dermot MacMurrough. When the latter died in 1171 Strongbow assumed his kingship. In 1170 a reinforced army of Anglo-Normans under Strongbow and an Irish army under Mac Murrough approached the gates of Dublin and naturally caused great alarm among the mixed Norse and Irish population. Hasculf Mac Torcaill, the Norse ruler of Dublin, sent out the Archbishop, Laurence O'Toole, to parlay. While the negotiations were going on a party of knights breached the walls and the town was soon captured. The Hiberno-Norse fled in their ships or else crossed the river to their suburb of Ostmantown (the town of the men from the east from which the name of modern Oxmantown is derived) where they were left in peace. Thus began for Dublin over 750 years of foreign occupation.

Photo: courtesy of Dublin Castle Conference Centre.

Above: During restoration work carried out by the Office of Public Works in the 1980s, the massive lower section of the Gunpowder Tower, one of Dublin Castle's medieval corner bastions, was discovered. The steps leading up to a postern gate, a section of the old town wall and the River Poddle itself are now also on view to the public.

Right: The Upper Yard of Dublin Castle today occupies the site of the original fortress and except for what lies underground little remains of the medieval structure. The entrance to the State Apartments is to the left of the picture. The building on the right, the Bedford Tower, was designed by Thomas Ivory as apartments for the Master of Ceremonies and was erected 1750 - 1760. It was extensively restored in 1988 during which a third storey, added in the 1820s,. was removed.

Below left: The Record Tower, although later modified, dates from 1205 and is the original south-eastern tower of the medieval castle. Now the home of the Garda (Police) Museum it served many roles in its historic past. It was once a state prison and more recently it served as the repository for State Papers - hence its name.

Below right: Interior of the Chapel Royal. Designed by Francis Johnston in 1807 the Chapel Royal is noted for its plasterwork, oak carvings, limestone heads (carved by Edward Smyth and his son John) and the coat-of-arms of all the Viceroys. Amazingly, that of the last Viceroy occupies the final available window space.

The erection of Dublin Castle was commissioned by King John of England in 1204 "...for the safe custody of our treasure, for the administration of justice and for the defence of the city." By 1230 the construction was completed. It was a medium-sized castle and surprisingly did not possess a fortified central keep. It was, however surrounded by a huge moat, 22 metres (72 ft) wide and 12 metres (39 ft) deep. The moat was filled on the two sides outside the adjoining city walls by the River Poddle. In 1684 the castle was virtually destroyed by an accidental fire but was largely rebuilt by the early 18th century (the architect for the first phase was Sir William Robinson). The new buildings provided a variety of administration offices, some richly decorated rooms for state receptions and residential apartments for the Lord Lieutenant. The latter usually lived in the Vice-Regal Lodge in the Phoenix Park but he did reside in the castle during the so-called Castle Season, a six week period of entertainment which reached its climax with a Grand Ball on March 17th, St. Patrick's Day. The area enclosed by the Castle was further extended over the years to provide additional facilities. During the Great War of 1914-1918 the apartments were pressed into service as a Red Cross Hospital. James Connolly, one of the leaders of the 1916 Easter Rising, was treated here for gunshot wounds before being taken away to Kilmainham Gaol to face a firing squad. On January 16th, 1922 the Provisional Government of the Irish Free State accepted the transfer of Dublin Castle from the last Lord Lieutenant, Lord FitzAlan. Since then the State Apartments, the ancillary buildings and the Castle's Conference Centre are used to host visiting heads of Government, meetings of the European Union, conferences, tribunals of enquiry and the inauguration of each new President of Ireland. The recent major restoration and the building of the new Conference Centre were carried out by a team of architects from the Office of Public Works under Klaus Unger, David Byers, Michael Carroll and Angela Rolfe.

Photo: courtesy of Dublin Castle Conference Centre.

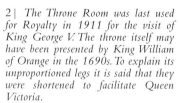 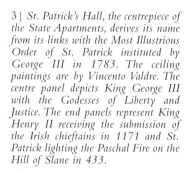
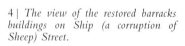
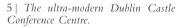

1 | The restored Lord Lieutenant's Coach House, now used for public and private functions. The castellated frontage was erected before a visit by Queen Victoria to disguise the unsavoury backs of nearby houses.

2 | The Throne Room was last used for Royalty in 1911 for the visit of King George V. The throne itself may have been presented by King William of Orange in the 1690s. To explain its unproportioned legs it is said that they were shortened to facilitate Queen Victoria.

3 | St. Patrick's Hall, the centrepiece of the State Apartments, derives its name from its links with the Most Illustrious Order of St. Patrick instituted by George III in 1783. The ceiling paintings are by Vincento Valdre. The centre panel depicts King George III with the Godesses of Liberty and Justice. The end panels represent King Henry II receiving the submission of the Irish chieftains in 1171 and St. Patrick lighting the Paschal Fire on the Hill of Slane in 433.

4 | The view of the restored barracks buildings on Ship (a corruption of Sheep) Street.

5 | The ultra-modern Dublin Castle Conference Centre.

Top right: St Michan's Church was built in 1095 and for 602 years it remained the only parish church in the town north of the River Liffey. Dedicated to a Danish martyr, it served the Norse suburb of Ostmantown whose population dramatically increased when the Anglo-Normans banished the Vikings from the walled city in 1170. The church was rebuilt in 1686 and extensively repaired in 1828. The orator, Edmund Burke, was baptised here as was the Duke of Wellington and Handel is said to have played the church organ in 1742. Some executed rebels from the 1798 Rising are buried here including Oliver Bond and the Sheares Brothers. A macabre tourist attraction is the presence in the vaults of four 17th century mummified bodies (above) preserved by the magnesium salts in the limestone which keep the air very dry.

Middle right: The crypt of Christ Church Cathedral dates from at least the 12th century and is the city centre's oldest surviving structure. It is one of the largest medieval crypts in Ireland or Britain and the rows of stone pillars and arches carry the entire weight of the cathedral above. Many interesting artefacts are stored in the crypt including the city stocks (see page 26), stone carvings made redundant in the cathedral's 1871-8 restoration, family monuments and the statues of Charles I and Charles II which once stood on the portico of the Tholsel or City Hall (demolished 1805). On view also are the tabernacle and brass candlesticks used for the Latin Masses said during King James II's brief sojourn in Dublin in 1689. The crypt underwent a major refurbishment in 1999-2000 under the guidance of Paul Arnold Architects. The concrete floor was replaced by stone flags, electrical and other services were hidden, uplighting was installed, the 19th century partition closing off the north aisle was removed and a new visitor entrance leading directly from the street was opened.

Bottom right: A drawing of Christ Church Cathedral taken from Charles Brooking's 1728 map of Dublin.

Photo: courtesy of Dublin Corporation Civic Museum.

Above: Christ Church Cathedral.

Christ Church Cathedral was founded c1030 by Bishop Dúnán with the support of the Norse King of Dublin, Sitric Silkenbeard. In 1163 Archbishop Laurence O'Toole (canonised 1225 and now Patron Saint of the Archdiocese of Dublin) replaced the secular clergy of Christ Church with Augustinian Canons Regular. The ruins of their priory Chapter House can still be seen outside the cathedral's south wall. Funded by Strongbow and his companion knights, work commenced in 1172 on replacing the Norse wooden structure with a stone cathedral built in the Norman tradition. Because it took several decades to complete the construction a variety of architectural styles, from Romanesque to English Gothic, were employed. In 1541 the Augustinian priory was dissolved by Henry VIII and the cathedral became part of the Anglican Community. For 700 years, until the Church of Ireland was disestablished in 1869, Christ Church was the State Church in which senior representatives of the crown swore their oaths of allegiance.

Photo: courtesy of Bert Keenan

Above: Alongside the existing twelve, seven new bells, cast at John Taylor's in Loughborough, Leicester, were hung in the tower of Christ Church Cathedral in September 1999. The complicated bell hanging was carried out by Hayward Mills Associates of Nottingham. Together, the bells now constitute possibly the largest ringing peal in the world.

Above: St Patrick's Cathedral.

Right: There is no mistaking the medieval and prayerful atmosphere of St Patrick's interior. There is a wealth of history present around its aisles and walls in the shape of carvings, memorials, tombs, windows and the like. Commemorated here are Jonathan Swift, Dean of St Patrick's 1713-45; Carolan, the famous blind harpist; composer Michael Balfe; Douglas Hyde, first President of Ireland and many more. Flags of old Irish regiments and those of the Knights of St Patrick add colour to the stonework. In the centre of the drawing are the magnificent choir stalls, a reminder that the cathedral's Choir School has been in continuous existence from 1432.

An ancient Celtic stone slab (preserved in St Patrick's Cathedral) is said to have marked the location of the well where St Patrick baptised converts in the 5th century *(see page 93)*. A church was erected here shortly afterwards and was still in use when the Anglo-Normans arrived to Dublin. Archbishop John Comyn replaced the old Celtic church with a stone one in 1191. He wished to wean himself away from the influence of the priory attached to Christ Church Cathedral. In 1219 his ambition was realised posthumously when St Patrick's was elevated to cathedral status under Archbishop Henry De Londres. From 1225 the cathedral was refashioned in the style that we see today. The design of the central part of the church is an almost exact copy of Salisbury Cathedral, which was being built at the same time. Ireland's first university was founded at St. Patrick's in 1320 and intermittently operated for 200 years. The cathedral's most famous dean was Jonathan Swift (1667-1745), creator of *Gulliver's Travels* and indefatigable champion of the underprivileged.

Centuries of financial deprivation and actual abuse (Oliver Cromwell stabled his horses here in 1649) seriously degraded the fabric of the building and it was in danger of imminent collapse until Benjamin Lee Guinness (he of the famous brewery) spent a large fortune on its restoration in the 1860s. The massive West Tower, rebuilt by Archbishop Minot in 1370 after a fire, houses the large peal of bells whose ringing tones are so much part of the character of this part of Dublin. One of the city's first public clocks was placed on the tower in 1560.

Dublin is uniquely a city of two cathedrals devoted to the same communion (both are Church of Ireland). Christ Church is the Cathedral of the Diocese of Dublin and Glendalough and Metropolitan Cathedral of the Southern Province while St Patrick's is the National Cathedral for Ireland.

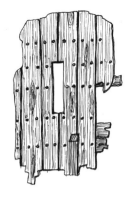

Above: Known as the Door of Reconciliation, this once belonged to the Chapter House of St Patrick's Cathedral. In 1492 Black Jack, nephew of the Earl of Ormond, took refuge in the Chapter House from his deadly pursuer, the Earl of Kildare. Kildare offered a truce and to prove his sincerity he cut a hole in the door with his sword and thrust his hand through to shake that of Black Jack. It is believed that this event could be the origin of the expression "to chance your arm".

Left: Dedicated to a Saxon abbess, St Werburgha, the Anglo-Norman church was built in 1178. After a major reconstruction in 1662 it was rebuilt again in 1715. A disastrous fire in 1754 resulted in yet another renovation and this time a very elegant tower and spire were added. In the unsettled political climate of the early 1800s the jittery authorities in neighbouring Dublin Castle feared that snipers would use the tower and ordered its demolition. In the late 1990's builders returned again to restore the building on behalf of its owners, the Church of Ireland. The world famous pianist and originator of the nocturne form of composition, John Field, was baptised here in 1782. Lord Edward Fitzgerald, leader of the 1798 Rising, is buried in the vaults.

Above: This 18th century fire pump is one of two preserved within St Werburgh's Church. They are reminders of the days when volunteer firemen operated from parish churches.

Right: Dvblinia (first opened in 1993 by the Medieval Trust) is a vivid and compelling exhibition of life and times in medieval Dublin. The exhibits include a large graphic model of the early 16th century city, recreations of buildings, docksides and markets, a walk-through-the-centuries display and archaeological artefacts. Dvblinia is housed in the former Synod Hall built in the 1870s around the medieval tower of St Michael's Church.

Above: St Audoen's Arch (1240) is the only gateway remaining from the medieval city walls. The gateway and the existing stretch of wall along Cook Street once lined the banks of the River Liffey but subsequent reclamation meant that new walls had to be built nearer to the river. Houses were built up against the Cook Street walls which in effect preserved them for future posterity.

Right: A section of the model on display in Dvblinia, St. Michael's Hill.

Photo: courtesy of Dvblinia and The Medieval Trust.

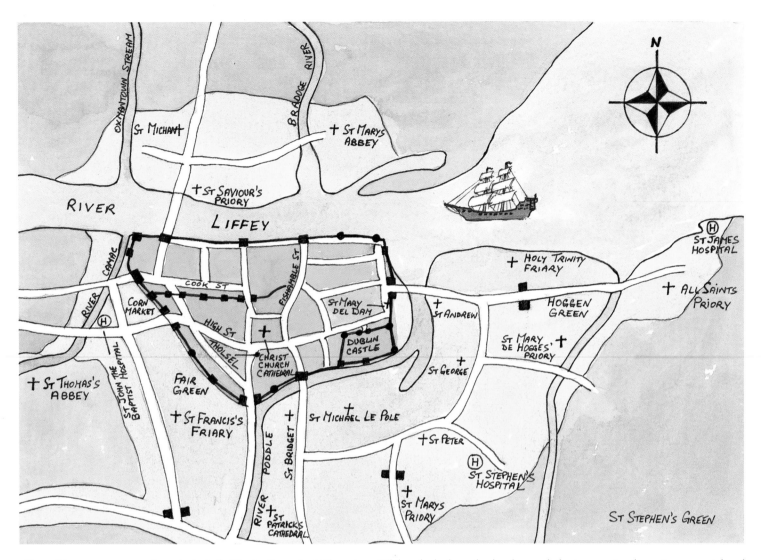

Above: The map represents the extent of Dublin in the early 16th century. While suburbs have developed around the town centre the main commercial and administrative activities were still located for security reasons within the defensive walls. The River Liffey has been further narrowed to increase its depth but silting and low tides remain problematic. Large and heavily laden ships have to use the port at Dalkey, 13km (8 miles) southeast of Dublin. The great abbeys continue to be a major presence in the landscape.

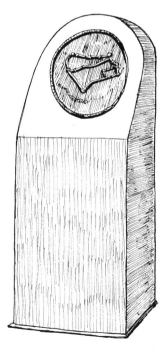

Above: Plaques, set onto stone pedestals such as this example, are to be found along the full length of the line of Dublin's medieval defensive walls. Each plaque by its siting indicates the position of a former tower or gateway as also indicated on the diagram sculptured on the bronze disk.

Picture: courtesy of Dvblinia and The Medieval Trust.

Above: The Dvblinia logo represents two foxes dressed as pilgrims with hats, staves and satchels. They feature on a 14th century two colour segmental floor tile from Christ Church Cathedral. The satirical use of animals dressed up as humans (here possibly friars begging for alms) was popular in medieval times.

Top right: The arrival of the Viceroy, Sir William Skeffington, in 1529 at the jetty of St. Mary's Abbey. Greeting him are the abbot and his community. Awaiting their turn at the gateway are the Mayor and members of the City Council (woodcut from Holinshed's "Historie of Irelande" 1577).

Centre right: In this somewhat exaggerated woodcut the historian Richard Stanyhurst colourfully depicts the abortive attack by Thomas Fitzgerald, son of Garret Og, the Earl of Kildare, on the walls of Dublin in 1534. Reinforcements sent by Henry VIII later defeated Fitzgerald, captured his castle at Maynooth and massacred the surrendering garrison. The young Earl was hanged, drawn and quartered at Tyburn, outside London.

Picture: courtesy of The National Library.

Picture: courtesy of The National Library.

Above: The stocks of the Liberty (jurisdiction) of Christ Church made in 1670, were in continuous use for over a century to punish offenders sentenced by the court of the cathedral's Dean and Chapter. They are now on view in the crypt of Christ Church Cathedral.

Bottom right: The substantial remains of the medieval city walls on Cook Street. They were restored in 1975 by Dublin Corporation for European Architectural Heritage Year.

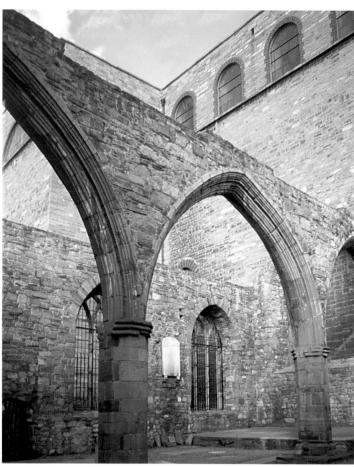

Above: Built between 1181-1212, St Audoen's Church is the only city centre medieval parish church retaining its original features that is still in regular use today. Dedicated to the patron saint of Normandy, St.Ouen, the fortunes of the church grew and diminished with the ebb and flow of its congregation. Large extensions were added in the 14th and 15th centuries but by 1773 the congregation was in serious decline so the roofs were stripped from the extensions. The western end of the north aisle is still used as a parish church. Dúchas The State Heritage Service, re-roofed the southern wing and in 1999 opened a memorable visitor centre here. The history of the church and parish is exhibited downstairs and included is the revealed excavation of a 12th century cobbled lane. Upstairs there is a graphic display on the history of the medieval trade guilds. The church tower still resounds to its peal of six bells, three of which date from 1423. Architects for the restoration were Willie Cummins (Dúchas) and Kevin Blackwood (Blackwood Associates) who worked in conjunction with the vicar of St. Audoen's, Canon Crawford.

Left: St. Mary's Abbey Chapter House and its adjoining slype (corridor) are all that remain of one of Ireland's largest, richest and most powerful monastic foundations. Founded in 1139 as a Benedictine Monastery it adopted the Cistercian rules in 1147. It was in the Chapter House in 1534 that Lord (Silken) Thomas Fitzgerald renounced his allegiance to Henry VIII and commenced his ill-fated rebellion. The rich assets of the abbey were eagerly confiscated by the authorities when St. Mary's was surrendered in 1539 under the directives of Henry VIII to close all monasteries. The stones from its buildings were used a century later to provide building material for a resurgent Dublin. The Chapter House Visitor Centre is under the care of Dúchas The State Heritage Service.

Photo: courtesy of Dúchas The Heritage Service.

Above: The Archbishop's Palace of St Sepulchre on Kevin Street was occupied by the Primate of Dublin from 1212 until 1806 when it was sold off for use as a police barracks.

Middle right: The present Garda Station retains little of the original palace except for the gate pillars, a vault, a small 16th century window and a 17th century internal double door with carved surrounds.

Bottom right: Rathborne Candles on East Wall Road, in business in Dublin since 1488, is believed to be the oldest firm of its kind in Europe. As well as using modern production methods it still employs ancient techniques for making special candles.

Below: The candlestick and snuffer are a reminder that for many centuries candles were the main means of illumination.

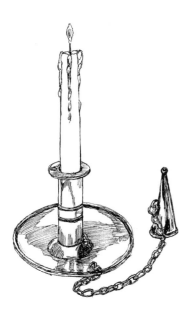

28

Picture: courtesy Dublin Corporation City Archives

Left: The Coat-of-Arms of the Guild of Goldsmiths, founded in 1637 and the only Guild still in existence.

Picture: courtesy Dublin Corporation City Archives

Above: The Coat-of-Arms of the Guild of Tailors and the Guild of Merchants.

Guilds were literally mutual benefit organisations which thrived throughout the towns of Europe from the 11th century. There were four types of guild. The merchant guilds regulated commerce and were deemed to be the most important. The trade or craft guilds set standards of workmanship and taught apprentices the secrets of their chosen trade. Religious guilds were formed for the spiritual advancement of members and military guilds provided army reserves in times of need. All four types existed in Dublin and they were first licensed under a charter issued in 1192 by Prince John. Dublin had twenty-five trade guilds including the merchant guild (the first to be formed), at least eleven religious guilds and two military guilds created in the late 15th century to ward off attacks on the Pale. The last guild to be formed was the apothecaries which was created in 1747. The members of the guilds enjoyed many privileges and added much ceremonial colour to the life of the city. From 1691 they had to take the Oath of Supremacy acknowledging the English monarch as head of the Church. This effectively meant that Roman Catholics were excluded from all but a compromise associate membership. They grew in political power but duly became irrelevant in a commercial sense and failed to adapt and welcome the newly enfranchised and liberated Roman Catholics in the 1830s. Their political base was removed by the Municipal Corporation Reform Act of 1840 and another fatal blow was delivered in 1846 when the Dublin Chamber of Commerce obtained an Act of Parliament which finally abolished the guilds. Thankfully one guild did survive and still functions in a most relevant way, the Guild of Goldsmiths.

Left: The Guild of Merchants may be defunct but their hall, built in 1821, still stands as testimony to their position and power. In the 18th century their wealth was displayed when they commissioned the Royal Exchange (now the City Hall) in which to conduct their business (see page 79).

1169: *Anglo-Normans land at Bannow Bay, Co. Wexford.*

1170: *Dublin falls to the Anglo-Normans and Dermot Mac Murrough, King of Leinster.*

1172: *King Henry II visits Dublin to assert his authority.*

1204: *Order issued by King John to build Dublin Castle.*

1215: *Magna Carta proclaimed by King John.*

1229: *First Mayor of Dublin elected.*

1275: *Marco Polo visits Kublai Khan in China.*

1317: *Edward Bruce's Scottish army poised to attack Dublin but decides to abandon the attempt.*

1347: *Black Death Plague kills up to a third of Dublin's population.*

1394: *Richard II visits Dublin with an army to ensure submission of the Irish Lords.*

1415: *Battle of Agincourt; English defeat the French.*

1440: *Gutenburg starts printing with movable metal type.*

1454: *All people of Irish blood banished from within Dublin's walls.*

1492: *Columbus reaches the West Indies.*

1487: *Lambert Simnel, Pretender to English throne, is crowned in Christ Church Cathedral.*

1509: *Accession of King Henry VIII of England.*

1534: *Failed rebellion of Silken Thomas Fitzgerald.*

1537: *Dissolution of Irish monasteries ordered by Henry VIII.*

The Office of the Chief Herald of Ireland has a long history. Armorial bearings or coats-of-arms originated during medieval days as a means of identifying armoured knights on the battlefield and at the tournament. To avoid any danger of duplication heralds were employed to regulate and record the issuance of coats-of-arms. The busy heralds also acted as kings' envoys, counted the fallen in battle, supervised the exchange of prisoners and assisted in the dubbing of new knights. When the military use of heralds became obsolete their expertise was directed to serve a wide range of formal and decorative uses in the civil and political life of Europe. Countries proclaimed their identity using the heraldic medium and this extended to flags, seals, coins, medals and the granting of coats-of-arms to territories, families and institutions.

Heralds have functioned in Ireland since 1382 and the situation was formalised when the post of Ulster King of Arms, Herald of all Ireland (now the oldest office of State in Ireland) was created by Edward VI in 1552 and continued under that name until 1943 when the Office of Arms was transferred to the Government of Ireland and renamed the Genealogical Office. One of the principal functions of the Office is the design, assignment and registration of heraldic property under the authority of the Government. It is open to civic and corporate bodies as well as individuals to petition the officers of arms for a formal assignment or grant of arms. The Office also operates a Museum and Archive, founded in 1909, in its headquarters at 2 Kildare Street. The Museum contains over 500 items including the Arms of Ireland that once hung over the Speaker's Chair in the 18th century Irish House of Commons.

Below: Example of heraldic calligraphy.

On Witness whereof I have hereunto subscribed my Name and Title and affixed the Seal of my Office this 31st day of October, One Thousand Nine Hundred and Seventy-five.

Picture: courtesy of the Office of the Chief Herald

Below: Two coats-of-arms. On the left is that of O'Murphy of Muskerry, Co. Cork: on the right is the coat-of-arms of the Office of the Chief Herald.

Chapter Three
Breaking Free

THE PERIOD immediately following the Norman conquest of Dublin was progressive but extremely volatile. Proper municipal regulation was introduced, the large abbeys around the little town flourished and new building works were undertaken. The defensive walls, towers and gateways were reconstructed, the area of the town was expanded and the River Liffey was further narrowed and deepened to facilitate shipping. The two great cathedrals of Christ Church and St Patrick were erected along with several smaller parish churches. Overlooking all this progress was the glowering strength of the newly built Dublin Castle. Elsewhere in the country the advance of the Normans was less sure. They did manage to initially subdue significant parts of Ireland which they struggled to hold by building immense castles such as those at Trim, Carrickfergus, Limerick and Dunluce. King John was unhappy with the obvious territorial ambitions of his knights and he effectively subjugated them, particularly in relation to Dublin, to the control of the crown.

The next few centuries saw the Norman noble families becoming more and more absorbed into the Irish community and they started to display very ambivalent attitudes towards the English crown and parliament. In the face of this situation and because of the increasing attempts by Irish chieftains to run their own affairs the sphere of English influence was gradually pushed back until, by the mid 15th century, the King's remit only counted in an area around Dublin called the Pale. This was an area following a line partially marked by earthen ramparts and ditches and guarded by a ring of castles which enclosed Dublin and parts of the counties of Meath, Louth and Kildare. Periodic incursions by the Irish or energetic sorties by the English led to fluctuating contractions and expansions of the Pale's borders. Apart from the almost routine dangers posed by local unrest there were occasions of widespread rebellion which threatened to sweep the English off the island altogether. England itself in the 15th and 16th centuries was engaged in its own wars elsewhere and its economy was shaky to say the least, but it always managed in the end to thwart the Irish menace. A succession of brutal campaigns during the Elizabethan period followed by the plantation of British settlers and the dismantling of the Gaelic chieftains' power base brought large parts of Ireland into direct English control.

During these periods of political and military instability Dublin's citizens were loath to abandon the security of their protective walls and castle which more than once warded off concerted attacks. However, by the middle of the 16th century the risks of assault in the Dublin region had become remote and the town at last broke free of centuries of constriction and malaise.

Below: The last example of a Dublin Elizabethan cage-work house. It stood in Castle Street and was demolished in 1813.

Bottom: A 20th century recreation in the Elizabethan style; the premises of Bord Gáis (Gas Board) on Leinster Market off D'Olier Street.

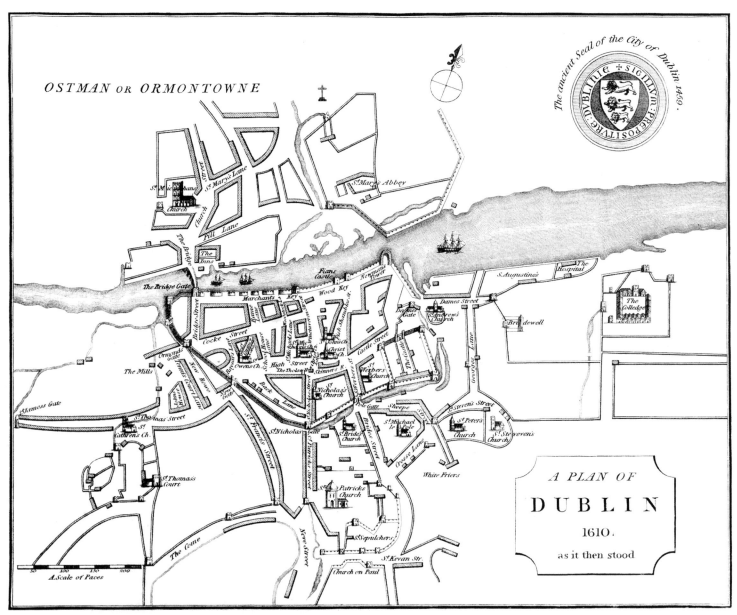

OSTMAN OR ORMONTOWNE

The ancient Seal of the City of Dublin 1459.

A PLAN OF

DUBLIN

1610.

as it then stood

Map: courtesy of the National Library of Ireland.

Above: Drawn by cartographer John Speed in 1610 and engraved in Amsterdam, this is the first known published map of Dublin. It has become an invaluable source of reference in the study of post-medieval Dublin. The city walls are still largely in place although there are some gaps in them along the quays to facilitate the movement of goods. In the more settled political climate suburbs have begun to appear outside the walls although the various outer watch towers and gates yet stand guard. The monasteries have all been closed down since Henry VIII's dissolution decree in 1537 but some of their sites are marked including that of St. Mary's Abbey and the White Friars. Another abbey, All Hallows Priory, has been rebuilt as Trinity College. Only part of Dame Street is laid down so Trinity College is somewhat out on its own.

In 1592 it was considered safe enough to build the new Trinity College which stood nearly 0.8km (half a mile) away from Dublin Castle. Fifty years earlier King Henry VIII had closed the monasteries and a programme of persecution against the "Popish" religion was actively followed by Queen Elizabeth I and her successor James I. In Dublin, Catholics could only practice their faith in secret and at great personal risk. Their religious and civil rights were gradually stripped away by a series of Penal Laws which reached a peak in the early 18th century.

The fabric of the medieval and the newer Elizabethan town was not in good shape by the end of the 1590s. To compound this state of affairs, in 1596 a terrible gunpowder explosion ripped the heart out of the town over a wide expanse around Winetavern Street. One hundred and twenty people were killed and many hundreds more were injured. The walled city was left to pick up the pieces (it could be argued that this devastated area never properly recovered until the 1990s!). Future development moved eastwards and, after a brief hiatus caused by the invasion of Oliver Cromwell in 1649, a new order emerged, under the leadership of the visionary Viceroy, the Duke of Ormond, and the first real flowering of a well planned city unfolded.

There had long been a need for a properly constituted university in Dublin. Earlier attempts had failed due to financial constraints or political opposition. In 1591 Archbishop Adam Loftus persuaded Dublin Corporation to grant the site of the dissolved Augustinian Priory of All Hallows together with an additional 9 ha (22 acres) to the new University of Dublin. Queen Elizabeth I granted the institution a charter in 1592. Its location was described as being "near Dublin" and it was washed (and sometimes flooded) on two sides by the estuary of the River Liffey. While it inherited the traditions of Oxford and Cambridge, Trinity College (founded as the "College of the Holy and Undivided Trinity") remains the sole constituent college belonging to the University of Dublin. It continues to maintain long established affiliations with St. John's in Cambridge and Oriel College in Oxford. Nothing now remains of the Elizabethan college which was swept away by the energetic building programmes of the 18th century. Each subsequent century brought a fresh expansion and today is no different. A generation after the college first opened only 200 students were enrolled. Now there are in excess of 13,000 full time undergraduates and 2,500 post graduates. Pressure on space is enormous and while on-campus opportunities are being fully exploited it has been necessary to acquire locations further afield but still in the neighbouring vicinity (see further entries in chapter 16). There is now a greater emphasis on developing Research and Development at the post-graduate level in association with industry as this is seen as vital to underpin Ireland's future relevance in the global economy. Trinity College will continue to preserve its rich heritage and traditions and at the same time grow, as it always has done, to meet contemporary challenges.

Above: The façade (West Front) of Trinity College stands amid the hustle and rush of busy city streets guarding a quieter world of scholastic endeavours within.

Above: Trinity College's campanile (1852, designed by Charles Lanyon) occupies the location where the medieval monastery of All Hallows had its bell tower.

1	2	3
7		
6	5	4

Trinity College is custodian to a legacy in art and architecture second to none in Ireland. Only a handful of examples are represented on this page.

1 | The elaborately crafted Irish Harp was presented to the College in the 18th century. Although legend ascribes it to King Brian Boru, who was slain at the Battle of Clontarf in 1014, it is generally believed to be between 500 and 600 years old. The official emblem of Ireland was copied from this harp (it appears, for instance, on the country's coinage).

2 | The Long Room in the Old Library is a direct descendant of Trinity's first library. The building was designed by Thomas Burgh and was formally opened in 1732. The Long Room contains over 200,000 volumes dating from the 16th century as well as ancient Greek and Latin manuscripts, Egyptian papyri and even a first folio of Shakespeare. Its greatest treasure is its collection of Irish early medieval manuscripts.

3 | The College Chapel, by William Chambers, was built between 1788 and 1798. It contains wonderful plasterwork by Michael Stapleton.

4 | The Rubrics, built about 1700, is Trinity's oldest surviving building.

5 | Deane and Woodward designed the Museum building which dates from the 1850s.

6 | Oliver Goldsmith was one of a long line of distinguished graduates. The statue, along with that of fellow graduate Edmund Burke, flanks the main entrance and is by John Henry Foley.

7 | The single greatest jewel in the possession of Trinity College must be the incomparable Book of Kells. Considered to be the most beautiful illustrated manuscript in the world, its 680 pages of vellum contain the Latin texts of the Four Gospels. It was written c 800AD in a monastery, probably either Iona or Kells. In any case it eventually ended up in Kells and from there it was deposited for safe keeping in Trinity around 1653.

Above: This aerial view of Trinity College (located in the centre of the photograph) captures the compactness of its campus situated right in the heart of Dublin, a fact that seems to preserve a unique sense of community among the students and teachers. The newer buildings, including libraries and science blocks, are situated to the south, (left hand side of the picture) and to the east of College Park and the Rugby Ground.

Below left: The Berkeley Library was designed by Paul Koralek and opened in 1967. Philosopher and historian, Bishop George Berkeley (1685-1753) was both a student and a teacher at Trinity. Berkeley Campus of the University of California is named after him. On the podium in front of the Library is a bronze sculpture entitled Sfera con Sfera (Sphere with Sphere) by Amaldo Pomodoro (1983).

Above: Exterior view of the Provost's House.

Above: The saloon in the Provost's House. Francis Andrews was a provost of great determination with influential political connections. He convinced the college authorities to provide a house worthy of the Provost's standing and £11,000 was spent in the 1760s in building, not the largest, but the city's most splendid 18th century residence. It is the only mansion built during the Georgian period in the city that's still being used for its original purpose. The stunning interior is a showpiece of Irish craftsmanship in masonry, plaster, wood and wrought iron and today is hardly changed from when it was first completed.

Left: The O'Reilly Institute for Communications and Technology, designed by Scott Tallon Walker and opened in 1989.

Above: Sir Henry Sidney, an able and energetic Lord Deputy of Ireland during Elizabeth I's reign, is shown in John Derricke's "Images of Ireland" (1581) setting out from Dublin Castle on a military campaign to quell truculent Irish chieftains. Note the grisly custom of displaying the severed heads of rebels over the castle gate. Derricke wrote: "These trunkles heddes do playnly showe each rebelles fatll end. And what a haynous crime it is the Queen for to offend".

Above: Coins as a means of exchange for goods were introduced into Dublin by the Vikings in the 11th century. The main unit of exchange for the Celts had been the cow, around which their barter system worked. Reading clockwise from the top the coins above are; Hiberno-Norse c 1035 (the top two coins), King John penny (1204), one shilling (1690), one shilling (1605).

O Sydney worthy of tryple re-
nowne,
For plaÿng the traytours that
troubled the crowne. 1581.

Above: The triumphant return of Sir Henry Sidney after his successful campaign. He is being greeted by the Council of State.

Left: Tailors' Hall, Back Lane was built in 1706 for the Guild of Tailors (see page 29) but the building was also hired out to other guilds and organisations. In 1792 the Catholic Committee passed through the gate (below) to discuss petitioning the Dublin Parliament to relax the Penal Laws. Their gatherings gave the place the sobriquet "The Back Lane Parliament". Revolutionaries planning the 1798 rising also gathered within its walls as did such diverse societies as the Freemasons and the Legion of Mary. Facing an uncertain future, Tailors' Hall in 1983 found gracious and caring new tenants in the form of An Taisce, The National Trust for Ireland. An Taisce have painstakingly restored the building and it now serves as their headquarters. Dublin Corporation are the owners of the building.

Left: Ormond Quay today. Note that the Presbyterian Church, as seen in the drawing below, has been modernised above ground level.

Left: An 1850 view of Ormond Quay, first laid down in 1662. It was named after James Butler, 1st Duke of Ormond, one of Dublin's most popular Viceroys. Ormond was instrumental in building the Royal Hospital, in laying out the Phoenix Park and in planning the quays. He displayed great vision when he insisted that the developer of the quays on the north side of the Liffey, Sir Humphrey Jervis, should face the houses to the river and not present their rear view as was more usual in 17th century cities.

Above: Chesterfield Avenue, Phoenix Park.

Above: The foundation stone of the Wellington Testimonial, designed by Robert Smirke, was laid in 1817, two years after the Dublin-born Duke of Wellington crushed Napoleon at the Battle of Waterloo. At 62.5 m (205 ft) it is the second highest obelisk in the world, being exceeded only by the Washington Monument.

One of the most unique and precious emeralds in Dublin's treasury is the Phoenix Park, larger than all the London parks combined and possibly the biggest urban park in Europe. A few short years after the Anglo-Normans assumed mastery of Dublin and its hinterland Hugh Tyrell, 1st Baron of Castleknock, granted a large swathe of land, including what now comprises the Phoenix Park, to the Knights of St John of Jerusalem. They established their great abbey at Kilmainham on the site now occupied by the Royal Hospital. The knights lost Kilmainham when King Henry VIII confiscated monastic properties in 1537 and eighty years later the lands passed to the ownership of the king's representatives in Ireland. On the restoration of King Charles II, his Viceroy in Dublin, James Butler, Duke of Ormond, turned the lands into a Royal Deer Park. He introduced a herd of fallow deer, a thousand pheasants and some partridge to provide hunting sport for the king and his retinue. In 1680 a boundary wall encircling the park's present 709 ha (1,752 acres) was constructed. The Phoenix Park remained the exclusive reserve of the British Royalty and its Irish court until the Viceroy, Lord Chesterfield, threw open the demesne to the public in 1745.

Huge improvements were carried out to the park during the 1830s and 40s under the very talented landscape architect, Decimus Burton. In 1860 it was placed under the care of the Commissioners of Public Works. Throughout the 18th and 19th centuries several magnificent mansions, lodges, institutions and memorials were erected in different corners of the park including, in 1831, the Royal Zoological Gardens, one of the oldest zoos in the world. In 1986 a major management plan was implemented and since most of its aspirations were fulfilled by 2000 a second strategic plan has been inaugurated under the direction of Dúchas The National Heritage Service, the current body responsible for the park. The new plan is designed to guarantee the Victorian integrity of the Phoenix Park and to enhance the natural and built legacies of a very remarkable place so important to the history and environment of Dublin.

Above: A bas-relief on the pedestal of the Wellington Testimonial depicts a battle scene from the duke's Indian Campaign. The Battle of Waterloo is featured on the opposite side of the pedestal. The reliefs were cast in bronze from captured enemy cannon.

Above: When the Papal Nuncio moved in 1978 from his house (formerly the Under Secretary's Lodge) in the Phoenix Park the structure was found to be irreparable due to dry rot. It was subsequently demolished whereupon the park authorities were astonished to find a small tower standing inside the rubble. It had obviously been incorporated in the old lodge and forgotten about. Dating from at least the 16th century it has been beautifully restored and Ashtown Castle now forms part of the excellent Phoenix Park Visitor Centre.

Above: Áras an Uachtaráin

Above: The 9.1m (30ft) tall Phoenix Monument was erected by Philip Dormer Stanhope, 4th Earl of Chesterfield and Lord Lieutenant in 1745. This energetic and humanitarian Viceroy undertook a major restoration of the Park and was responsible for planning the long main avenue which today bears his name.

From 1668 the Phoenix Park Ranger lived in Newtown House, the location for the future Áras an Uachtaráin (Residence of the President). The present house, or at least the centre portion of it, was built in 1751 after Newtown House was demolished. The Park Ranger lost his stylish accommodation when the Government bought the house in 1782 and attempted to bribe the obstinate Henry Grattan, leader of the opposition in the Irish Parliament, by offering the house to him. He refused the overture and so five years later it was decided to convert the house into the new Viceregal Lodge, a summer residence for the Lord Lieutenant. It was lavishly enhanced and greatly extended, work that included the addition of the north Doric portico and a south Ionic portico complete with massive columns. Further wings were added in 1848 and 1911. George IV, Queen Victoria, Edward VII and George V all stayed here at one time or another. The gardens were landscaped by Decimus Burton, famous for his work in London's Hyde Park, Kew Gardens and Regent's Park. Ninian Niven, who was curator of the Royal Dublin Society's Botanic Gardens from 1834 and also designed the Iveagh Gardens in 1863, redesigned the formal gardens of the Viceregal Lodge. With the establishment of the Free State in 1922 the lodge became the residence of the Governor General and since 1938 the President of Ireland has lived there. In the intervening years many additional improvements have been carried out to the house including the erection of decorated plasterwork ceilings rescued from houses demolished in the 1960s.

Above: One of the many park lodges designed by Decimus Burton in the picturesque cottage orné style.

Above: All of the park's ornamental lamps are still lit by (natural) gas.

Below: A section of the lovely iron gates at the North Circular Road entrance which were restored in 1999.

Above: Map of the Phoenix Park.

Below: The famous herd of fallow deer number around 500 today. Their ancestors were first introduced to the park in 1662. They are highly social animals and will be seen in large groups mainly, but not exclusively, around the Fifteen Acres. They are cared for by park rangers in conjunction with the Department of Zoology, University College, Dublin.

"Behold the proof of Irish sense, here Irish wit is seen:
When nothing's left that's worth defence, we build a magazine"

These words by Jonathan Swift greeted the building of the Magazine Fort (above), a munitions storage compound, in 1734. It stands on St. Thomas's Hill, the site originally of Phoenix House, a residence which gave its name to the whole park. The name Phoenix is a corruption of Fionn Uisce, the Gaelic words for clear water, which is a reference to a well once located near Áras an Uachtaráin. No munitions were stored in the Magazine Fort subsequent to 1939 and it is now hoped to turn it into a military museum.

Above: The Papal Cross was erected as the centre point for the concelebrated Mass offered on the occasion of the visit of Pope John Paul II to the Phoenix Park in 1979. Over 1.25 million people attended the ceremony.

Above: A polo game in the Polo-Grounds of the Phoenix Park. The game was introduced into Ireland during the 19th century by officers serving in the British Army who first saw the game being played in the North West and North East Frontiers of India.

Above left: The Victorian Bandstand which is still very much in use during summer weekends. It is located in a picturesque depression known as "The Hollow".

Above right: The People's Gardens are a 8.9 ha (22 acre) enclosed park within a park that are landscaped in the style of Victorian ornamental horticulture.

Above: A princely peacock struts around the zoo as if he was the centre of attraction.

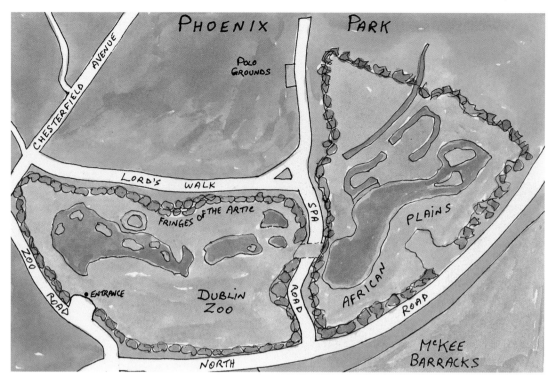

Above: A map showing, on the left of Spa road, the former area of the Zoo before the enlargement in 1999 and, on the right, the new "African Plains".

Above: A polar bear frolicking in his pool in "The Fringes of the Arctic", that part of the zoo dedicated to animals who normally inhabit regions near or in the Arctic. Polar Bears, who live along the shores and open icefields of the Arctic Ocean, are extremely dangerous creatures and will even attack small boats without provocation.

Dublin Zoo was opened to the public on 1st September 1831 and on show was a very small group of animals consisting of a few deer, a couple of emu, a pair of ostriches, a hunting panther, a bear, a wild boar (the first resident), a single fox, a racoon and an assortment of exotic birds. There were very few specialised buildings at first but at least the 2.2 ha (5 and a half acres) of undulating ground bordered by 1.6 ha (4 acres) of water, landscaped by Decimus Burton, offered an exceptional setting. The original landscape designs are still more or less in place as are several of the stylish Victorian animal houses but beyond that there is little similarity between the zoo today and times past. No longer are animals kept in cages too small for their needs nor are they trained to perform antics solely for the amusement of visitors. Zoos are now serious places for research and breeding and animal welfare supersedes all other considerations. A subvention of £15 million and a grant of land from the Irish Government have allowed radical changes to be made at Dublin Zoo. The addition of 12 ha (30 acres) taken from the lake area of Áras an Uachtaráin in 1999 has effectively doubled the size of the zoo. This new enclosure has become the "African Plains" and accommodates the larger animals such as the rhinoceros, giraffe and hippopotamus. Not only have these animals a more natural habitat but their personal enclosure space been greatly increased. The rhino enclosure, for example, has expanded by a factor of 32. The creation of the "African Plains" allowed extra room to be set aside for those animals staying in the older part of the zoo and for those a number of redesigned areas were laid out including the "World of Primates", "The Fringes of the Arctic" and "The World of Cats".

Above: An early landmark, the thatched gate lodge, dates from 1832.

Throughout the world traditional habitats are being destroyed daily and so Dublin Zoo has become increasingly involved in the protection of endangered species. It has implemented co-operative projects with other zoos, wildlife groups, the Smithsonian Institute and the European Breeding Programme. The Rodrigues Fruit Bat was facing extinction but successful breeding will now allow a large contingent to be released again into the wild. Other endangered species such as the Celebes Macaque, the Ground Hornbill, the Banded Mongoose, the Forest Antelope and an endearing little monkey, the Golden Lion Tamarin, are being given the same scientific and loving attention with a view to their reintroduction into their natural environment. The zoo, under the auspices of the Zoological Society of Ireland, is no longer just a wonderful and educational place to visit but performs an invaluable service in the protection of our natural heritage.

Above: The Irish Museum of Modern Art, Royal Hospital, Kilmainham.

The Irish Museum of Modern Art (IMMA) is based in the former Royal Hospital, Kilmainham which was built between 1680-84 as a retirement home for veteran soldiers. It was the world's second oldest such institution after Les Invalides in Paris upon which the layout of the Royal Hospital was based. While the architect was Sir William Robinson the inspiration for the design came from James Butler, Duke of Ormond and Viceroy in Ireland for Charles II. Butler had seen Les Invalides and was moved to provide something similar in Dublin. His legacy is Dublin's finest 17th century building although it nearly fell into ruin some years after the final old soldier left in 1928. In the late 1970s the Government decided to reverse the decline. Restoration of the Hospital was carried out with great integrity and with over 300 rooms involved, from the Great Hall to the humblest dormitory, the task was singularly difficult. Fortunately Robinson's plans and all subsequent records were still extant and during work on the Great Hall itself the original oak floor and panelling were uncovered. Innovative work to conceal modern facilities was carried out and included concealing the ultra modern kitchen in the basements, the heating under the floor and the lifts in the chimney shafts. The huge restoration task took from 1980 to 1984 and cost £20 million (construction 300 years earlier had cost £24,000). In recognition of the achievement and its "distinguished contribution to the conservation of Europe's architectural heritage", the Royal Hospital was awarded the prestigious Europa Nostra award for 1985. The building is especially important as it was Ireland's first classical building and marked the real beginning of Dublin's architectural development. The IMMA has built up its own collection of modern works of art and also organises regular visiting exhibitions across the several galleries available for the purpose. Valuable additional space to the amount of 3,048sq m (10,000sq ft) was gained in November 1999 with the renovation of the former mid 18th century Deputy Master's House which is situated at the north-east corner of the restored formal garden.

Above: The West Gate entrance to the Royal Hospital, known as the Richmond Tower and designed by Francis Johnston (1760-1829), originally stood at the Watling Street junction with Victoria Quay. When Kingsbridge (Heuston) Railway Station was opened in 1844, traffic along the quays increased to the extent that the gateway became a traffic obstruction. It was removed to its present site and re-erected in 1846.

Photo: courtesy of The Irish Museum of Modern Art.

Above: A general view of the Chapel, Royal Hospital, Kilmainham.

Photo: courtesy of The Irish Museum of Modern Art.

Above: The Great Hall of the Royal Hospital where the former residents dined and relaxed.

1st October 1741.   **Dublin News Letter**   Issue No. 23546.

Deserted in September 1741, from the Right Hon. The Lord Viscount Molesworth's Regiment of Dragoons and Captain Allen Johnston's Troop JOSEPH MARSHALL five feet ten inches and a quarter high without shoes, 23 Years of Age, by Trade a Weaver, thin faced, with a Mark on the Top of his Forehead of a Cut joining the Hair, which is brown. He went off in a brown Wigg, and brown Clothes, full and well limb'd, having a Scotch Accent in his Speech, and is suppos'd to be born in the County of Cavan, where it is thought he skulks. Whoever seizes him and gets him lodged either in Cavan or Enniskillen Gaol, giving Notice thereof to the Commanding Officer at Ballyshannon, he shall have Twenty Shillings Reward, to be paid by the said Capt. Allen Johnston, besides the King's Allowance of Forty Shillings.

Photo: courtesy of The Irish Museum of Modern Arts.

Above: View of an installation by Juan Munoz entitled Conversation Piece (1994) in the courtyard of the Irish Museum of Modern Art, Royal Hospital.

Photo: courtesy of The Irish Museum of Modern Arts.

Above: Detail of a stained glass window composed of the coats-of-arms of various masters of the Royal Hospital.

Chapter Four
Georgian Inspirations

FROM THE first confident steps taken by a new breed of property speculators in the 1660s, under the guidance of the Viceroy, the Duke of Ormond, the form of the present-day centre of Dublin began to emerge. The River Liffey was further tamed and deepened by the building of stone quays, St. Stephen's Green was laid out by Dublin Corporation and many new neighbourhoods took shape. Public cultural life was attended to by the opening in 1662 of the Smock Alley Theatre on the site where the Viking Adventure on Essex Street West now stands. Developers such as Aston, Hawkins, Jervis, Amory, Aungier and Ellis left their mark with, and often their name on, their networks of new streets. The city grew from a population of around 10,000 in the 1640s to almost 60,000 by 1682. This was a process that would accelerate in the next century. Dublin developed fairly equally on both sides of the river necessitating the building of additional bridges. In the absence of a permanent crossing, ferries usually filled the gap and the site of a new bridge often coincided with the direct line previously taken by the ferries, much to the vexation of their operators. When a wooden span was opened in 1670, connecting present-day Ellis Street to Watling Street, it occasioned a riot instigated by ferrymen in which four young lads were killed. The bridge thereafter became known as Bloody Bridge. The first major public building to be erected since the two great cathedrals was the Royal Hospital at Kilmainham. Work commenced in 1680 and the first retired soldiers moved in four years later. Soldiers of a more active vintage were billeted in the huge new Royal Barracks from 1704, a sign that England intended to constantly remind Ireland of who was in charge.

In the 1720s the city was poised for the rapid expansion that would soon take place. Known as the Georgian Period (after the line of Georges on the English throne) or as the Age of Enlightenment, the rest of the 18th century saw a succession of inspired developers, gifted architects and an increasingly independent Irish Parliament push Dublin to the very forefront of stately European capitals. A new wave of property developers such as the Gardiners, the Dominicks, the Fitzwilliams and the Pembrokes reclaimed eastern Dublin from the estuary of the River Liffey and planned the impressive Georgian squares and boulevards. They found ready occupants for their terraces and great houses and the richer nobles commissioned their own palatial mansions that for the most part still adorn the city. Great institutions such as the Royal Irish Academy (1785) and the Dublin Society (1731) were founded and growing concern for the disadvantaged led to the opening of many hospitals and charitable centres. External communications were enhanced with the opening of the canals, the inauguration of mail-coaches and the improvements to Dublin Port. The only fly in the Protestant Ascendancy ointment was the burgeoning Roman Catholic population and the increasing misery of their underprivileged condition.

Above: Jonathan Swift (1667 - 1745), in his long lifetime, saw the transition of Dublin from being a small post-medieval town to a city of mansions, grand Georgian terraces and notable institutions. He became Dean of St Patrick's Cathedral in 1713 and spent much of his later years helping the many distressed poor in the locality. He bequeathed his modest fortune to the founding of St Patrick's Psychiatric Hospital which still operates as such today. Dean Swift is probably best remembered as the author of "Gulliver's Travels".

Above: Marsh's Library on St. Patrick's Close was founded by Archbishop Narcissus Marsh in 1701. Now the oldest public library in Ireland, it contains over 25,000 volumes, some dating from the 15th century, and subjects range from liturgical works and classical literature to science and exploration.

Right: The interior of Marsh's Library has changed little since the 18th century and the cages, where readers were locked in to safeguard rare books, are still in place. The library was restored in 1986 by the American Irish Foundation and since then the Delmas Bindery has been added thanks to a philanthropic donation.

Below: St. Mary's Church (1702), designed by Sir William Robinson, resulted from the sub-division of the old parish of St. Michan in 1698. The Earl of Charlemont and Wolfe Tone were baptised here. It closed as a parish church in the 1970s and was converted in 2000 for use as a public house.

Parliament did begin to introduce a programme of relief acts but these efforts were overtaken by the cruelties and misery emanating from the aftermath of the 1798 Rebellion and the Parliament's own abolition in 1800. Bribery, corruption and just plain indifference all played an ignoble part when the Irish members of Parliament voted in favour of the Act of Union with Britain. Dublin, whose population had now grown to well over 150,000, found itself without a central focus although the construction, commercial and cultural momentum already in motion obviously did not come to an abrupt halt. In time Dublin adjusted to its reduced status but the refinements of its Georgian hey-day were gone forever. Thankfully, however, much of the built legacy from the period still remains.

---

20 -23 January   **Freeman's Journal**   Issue No. 2687

Corporation House, 19th January, 1787

The Paving Board finding with concern that the remitting of Fines for not scraping, sweeping and cleaning the footways, on the oath of one witness, has been, as they fear, in many instances productive of perjury, think it necessary to apprize all persons concerned, that henceforward they will remit no Fines for not sweeping of footways, unless the fact be attested by two credible witnesses. By the Act the front of all houses, &c. must be swept, from the 1st September to the 1st May before ten o'clock, and in the other months before 8 o'clock in the morning.

Signed by order,

The eminent Dr Steevens stipulated in his will (he died in 1710) that his twin sister, Grizel, was to benefit from his wealth in her lifetime but upon her demise it was to be used to build a hospital "for maintaining and curing such sick and wounded persons whose Distempers and Wounds are curable". In a city that had lamentably few medical facilities Grizel lost no time in fulfilling her brother's wishes. By 1733 the first patients, eight men and two women, were admitted to the new hospital which was built outside the city limits to distance it from the sources of rampant plagues and diseases, It was designed free of charge by one of its trustees, Thomas Burgh, who was Surveyor-general of his Majesty's Fortifications in Ireland. The building has a layout and an arcaded courtyard much like that of the Royal Hospital in Kilmainham. From a humble start of 40 beds and a medical staff consisting of a matron and four nurses (the latter earning £1 a month) the hospital went on to distinguish itself in fields such as nurse training, anaesthetics, X-ray technology, burns treatment and plastic surgery. However, following the rationalisation of hospital coverage in the city, Dr Steevens', was finally closed in December 1987.

In July 1988 the Eastern Health Board purchased the hospital on the open market for £800,000 and then spent a further £4.2 million on refurbishment. Architects Arthur Gibney & Associates and main contractor John Paul Construction cleared away the old Nurse's Home and opened a new main entrance on the north-facing façade, replicating the original stone-surrounded doorway on the east side. The former wards lent themselves easily for conversion into offices totalling 9290sq m (100,000sq ft). The old operating theatre was re-fashioned into a boardroom. The wonderful rococo-styled plastered ceiling hanging over the new entrance vestibule came from the now-demolished Newtown House in Rathcoole. Dating from the 1740s, it was re-hung by Tommy Lydon. The former hospital's historic links with the medical profession were then assured when it became the headquarters for 400 Eastern Health Board staff. The Board's many community services and the Health Research Department are also co-ordinated from here. In March 2000, the Eastern Health Board was re-organised into three separate regions to respond to the growing population of Dublin. Dr Steeven's is now the Eastern Regional Health Authority's Shared Service Centre.

Above: The photograph shows the impressive north façade of Dr. Steevens', where a new main entrance, in the style of the north-facing original, was inserted under the existing pediment.

Below: A view down Steevens Lane showing, on the right, the rather grim 19th century Nurse's Home which was demolished to open up the aspect to the north and now main façade of Dr Steevens' Hospital.

Above: The arcaded courtyard of Dr Steevens' Hospital echoes that of the Royal Hospital in Kilmainham from where the inspiration for this design is drawn. The bell in the old clock tower used to be rung when consultants entered the hospital.

Above: Sir Patrick Dun's Hospital, Grand Canal Street, was opened in 1808 following the bequest of its namesake, a Scottish doctor based in Dublin. Closed as a hospital in 1986 it was lavishly restored by Professor Austin Darragh for his drug research company, the Institute of Clinical Pharmacology. It was then bought by the Eastern Health Board and the building now houses the Public Analyst Laboratory, a home for older persons and the Registry Office for Civil Marriages.

Above: Grizel Steevens by Michael Mitchell.

Above: The Worth Library at Dr Steevens' dates from 1742 and was donated by physician Edward Worth. It contains many rare classical, scientific and medical volumes including 21 books printed before 1500.

Photo: courtesy of The Irish Architectural Archive.

Above: The once fine Henrietta Street may be looking sad and dilapidated now but the example set at number 13 (built c. 1740) may indeed be a catalyst for the renewal of the remarkable street. Typically, this house became a tenement accommodating eleven families comprising thirty-seven people. In the mid 1970s the house was purchased by Michael Casey and his wife Aileen and since then they and their children have discovered the hidden grandeur and beauty of the former mansion. Funded from his own modest resources, Michael and his family singlehandedly began to painstakingly and authentically restore the interior decoration and fittings. The Irish Georgian Society generously funded the re-instatement of the magnificent staircase. This is a work in progress that will take several more years. Michael Casey has already revealed the social organisation of the house from the public reception rooms and the entertainment suites to the inner sanctum of the state bedroom and the cabinet (a small private room). Despite its potential splendour it is above all a family home that is being transformed into one of Ireland's great treasures.

Far left: Henrietta Street (named after Henrietta, Duchess of Grafton and the wife of the Viceroy), laid out by Luke Gardiner between the 1720s and 1740s, was the finest Georgian Street on Dublin's northside and remained the city's most fashionable address until the Act of Union in 1800. Each of the massive houses was individually designed by notable architects such as Sir Edward Lovett Pearce and Richard Cassels. The Primate of Ireland's mansion was demolished in 1827 to make way for the King's Inns Library designed by Frederick Darley. The King's Inns itself closes off the end of the street. Bishops, earls, judges and Members of Parliament made up the distinguished list of residents. Luke Gardiner lived in Number 10. When built, the street was the broadest in Dublin, part of a carefully designed plan to allow sunshine to fall on the south-facing terrace. Alas, after 1800 many of the houses were converted into tenements and features such as grand staircases and splendidly carved fireplaces were removed.

Left: The Casey Family outside No. 13 Henrietta Street. From left to right: James, Aileen, Sarah, Michael, Edward, William, Patrick and Christina.

49

Above: Known as Mornington House No 24 Upper Merrion Street was the birthplace of Arthur Wellesley, the 1st Duke of Wellington and the victor over Napoleon at the Battle of Waterloo. Mornington House and the rest of this impressive block, all listed for preservation, were fastidiously converted in 1996 into the luxury 5-star Merrion Hotel.

Top right: An example of a grand Georgian House on St. Stephen's Green showing off its blanket of autumn-hued Virginia Creeper.

Bottom left: A view down Fitzwilliam Place continuing into Fitzwilliam Street. Apart from the intrusion of a dismal 1960s office block, this almost 1 km (0.6 mile) long boulevard offers the longest straight stretch of unbroken Georgian streetscape in the city. Fitzwilliam Street was laid out in 1792 and Fitzwilliam Place in 1807 by the Fitzwilliam family, one of the prominent developers of the southside.

Bottom right: A quiet Sunday aspect up Mount Street Upper. The church at the street's end is St. Stephen's, designed by John Bowden and consecrated in 1824. Its cupola-topped tower inspired the church's popular name "The Pepper Canister".

Photo: courtesy of Dublin Tourism

1	3
	4
2	5

Some distinguishing features of typical Georgian houses are:

1| Doorways - they provided an opportunity for individualism in an otherwise fairly rigid exterior treatment. This distinctiveness was expressed through fanlights, pillars, door panels, side windows and architectural surrounds.

2| Interior decoration was not constrained in any way and major stuccodores, several of whom were from Italy, found generous patrons among the aristocracy of Dublin. This example is from the Writers' Museum on Parnell Square.

3| One of the many decorative door knockers.

4| Intricately shaped wrought-iron foot scrapers, a necessary furnishing in the days of horse transport and filthy pavements.

5| Coal cellar covers, a surviving feature of Dublin's Georgian pavements, usually displayed the iron foundry of their origins.

51

Above and right: No. 85 and 86 St Stephen's Green, collectively known as Newman House, are among the finest Georgian houses in Dublin. Each house contains spectacular stucco interiors. No. 85, formerly known as Clanwilliam House (designed by Richard Cassels in 1738), contains some of the finest plasterwork of the Francini Brothers while No. 86 (in the centre of the drawing) boasts the work of stuccodore Robert West. The newly formed Catholic University commenced lectures here in 1854 under its first rector John Henry (later Cardinal) Newman. The buildings, now in the ownership of University College Dublin, were restored to their original Georgian splendour in the early 1990s through the financial aid of Bórd Fáilte and Gallagher (Dublin) Ltd. Newman House is also the administrative and teaching base for the Keough-Notre-Dame Study Centre, a co-operative student exchange arrangement between the University of Notre-Dame in the USA and Trinity College Dublin and University College Dublin.

Right: Powerscourt House, designed for Richard Wingfield (1730-1788), the 3rd Viscount Powerscourt, by Robert Mack, was completed on William Street South in 1774. It boasts a great staircase by James McCullagh and fine plasterwork by Michael Stapleton. The left-hand side entrance led to the kitchens while the one on the right opened into the stables. Since the late 1970s Powerscourt House has been tastefully absorbed into the Powerscourt Townhouse Centre, an upmarket shopping centre, (see page 139).

Above: The Casino, Marino

The Casino, in Dublin's northside suburb of Marino, is considered to be the finest example in Europe of neo-classical architecture in miniature. Inspired by his Grand Tour of Italy James Caulfeild, 1st Earl of Charlemont, one of the most enlightened and cultivated men of 18th century Ireland, set about designing his estate in the Italian style. He enjoyed a panoramic view of Dublin Bay and so named his estate Marino. His chief ornament on the demesne was his exquisite Casino, a triumph of his classical tastes. Actual work commenced on the building c.1760 and it took nearly twenty years to complete at a cost then of £20,000. The architect was the renowned London-based Sir William Chambers and the construction was supervised by sculptor, Simon Vierpyle. The Casino was placed on the highest point of the Charlemont property so that the good earl could take in the best views of the sea, the distant mountains and his rolling 202 ha (500 acre) estate. The earl's grandnephew sold the estate, including the Casino, to the Irish Christian Brothers in 1881. By 1930, when it was declared a National Monument, the Casino was in some decay. Essential works were then carried out but a comprehensive restoration, undertaken by the Office of Public Works, had to wait until 1974. Painstaking work over the next ten years has restored the masterpiece to its original glory.

Based on the plan of a Greek cross each façade is of a slightly different style. The size of the building is deceptive; it appears at a distance to be a single storey structure where in fact it is a two storey building over a basement and contains no less than 16 rooms. The external decorations, carved from Portland stone, set a new standard for such work in Ireland. Internally, the four ground floor rooms and the State Room display a supreme artistry in plasterwork and inlaid floors that rival anything found elsewhere. The small spaces are cleverly arranged, sometimes with concealed doorways. Lions, urns, a frieze of ox-sculptures and shields and four gods, Bacchus, Ceres, Apollo and Venus, were sculpted by Vierpyle, Joseph Wilton and Giovanni Battista Cipriani. To maintain and preserve the visual integrity of the building several clever innovations were employed. The down-pipes from the gutters travel inside four outer columns. In the basement the pipes can be checked for any blockages by opening curved wooden doors in the columns. The urns at roof level are disguised chimneys and bedroom windows are concealed behind balustrades. The lower step at each flight is channelled to drain away water, helping to keep the approach to the Casino dry. The service areas, including the large kitchen, are located in the basement. A central heating system served by the fireplaces was built into the walls.

Photo: courtsey of Dúchas The Heritage Service . Photographer: Con Brogan.

Photo: courtsey of Dúchas The Heritage Service . Photographer: Con Brogan.

Top: The Saloon, with its intricate parquet floor and coffered ceilings.

Above: The Casino's State Room where Lord Charlemont formally received visitors.

53

Right: Following its medieval tradition, Dublin, in the early 18th century, grew to be a very congested city of dense housing and narrow streets. Architect George Semple designed and built a new and wider Essex Bridge across the River Liffey in 1755. His proposals for opening an additional street leading directly from the bridge to Dublin Castle led to the formation in 1758 of Dublin's first statutory planning body, the Commissioners for Making Wide and Convenient Streets. The Commissioners were empowered to buy property by compulsion and this they did with some gusto when they sliced through blocks of houses to open up Parliament Street in 1762. The Wide Streets Commission, as the planning body became popularly known, went on to lay down or influence the creation of broad streets, avenues and squares that are now so much part of the legacy of Georgian and Victorian Dublin. The Commission was disbanded in 1851 when Dublin Corporation took over its functions.

Middle right: The current Essex Bridge was opened in 1875 and is now named Grattan Bridge in honour of Henry Grattan (1746 - 1820), patriot and member of the Irish Parliament who voted against the Act of Union in 1800. This latest bridge, designed by Bindon B. Stoney, was actually built on Semple's foundations. The new carriageway was then made the full width of the old bridge and the footpaths were cantilevered out on girderwork from the masonry wall.

Above: A view to Westmoreland Street as widened by the Wide Streets Commission in 1801. Carlisle Bridge (now O'Connell Bridge) was not widened to its present expanse until 1880.

Above: The King's Inns was architect James Gandon's last great public building in Dublin. Standing with Henrietta Street to its rear and Constitution Hill to its elegant front it was built between 1795 and 1827. It has recently been extensively restored by the Benchers of the Honorable Society of King's Inns (the governing body for barristers in Ireland). The dining room in the King's Inns now contains the only Gandon interior (apart from some rooms inside the east portico of the Bank of Ireland building) to survive intact in a major public building. All the others have been burnt or bombed during the wars of the early 20th century or have since been radically altered.

Left: The main façade of the Rotunda Maternity Hospital on Parnell Square South has changed little since it was opened in 1757. However the hospital has expanded hugely since then with new buildings gradually filling the space occupied by the Pleasure Gardens. The latest, now the main wing, was added to the west side in the 1990s.

Poor women, living in appalling circumstances in 18th century Dublin, ran a high risk of losing not only their infants but also their own lives in childbirth. Dr. Bartholomew Mosse, a barber-surgeon who also practised the disdained profession of mid-wifery, was moved to do something about their plight. He set up, in 1745, a small Hospital for Poor Lying-In Women in George's Lane which became "the first and only public one of its kind in his Majesty's Dominions" if not in the world. Another first was performed in the Musick Hall in Fishamble Street in aid of the hospital. The Musick Hall, where Handel had earlier conducted his first public performance of the "Messiah" in 1742, again resounded to the British Isles' premier of Handel's oratorio "Judas Maccabaeus" (this time without the personal appearance of the composer). Mosse realised that he needed bigger premises for his hospital and so 1.6 ha (4 acres) of land were bought on the north side of the Liffey. His architect, Richard Cassels, supplied drawings based on a modified design of Leinster House. The foundation stone was laid in 1752 and it received its first patients in 1757. To fund his venture Mosse opened pleasure gardens behind the hospital which became a very fashionable resort with the upper classes. The Rotunda Room (architect John Ensor) was built in 1764 (giving the hospital its familiar name) and the new Assembly Rooms (architect Richard Johnston) were erected between 1784 and 1786. These entertainment centres gained further income for the hospital.

Above: The Gate Theatre was founded in the former Grand Supper Room of the Rotunda's New Assembly Rooms in 1928 and in a short time achieved international fame under the direction of Micheál MacLiammóir and Hilton Edwards. Orson Welles and James Mason cut their acting teeth on the stage of the Gate.

Left: Bartholomew Mosse died in 1759 before he was able to realise all his plans for the decoration of the Rotunda's chapel. Notwithstanding this the rococo plasterwork of Frenchman, Barthelemi Cramillion, is of a scale and refinement not to be seen elsewhere in Dublin.

Above: Public fountains, which supplied drinking water to rich and poor alike and to passing horses, were a prominent and necessary feature on Dublin streets in bygone days. Reading from the top, the three examples above are; Cavendish Row, the Rutland Fountain on Merrion Square and the fountain inset into the wall of the Rates Office on Lord Edward Street.

Right: Map of Dublin from the 1760's by Bernard Scalé.

Above: Bank of Ireland, College Green with the memorial to Thomas Davis, (1814 - 1845) poet and patriot, in the foreground. The sculptor was Edward Delaney.

Above: The statue by John Foley to Henry Grattan (1746 - 1820) who entered the Irish Parliament in 1775. He distinguished himself as an able and fiery orator and became leader of the Liberal Party. He opposed the Act of Union and thereafter worked for Catholic Emancipation.

The Bank of Ireland occupies perhaps one of the most prestigious and historic buildings in Dublin, the old House of Parliament. Parliament had been meeting in Chichester House, on the same site, since 1661 but the accommodation there was both inadequate and in decay. A decision was made in 1727 to demolish Chichester House and build a new Parliament House. Sir Edward Lovett Pearce was selected as the architect for what was to become the world's first building designed as a two-chamber legislature. The foundation stone was laid in 1728 and the work was substantially finished by 1733, the year Pearce died. The House of Commons occupied the centre of the arrangement under a Pantheon-style dome. A public gallery could and often did accommodate up to 700 spectators. The House of Lords was much smaller but no less elegant. The first session of Parliament took place in its new quarters in 1731 and its last was held in 1800 when the infamous Act of Union with Great Britain was ratified.

Founded in 1783 the Bank of Ireland had outgrown its premises in Mary's Abbey, near the Four Courts, and had already decided to move to College Street at the corner with D'Olier Street and Westmoreland Street. When the now redundant Parliament House came on the market in 1801, the bank showed interest and eventually became the new owners in 1803 for the sum of £40,000. A stipulation of the sale required that all evidence of the building's former use was to be removed so the House of Commons disappeared, but the House of Lords was surreptitiously saved preserving for posterity the most unique chamber of its kind to be found anywhere in the world. Under architect Francis Johnston the complete range of buildings was unified as one on the outside. Work to the interior was finished by 1808 when the bank opened for business. College Green was headquarters of the bank until 1972 and is still the principal Dublin branch. A monumental task of restoration to the granite exterior was carried out between 1971 and 1981. Damaged stones were replaced as were the weatherworn heads of Edward Smyth's statues of Fidelity, Hibernia and Commerce over the front portico which were re-carved by sculptor Paddy Roe.

1 | The preserved chamber of the House of Lords. The two tapestries, first hung in 1733, represent the Valiant Defence of Londonderry and the Glorious Battle of the Boyne. Their designer was Johann van der Hagen and the weaver was John van Beaver, Dutch craftsmen then living in Dublin. The fireplace surround was carved in oak by Thomas Oldham in 1748. The chandelier dates from 1788 and consists of 1,233 separate pieces of glass. It was made by Chebsey's Glass Works near Ballybough Bridge.

2 | This tapestry shows King James II surveying what would prove to be the failed Siege of Londonderry.

3 | The entrance portico to the former House of Lords was designed in the Corinthian Order by James Gandon and erected in 1785. The statues over the pediment are Wisdom, Justice and Liberty.

4 | The Mace of the House of Commons was made in England in 1765. The descendants of the last Speaker, James Foster, sold it on and it was repurchased, in 1937, by the Bank of Ireland at a sale in Christie's for £3,100.

5 | The Cash Office was constructed on the site of the Hall of Requests and the old lobby leading to the House of Commons.

Above: courtsey of Bank of Ireland

Above: courtsey of Bank of Ireland

Above: The Royal Coat of Arms carved into the tympanum over the main portico of the Bank of Ireland, College Green.

Middle left: Two cannon guns standing under the front portico bear witness to the time when the bank had its own yeomanry to guard against possible assault in the troubled years of the early 19th century.

Below left: This building stands near the opposite corner to the Bank of Ireland on Foster Place. Somewhat altered from the original design it once housed the famous Daly's Club which functioned here from 1789 until 1823. A private underground passage connected the club with the Parliament House. This proved to be a great convenience to the members for the discreetness it offered as the club had a reputation for its round-the-clock gambling and other nefarious goings-on.

Below right: The Bank of Ireland Arts Centre occupies the former armoury of the bank at the end of Foster Place and was designed by Francis Johnston as part of his brief to convert the old Parliament House. The Armoury now contains "The Story of Banking", an interactive museum which reflects both banking and Irish history over the past 200 years. It also traces the history of the adjoining Bank of Ireland building from its earliest days as Parliament House. Since 1995 the Arts Centre has become a significant venue for the living arts and hosts a variety of events from free classical recitals to exhibitions, theatre, launches and conferences.

Above: The Four Courts

Property owners and business people with vested interests in the area around the Old Custom House vociferously and sometimes violently opposed its replacement by a new and grander version downriver. Their anger was somewhat assuaged by the promise to situate on Inns Quay an equally imposing edifice. This was to accommodate the Four Courts which badly needed to relocate from entirely unsuitable premises beside Christ Church Cathedral. Design would be in the hands of James Gandon, the same architect in charge of the new Custom House. Thomas Cooley, architect of the Royal Exchange (now the City Hall), had already built a public office on Inns Quay which Gandon proceeded to incorporate with some modifications as his West Wing, then built a similar East Wing and joined the two to a central domed core with arches and arcades. The foundation stone was laid by the Viceroy, the Duke of Rutland, in 1786. The first court sessions took place ten years later and by 1802 the whole splendid array was completed. The portico contains six Corinthian columns and over the front stand five statues; Moses, Justice, Mercy, Authority and Wisdom. Five courts, not four, sat in Gandon's masterpiece and these were: the King's Bench, the Chancery, the Exchequer, the Common Pleas and the Judicature.

In 1922 the Four Courts were occupied by Anti-Treaty forces and were bombarded by Government troops using borrowed British Army field guns. The accidental explosion of a mine then shattered the central block and also destroyed the irreplaceable collection of 700 years of accumulated historical documents held in the adjoining Public Record Office. Within nine years of the disaster a complete restoration by the Office of Public Works was expertly concluded. The exterior was unchanged from the original except for alterations to the dome, which had to be replaced in its entirety. More recent additions to the complex include the building of an office annexe on the site of the old Four Courts Hotel. The resultant release of office space within the Four Courts itself has allowed for extensive refurbishment to be carried out including the provision of additional courtrooms and ancillary accommodation.

Above: A restored sculptural detail from the Four Courts.

Above: The Custom House.

Above: James Gandon (1743-1823) was born in London and studied architecture under Sir William Chambers. His extant works include the Four Courts, the Custom House, the King's Inns and additions to the Parliament House (now the Bank of Ireland).

Before the foundation stone of the present Custom House was laid in 1781 there had been four predecessors. The first was built in 1620, followed shortly in 1637 by another, the third arrived in the 1660s and the Wellington Quay version was erected in 1707. Moving further downriver with each succeeding Custom House, Wellington Quay was still found to be unsuitable for deep draught vessels and the quayside itself could accommodate only one ship at a time. John Beresford, the Revenue Commissioner, was determined to build a new Custom House nearer the mouth of the River Liffey and persuaded one of England's most promising architects to pass over an invitation to Russia and come to Dublin instead. James Gandon was to leave to Dublin a number of important architectural legacies, not the least of which is the Custom House which was completed by 1792 at a cost of nearly a quarter of a million pounds. Laid on a bed of wool and wickerwork to counteract the marshy ground, the building of the Custom House was not without incident. Mobs, in the pay of merchants who opposed the relocation of the old Custom House, harried the construction workers. For personal protection Gandon himself constantly carried a sword. To add to these difficulties a fire broke out in 1789 and destroyed some of the completed work. Another fire in 1833 fairly gutted the Custom House but fortunately it was thoroughly reconstructed, although Gandon's original interior was largely altered.

In 1921, during the War of Independence, the Custom House fell prey to fire once more only this time on a more disastrous scale. The conflagration was so intense that the stone rubble was still cooling weeks later. Reconstruction appeared hopeless and the building that had inspired Lutyen's Viceroy's Palace in New Delhi seemed doomed. However, the basic walls were still standing so it was decided to go ahead. The dome and drum had to be totally rebuilt.

Ireland's best known architectural glory was saved but in the late 1970s and 80s it became apparent that there was serious deterioration to the fabric resulting from the last fire. Major repair, replacement and conservation works were undertaken from 1984 to 1991 at a cost of around £6 million. Each of the Royal Arms of Ireland, weighing about twelve tons each, was in need of restoration. The four roof urns, whose function was to mask the chimney flues, and the four Portland Stone statues were also carefully restored. The restoration work, overseen by the Office of Public Works and its architect, David Slattery, was awarded the Europa Nostra Diploma of Merit in 1989.

The bas-reliefs in the Tympanum (top), the Royal Arms of Ireland (left) and the fourteen Riverhead sculptures representing the main rivers of Ireland and the Atlantic Ocean (Anna Livia, or the River Liffey [far left] is the only female head) were all carved by Edward Smyth, Ireland's greatest 18th century sculptor. Smyth also carved the figures of Industry and Plenty above the pediment and that of Commerce on top of the dome. Italian Agostino Carlini carved Neptune and Mercury and designed the scene inside the tympanum of Neptune on his chariot banishing famine and despair, a sentiment which would be echoed fifty years later when the Custom House would become the main centre organising the relief during the Great Famine of the 1840s.

Left: A nighttime view of the north façade of the Custom House. The bronze statue group to the front is a memorial to the Dublin Brigade of the old Irish Republican Army. It shows Erin (Ireland) comforting one of her fallen sons and was sculpted in 1956 by Brittany-born Yann Renard Goulet.

Above: St Patrick's Hospital, at the corner of Bow Lane and Steevens Lane, is the oldest psychiatric hospital in Ireland and only Bethlem (Bedlam) Hospital in London is older in all of Britain. Jonathan Swift, author of Gulliver's Travels and Dean of St Patrick's Cathedral, was a member of the board of governors of Bethlem and abhorred the cruel methods used there to subdue patients. He spent the last 14 years of his life preparing the foundation of a more enlightened hospital in Dublin "for the reception of aged lunaticks and other diseased persons". Inmates were to be treated as patients and not as criminals. The hospital was founded in 1745, the year of Swift's death, and his will provided the finances necessary to build St Patrick's on land donated by the trustees of adjoining Dr Steevens' Hospital. The original building, which is still in use, was designed by George Semple and opened in 1757. Over the years several major extensions have been added. A board of governors, made up of Swift's trusted friends, administered the hospital, a system that kept control at a local level and avoided state bureaucracy. Today it is managed in the same way and run as a charitable institution much as envisaged by its founder. St Patrick's, a teaching centre for Trinity College, is one of the country's foremost psychiatric hospitals and is renowned for its treatment of alcoholism, phobias and psycho-sexual disorders.

Above: Francis Johnston's St George's Church in Hardwicke Place is as exquisitely designed as any of Christopher Wren's London churches. In 1814, when the church was completed, there was a huge Protestant population in the parish but by the 1970s it had all but disappeared. Already suffering some structural decay (the fine tower and steeple are still encased in scaffolding) the church was closed down and sold on. It is now operating as the Temple Theatre, a venue for popular music.

Below: Dublin Corporation received a charter in 1670 to erect a school for the care and education of children from families found to be in reduced circumstances. It was officially known as the Hospital and Free School of King Charles II, generally shortened to the King's Hospital or the Blue Coat School (from the colour of the boys' uniform). The present building on Blackhall Place was erected between 1773 and 1783. Thomas Ivory's original ambitious design was not completed due to a shortage of funds. The tall elegant central tower shown rather previously in Malton's 1790s "Picturesque and Descriptive Views of Dublin" was never realised. The students of the Kings Hospital (which still exists) moved out to Palmerstown in 1970. The new owners of the Blue Coat School, the Incorporated Law Society, carried out a major refurbishment of the building in the 1970s using the services of architects Nolan and Quinlan and contractors G. & T. Crampton.

Left: A view up D'Olier Street, one of the streets laid down (in 1801) by the Wide Streets Commission. The block on the left belongs to "The Irish Times" newspaper which has been in publication since 1859. In 1991 "The Irish Times" undertook an extensive remodelling of its premises' exterior to authentically recreate what it would have looked like when it was built at the turn of the 19th century.

Middle left: The D'Olier Street block as mentioned above, taken from the 1850 edition of Shaw's Pictorial Guide & Directory. All the buildings on the street were designed by the one architect, Henry A. Baker.

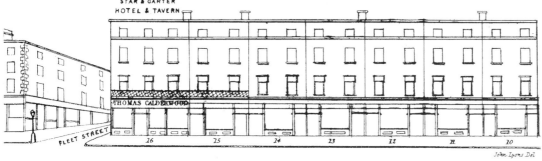

Below: Around 1720, William Conolly, the Speaker of the Irish Parliament, built a hunting lodge on Mount Pelier Hill in South County Dublin. Upon his death in 1729 it was sold and in 1735 it was bought by the notorious Hell Fire Club. This was a gathering of young bucks from the nobility and the officer corps who were celebrated for their excesses during evenings of licentiousness, blasphemous toasts and devil worshipping. With the demise of the club in the 1740s the sturdy lodge was abandoned. Today the substantial ruin provides an unrivalled viewpoint over the whole city.

1714 George I ascends to the English throne, ushering in the Georgian Period.

1721 Johann Sebastian Bach completes the Brandenburg Concertos.

1722 Henrietta Street first developed.

1729 Parliament Buildings, now the Bank of Ireland, College Green, built.

1742 Handel's Messiah first performed in the Musick Hall, Fishamble Street, Dublin.

1756 Birth of Mozart.

1757 The Wide Streets Commission established.

1762 Merrion Square laid out.

1771 Bogland Act brings first relief to Roman Catholics.

1776 American Declaration of Independence.

1782 Establishment of Irish Parliamentary Independence.

1789 French Revolution begins.

1791 Society of United Irishmen founded.

1795 Orange Order founded.

1798 Rebellion in Ireland crushed.

1800 Act of Union joining Ireland with Great Britain.

1807 Daniel O'Connell becomes leader of Catholic Emancipation Movement.

1829 Emancipation Bill passed.

1830 George IV dies, ending the Georgian Period.

Top and above: Despite the great progress of Dublin in the 18th century the pathetic state of the disadvantaged majority would continuously present a potential for destabilisation. The ideals expressed through the French Revolution of 1789 sent shudders of anxiety through the authorities in Ireland who, as one countermeasure to any revolt, began to build a series of prisons throughout the land. Kilmainham Gaol was opened just two years before the disastrous rising of 1798. From then on, until the release of its last prisoner, Eamon de Valera, in 1924, the jail was at full stretch accommodating insurgents from the uprisings of 1803, 1848, 1867, 1916, the War of Independence and the Civil War. In 1960 an enthusiastic group, including some former inmates, came together to begin the restoration of the near ruinous prison. Their trojan work was recognised in 1986 when the Office of Public Works took over the project on behalf of the nation. Today, under the care of Dúchas The Heritage Service, the jail is presented just as it would have looked in the 19th century.

Below left: The grim Debtors Prison on Halston Street is long closed and now awaits a new use as offices for the Court Services (it is owned by the Office of Public Works).

Below right: Opened in 1797 Green Street Courthouse heard the pleas and speeches of many revolutionaries. It is now the seat of the Special Criminal Court.

Chapter Five
Victoriana

QUEEN VICTORIA ascended the throne in 1837 and remained there until her death in 1901. The period of her reign was a time of mixed blessings for Dublin. The air of independent pride prevalent in the latter half of the 18th century was initially replaced by a disoriented acceptance of the city's downgrading following the Act of Union with Great Britain in 1800. The people got on with life and those who felt downtrodden found a new hero in Daniel O'Connell who knew how to play the political game. He succeeded by 1829, through the Act of Emancipation, in removing legal discriminations against Roman Catholics and Dissenters. In 1841 he became Dublin's first Catholic Lord Mayor in over 150 years and he continued right up to his death in 1847 in his attempts to repeal the Act of Union.

Business in Victorian Ireland boomed and a strong new merchant class, mostly Roman Catholic, emerged, The economy was fuelled by the introduction of railways, tramways and fast steamships between Dublin, Holyhead and Liverpool. Agricultural and manufactured goods found ready export to an England whose own population was growing commensurate with its rapidly expanding empire. Major industrial exhibitions promoting Irish products were the order of the day from the 1850s to the 1870s. Many learned institutions were founded as were the Royal University and the Catholic University. Growth and progress were counterbalanced and often pulled back by calamitous events. The Great Famine of the 1840s devastated the rural community and caused an influx of wretched souls to a city that already supported a huge volume of destitute people. Disease and overcrowding were rampant and the oversupply of labour kept wages appallingly inadequate for those lucky enough to find jobs.

The higher social orders took advantage of the mobility offered by trains and trams and surrendered their town houses to tenement lettings. Centre city slums achieved the reputation of being the worst in Europe. Social unrest was inevitable and this led to several failed attempts at revolution culminating in the more nationally widespread War of Independence of 1919 – 1921 and eventual nationhood.

Above: One of the finest but least observed memorials in Dublin is that erected in 1871 to Prince Albert, the late husband of Queen Victoria. Sculpted by John Henry Foley (1818-1874) the statue group is tucked away in the grounds of Leinster House next to the Natural History Museum.

Above: These elegant cast-iron circular frames off the South Lotts Road once supported expanding gas storage tanks. Since the introduction of natural gas the old tanks became redundant and were dismantled. Their frames, now on the preservation list, will be included in the designs for the site's redevelopment.

Left: A showpiece of Victorian architecture, the Royal Victoria Eye and Ear Hospital on Adelaide Road was designed in 1901 by the firm of Carroll and Batchelor.

Above: John Henry Foley designed the memorial to Daniel O'Connell which was unveiled to admiring crowds gathered in the pouring rain on 15 August 1882. O'Connell, known as "The Liberator", had achieved religious freedom in Ireland through his 1829 Act of Emancipation. His further efforts to have the Act of Union rescinded met with no success and he died on his way to Rome in 1847. The figures around the drum of the memorial under the 3.6m (12ft) bronze of O'Connell represent the church, the professions, the arts, the trades and the peasantry. Erin (Ireland) is trampling her cast-off shackles while holding the Act of Emancipation. The four winged Victories stand for O'Connell's virtues of Patriotism, Fidelity, Eloquence and Courage. A neat bullet hole over the right breast of "Courage" is a legacy from the Rising of 1916.

Above: The Royal City of Dublin Hospital, Baggot Street, commenced operations from its splendid new premises in 1892. Designed by Albert E. Murray, it is embellished with design details on ruabon brick and buff-coloured terracotta. Presently it operates as a community hospital offering drug and alcohol abuse treatment and geriatric care including respite for carers.

Below: Edward Cecil Guinness, through his philantrophic organisation, the Iveagh Trust, rehoused many of the poor, then living in slums around St. Patrick's Cathedral, in a group of blocks known as the Iveagh Buildings. The Iveagh Trust built the Bull Alley Play Centre in 1915 to offer underprivileged children an enlightened trade and general education along with nourishing meals. The building is now used by the Dublin City Vocational Education Committee to house the Liberties College. The façade of the college, which forms an impressive backdrop to St. Patrick's Park, was restored in 1999 by T. C. Walsh & Son Ltd., under the guidance of stone consultant David Slattery.

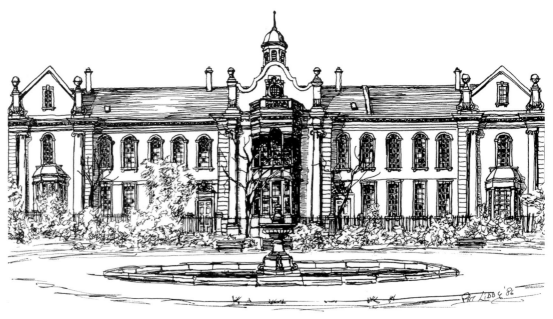

Left: The Shelbourne Hotel (now officially known as the Shelbourne Meridian Hotel, part of the Granada Group) has graced the north side of St. Stephen's Green since 1867. The sumptuous façade and the mid-Victorian interior have recently been refurbished to their former glory. John McCurdy designed the hotel to the very latest specifications of the day and the studio of M. M. Barbezet of Paris cast the four external statues; two Nubian Princesses and their shackled slave girls.

Above: By the end of 1999 the Halfpenny Bridge was due a complete overhaul and who would deny this to the venerable old crossing much loved by Dubliners and popular symbol of the city since the destruction of Nelson's Pillar in 1966. Long the sole footbridge along the city centre stretch of the River Liffey, it was carrying up to four thousand people an hour causing potential hazardous congestion at the exits. The situation was eased on 20 December 1999 when, a short distance upriver, the new pedestrian Millennium Bridge was officially opened by the Lord Mayor, Councillor Mary Freehill. Restoration work commenced on the Halfpenny Bridge in mid-2000.

Up to 1816, the year the Halfpenny Bridge was erected, no other bridge existed between Essex (now Grattan or Capel Street) Bridge and Carlisle (O'Connell) Bridge. There was a ferry from the Bagnio Slip (at the bottom of Fownes Street) operated by one William Walsh. He owned seven leaky ferries and was under pressure from Dublin Corporation to repair them or replace them. He baulked at that idea, preferring instead to build a bridge. Besides, he was encouraged to follow this latter course by the owners of the Theatre Royal in nearby Crow Street who were anxious to attract more north-side patrons. His proposal to Dublin Corporation was adopted and he was allowed in a hundred year lease to charge a halfpenny toll. Designed by John Windsor and costing £3,894.7s.11½d., the bridge was manufactured in Coalbrookdale in Shropshire, the first centre of iron casting in Britain. Now one of the oldest cast-iron bridges in the world, it was originally named Wellington Bridge after the Dublin-born duke who had trounced Napoleon at Waterloo. Renamed Liffey Bridge, it is more commonly known as the Halfpenny or Ha'penny Bridge. It was not always held in high regard. In 1913, one entry from the records of Dublin Corporation states: "Wellington Bridge is an unsightly structure. It is a narrow footbridge with a steep gradient and a toll of one halfpenny is made for crossing it. The lease will expire in a few years when a suitable new bridge will be built". Various suggestions followed including a Porte Vecchio style art gallery (designed by Sir Edwin Lutyens) to house the Hugh Lane Collection. Fortunately, the Halfpenny Bridge is still serving the people of Dublin and looks assured to continue as an intrinsic part of the city's soul.

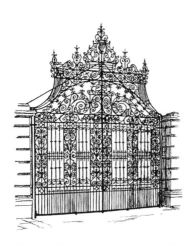

Above: Nineteenth century Dublin was famous for the production of wrought iron gates. This example, fronting Leinster House, was built at the turn of the 20th century by the Art Iron and Brass Works of J. & C. McLoughlin Ltd.

Above left: The former Dublin Exhibition Palace on Earlsfort Terrace was constructed in 1865 but is shown here just before it was rebuilt in 1914 for University College Dublin (UCD). The new design was in the hands of R. M. Butler and the building contractor was G. & T. Crampton. The tower on the right of the picture was re-erected as a boiler chimney at the back of Government Buildings. Also relocated were the three statues which now stand in the Millennium Garden (see page 71).

Above right: The remodelled UCD building on Earlsfort Terrace as it appears today. The Great Hall, in the centre of the complex, was converted into the National Concert Hall in 1981 to great acclaim.

Below left: The exterior of the former Kildare Street Club still possesses a fine Venetian appearance. Also worth noting are the exquisite sculptures at the base of the columns, carved by Charles W. Harrison. They feature animals engaged in odd pursuits as in the example below where monkeys are arguing over a game of billiards.

Below right: Gentlemen's clubs blossomed during the Victorian era, none more so than the famed Kildare Street Club which was founded in 1782. The club built their premises in the 1860s employing the renowned architects Benjamin Woodward and Thomas Newenham Deane. In 1954 the Kildare Street Club sold off its club house and the membership has since amalgamated with the University Club on St. Stephen's Green. Tragically a substantial part of the wonderfully carved stone interior was gutted in the early 1970s, a high point of philistinism among Dublin's development fraternity. Today, the building is partitioned and shared between the Alliance Francaise, the Heraldic Museum and the Office of the Chief Herald.

Above: The Millennium Garden was opened in 1987 and named a year later during the celebrations marking Dublin's millennium as a town. Splashed by gentle fountains the three statues, representing the crafts of stonework, woodwork and ironwork, once stood on top of the Dublin Exhibition Palace on Earlsfort Terrace (see page 70).

Above: Martello towers were built around the coasts of Ireland and Britain in 1804 to frustrate any plans Napoleon had to invade these islands. Named after their prototype at Cape Mortella in Corsica these formidable bastions possessed 2.4m (8ft) thick walls. A large cannon was mounted on a traversing carriage on the roof. The towers never did fire a shot in anger and they fell into disuse. Some 39 still survive in Ireland and the one shown above stands in forlorn but splendid isolation on Ireland's Eye, an island off Howth Harbour.

Below: It might not look much from the outside but the chief glory of the Olympia Theatre is the interior, a riot of Victorian embellishment. Dan Lowry opened his new Star of Erin Music Hall in 1879 with the main entrance off Crampton Court. In 1897 the theatre was reconstructed, the Dame Street entrance was added and the name was changed to the Empire Theatre of Varieties. The last century saw the name finally change to the "Olympia". Many Irish artistes made their debut on the stage of the Olympia and its old-world interior still resounds to musicals, revues, plays, pop concerts and seasonal pantomimes.

Below: Several large military barracks were built for the British garrison in Dublin but none were as architecturally ornate as McKee (then called Marlborough) Barracks, built between 1888 and 1892 on the northern fringes of the Phoenix Park. The red-bricked exteriors, topped by turrets, towers, spires, cupolas and tall chimneys were extensively restored for the army in recent years by the Office of Public Works (see also page 113).

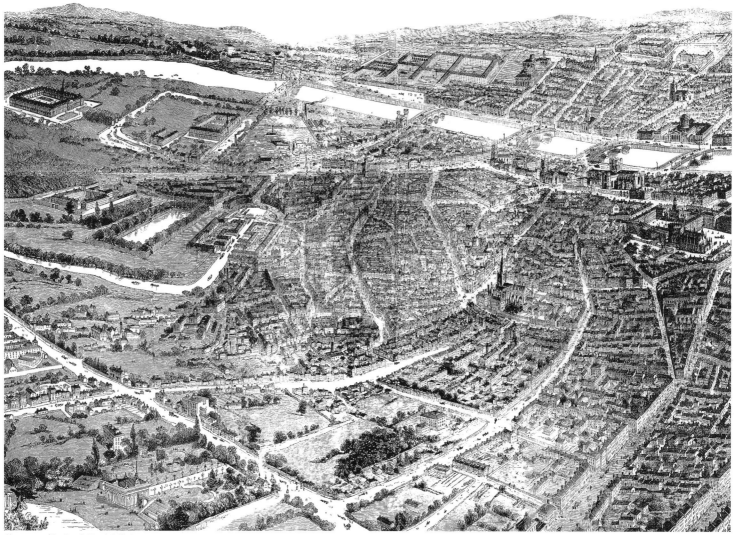

Photo: courtesy of Tom Kennedy, Kennedy Publications.

Far left: Recently restored by Dublin Corporation this fountain along St. Stephen's Green North dates from 1880 and is an example of a dual-purpose water supply; one for people and one for horses.

Left: Long before the invention of refrigerators well-off society kept its perishables in cool underground chambers called ice-houses. Large blocks of ice from frozen ravines in the Dublin and Wicklow mountains were carted down to the city and stored in these chambers to keep them extra cool. The ice house in the drawing can be seen in the grounds of the Dublin Zoological Gardens.

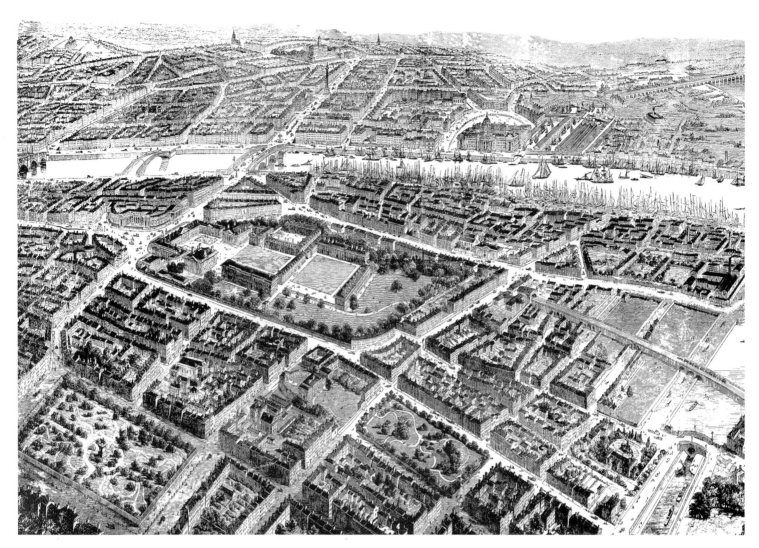

Above: This aerial-view drawing of Dublin was made in 1846 for the London Illustrated News. Note the recently imposed presence on the landscape of two railway lines and their viaducts. The Liffey and the Grand Canal are choked with traffic. The present location of Dublin Port is still under water. The Royal Hospital and Dr Steevens' Hospital lie in a well-cultivated pastoral setting, There is an apparent air of organisation and prosperity which camouflages the misery of the poorer classes especially at this time, the height of the Great Famine.

Left: In contrast to the great marching terraces of Georgian Dublin individualism marked the design of grand Victorian houses. The example shown here, "Glena" on Rock Road in Booterstown, was the home until his death in 1945 of Ireland's greatest international tenor, Count John McCormack.

Time Watch

In 1795 the Royal Dublin Society was appointed by the Irish Parliament to open a botanical gardens where experiments and research in Irish horticulture and agriculture would be undertaken. Portion of the Glasnevin estate of poet Thomas Tickell was purchased and this land formed the basis of today's 19.5ha (48 acres) site. In 1877 the gardens came under state control. Within the grounds there are four ranges of large glasshouses including the Orchid House, the Palm House (bottom left) and Dublin ironmaster Richard Turner's celebrated Curvilinear Range (below). Built between 1843 and 1869 the Curvilinear Range was magnificently restored in the 1990s. Turner was also responsible for the main glasshouse in London's Kew Gardens. Over 20,000 species and cultivars are spread around herbaceous borders, rockeries, arboreta, woodlands, lawns, walled enclosures, glasshouses and lakeland settings (bottom right). In 1844 The Botanic Gardens carried out what is believed to be the world's first attempt to raise orchids from seed to full flowering stage. Other firsts include the hybridisation of insectivorous pitcher plants and the introduction of Pampas Grass to European gardens. Under the management of Dúchas The Heritage Service, the National Botanic Gardens will be undergoing a continuing and active programme of refurbishment and renewal to ensure its role as a primary research and training centre as well as providing the most satisfying public formal gardens to be found anywhere in these islands.

Part Two
EBLANA
IN COMPLEXITY

*They pressed upon my banks and sailed their commerce o'er
my waters, the sustaining lifeblood of their being.*

*And then a kinship grew of learned respect and mutuality.
My lapping shores they swathed with encasing walls of stone*

*To allow me run and tumble with greater zeal to greet the tide.
Yet, in time, the fledgling town so grew beyond my sight.*

They call it History, they call me Anna Livia.

Chapter Six
Metropolitan Governance

Above: The Coat-of-Arms of Dublin Corporation was first formally granted in 1607 by Daniel Molyneux, Ulster King of Arms and Principal Herald of All Ireland. The Three Castle symbol of the city, however, is a much more ancient device and goes back to the Middle Ages. It represents three watch towers of the walled city and the leaping flames symbolise the zeal of the citizens to defend Dublin. This version of the Coat-of-Arms also shows the City Mace and the City Sword. The Latin inscription is the city motto and translates as "Obedient Citizens make for a Happy City".

Right: The Royal Charter, issued by King Henry II in 1172, granted Dublin to the citizens of Bristol. Its purpose was to assert the King's authority over the Norman knights who had captured Dublin two years earlier. This remarkable document, along with other ancient city muniments and treasures, is on display in the City Hall Exhibition Centre.

Photo: Dublin Corporation Archives Collection.

BEFORE THE coming of the Anglo-Normans there was little in the way of formal government in Dublin. The Celts had their Brehon Laws but the urban environment was alien to these codes. The Vikings set up a number of practical principles by which property boundaries and other issues were regulated. Disputes were settled and new laws enacted during meetings of the town leaders at the Thingmote, a mound which the Vikings erected off College Green opposite today's Dublin Tourism Centre, the former St Andrew's Church.

The arrival of the Anglo-Norman knights in 1170 also brought in train the first semblance of a proper local government system which was augmented by the issuance of Royal Charters granted to the City of Dublin by various Kings and Queens of England from 1172. Dublin Corporation still has in its possession 102 of those charters dating from 1172 to 1727. Their purpose was to secure the loyalty of the citizens by granting various rights and privileges and they formed the basis of municipal legislation in Ireland. The administration of the medieval city was, in effect, carried out by a City Council composed of members from the powerful trade guilds presided over by the annually elected Mayor, an office established in 1229.

Today's Corporation is a large organisation employing over 6,200 people. It provides around 500 different services to a population of 500,000 (the Greater Dublin Area has a population of around 1 and a quarter million) over a region of 115sq km (44sq miles). Overall responsibility for all the functions of the Corporation, including the implementation of the decisions of the City Council, rests with the City Manager.

Above & below: The Dublin City Seal dates from the 13th century and is the earliest item in the City Regalia. Showing the city under siege, two sentries on the central watchtower are sounding the alarm, two heralds on the walls are doing likewise and on top of the gate tower two archers are aiming their crossbows. A sentry holds the gate and above him the decapitated heads of three transgressors are impaled over the gate as a grisly warning to lawbreakers. The craftsmanship of the seal is remarkable considering it is only 8.5cm (3 inches) in diameter. The reverse side depicts a scene of Dublin at peace enjoying the pursuit of commerce, symbolised by a merchant ship at sea. A passenger quaffs a goblet of wine and the seas beneath teem with fish.

Every July, the Lord Mayor, who is the first citizen of Dublin, has been elected for a one-year term by the City Council from among its members. However, new legislation is now being prepared which will soon allow the general electorate to nominate the Lord Mayor. The 52 members of the City Council are formed through the Local Government elections which are generally held every five years. Each Councillor also sits on one of the five Area Committees which deal with all aspects of delivery of services and the handling of issues at a local level.

Above: The Lord Mayor's Great Chain was given to the city by King William III in 1698. The medallion carries the effigy of the King.

Above: The Great Mace was made in 1665 for the first Lord Mayor, Sir Daniel Bellingham. At one time his own personal weapon, the Dublin Civic Sword, was presented by Henry IV of England in 1409.

Photo: Dublin Corporation Archives Collection.

1.   4.
2.   5.
3.   6.

1 | Daniel Bellingham, Lord Mayor 1665-1666, was the first person to bear the prefix "Lord" in front of the title "Mayor".

4 | Alfie Byrne (1882-1956), one of Dublin's most popular Lord Mayors, held the position more often than anyone else. (Thomas Cusack was Mayor – without the "Lord" - on 19 occasions between 1390 and 1430). Byrne served from 1930 to 1939 and again from 1954 to 1955. He was loved for his untiring work on behalf of the poor, especially underprivileged children.

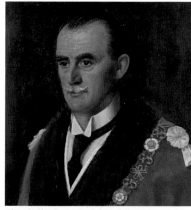

Photo: Dublin Corporation Archives Collection.

Photo: Dublin Corporation Archives Collection.

2 | Daniel O'Connell, known as "The Liberator" for his role in achieving the Act of Emancipation in 1829, was elected Lord Mayor in 1841. He was the first Roman Catholic to hold office since the enactment of the Penal Laws. The portrait is by Stephen Catterson Smith, PRHA.

5 | Alfie Byrne's imaginative memorial, next to the road which bears his name at Clontarf, was unveiled by another Lord Mayor, Joe Doyle, on 3 June 1999. Exquisitely carved in wood, the panels leading out from the central chair describe the achievements of Byrne.

Photo: by kind permission of Dr Emmet Clarke.

3 | The City's first female Lord Mayor was Caitlín Bean Uí Chléirigh (Kathleen Clarke) who served 1939-41. She was the widow of Thomas Clarke, the executed 1916 leader.

6 | In 1927, Gerald J. Sherlock became Town Clerk of Dublin and three years later he was appointed as Dublin City Manager, the first to hold this new post created under the Local Government (Dublin) Act of 1930. The portrait is by Sarah Cecilia Harrison.

Photo: Dublin Corporation Archives Collection.

Photo: Dublin Corporation Archives Collection.

Above: Determined not to be upstaged by the City of London, which had recently provided its Lord Mayor with a resplendent carriage, the Aldermen, Sheriffs and Commons of the City of Dublin appointed a committee in 1763 to ensure that the First Citizen would henceforth appear on public occasions in a "befitting state". The original budget was £400 but years of procrastination meant that when the new Lord Mayor's coach finally rumbled out of Mr William Whitton's coach-building yard in Dominick Street in 1791, the cost had risen to £2,690.13s.5d. The body of the coach is elaborately carved and richly gilded. The front, rear and side panels are painted in allegorical subjects. Retrieved after years of obscurity it was restored in 1975 and from 1976 it has annually rolled along the streets of Dublin in the St Patrick's Day Parade.

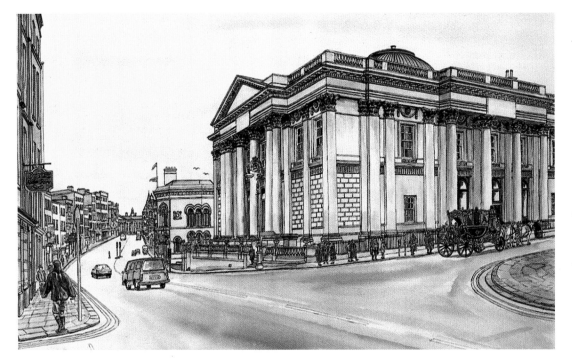

Left: A 1991 view of City Hall taken from Lord Edward Street and showing the entrance portico facing Castle Street. Dublin is a city with a rich historic past spanning two millennia. To protect the archaeology both above and below ground Dublin Corporation employs a full-time archaeologist who investigates all sites being developed in areas where finds are likely. In consultation with the planners and the developers the City Archaeologist advises the course of action which must be taken to investigate and protect sensitive sites before permission is given to proceed with building. A Conservation Officer was appointed by Dublin Corporation in 1998 to ensure that listed and historic buildings are protected and to assist owners of such buildings to conserve their properties. Another duty of the office is the administration of the Conservation Grant Scheme for Dublin city.

An architectural competition was announced in 1768 by the Merchants' Guild of Dublin for a new Royal Exchange on Cork Hill opposite recently opened Parliament Street. A Londoner, Thomas Cooley, won the first prize of £100 (and the commission). James Gandon won the second prize of £60. Construction work started in 1769 but it would take 10 years before the building was completed. The finished work was greeted with great enthusiasm and praise. In 1851 the Merchants' Guild vacated the building in favour of Dublin Corporation. The upstairs Coffee Room was converted into the Council Chamber (in which function it still serves) and the Rotunda area was made smaller by the erection of screen walls and partitions around the ambulatory. Cooley's original forecourt balustrade collapsed in 1814 with the loss of nine lives. The replacement by a railings was unsatisfactory and a new balustrade, designed by Thomas Turner and the one we see today, was erected in 1866.

Left: A drawing of the façade of the City Hall restored in 1999/2000. It was not possible to reinstate the main entrance podium facing Parliament Street to the original design of Thomas Cooley because of road widening subsequent to the erection of the building. The existing 19th century balustrade and wall have been retained and repaired.

Above: The Civic Exhibition is housed in the lower ground floor of City Hall (which has its own same-level entrance from Exchange Court). When the partitions were removed during the recent renovations a series of wonderful vaulted spaces was revealed which now provide the backdrop for the Civic Exhibition. Design for the exhibition was carried out by Orna Hanley Architect, who was advised and directed by the staff of the Public Library and Archive Services of Dublin Corporation. The City Architect's Division of Dublin Corporation played a vital role in the refurbishment of City Hall. Its team included; City Architect: James Barrett, Project Architect: Ronan Boylan and Assistant Architect: Eileen McNamara. The Quantity Surveyor's Division was led by John Callaghan with David O'Brien as Project Surveyor. Outside consultants were; Historic Buildings Consultant: Paul Arnold Architects, Structural Engineers: Barrett Mahony Engineers, Electrical Contractors: Patrick Dunphy & Associates and Stone Restoration: Conservation and Restoration Ltd. The main contractor was Dunwoody & Dobson Ltd.

Above: An internal view of City Hall by Patrick Byrne (1783-1864) painted in 1834 while it was still the Royal Exchange. This was before the various partitions were erected. They have now been demolished and the interior refurbished down to the finest detail to restore the rotunda to the condition and ambience intended by Thomas Cooley and his clients, the Merchants' Guild. Gold leaf was restored to the interior elements of the dome, the internal Portland stone walls and pillars were refurbished and the external stonework, especially the carved sections, was cleaned with almost surgical precision.

Below: A "before" and "after" ground floor plan illustrates the removal of office partitions and the reinstatement of the encircling ambulatory.

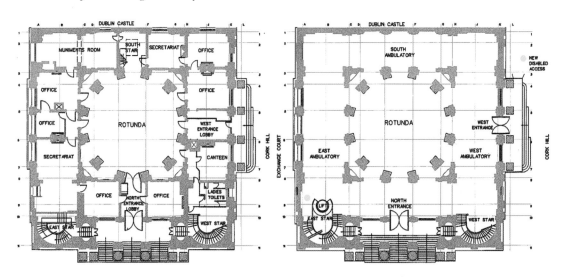

Above: The Mansion House was originally built in 1705 for Joshua Dawson who was the developer of Dawson Street and Nassau Street. Dawson's townhouse, partly unfinished and seldom lived in, was sold to the Corporation in 1715 for £3,500. The Lord Mayor of the day took up residence and thus Dublin preceded the City of London by some 15 years in providing an official house for its Mayor. The house was originally faced in brick but was later plastered and the city Coat-of-Arms was added to the pediment. A further embellishment, the metal canopy at the front entrance, arrived in 1896. The Round Room beside the Mansion House was built in 1821 for a visit by King George IV and it was here that the adoption of the Declaration of Independence in 1919 and the signing of the Treaty took place. Dublin has had civic government since 1172 and the office of Mayor was instituted in 1229 by Henry III to act as a form of city magistrate. The first Mayor in 1229 was Richard Moulton. Sir Daniel Bellingham became the first to hold the new title of Lord Mayor in 1665 and in 1841 Daniel O'Connell was the first Lord Mayor under a newly reformed Dublin Corporation. The Lord Mayor presides at the meetings of the City Council, signs its record of proceedings and is present when the City Seal is affixed to municipal documents.

Photo: Dublin Corporation Press Office.

Photo: Dublin Corporation Press Office.

Far left: The Drawing Room of the Mansion House.

Left: The Oak Room, built in 1715, still retains much of the original oak panelling. Used for civic receptions it contains a number of portraits including that of Charles Stewart Parnell, founder of the Home Rule Party. Additional portraits from the Civic Collection, mostly of historic Lord Mayors, hang throughout the house. The walls of the Oak Room bear the family crests of former Lord Mayors.

Above: The original twin blocks from 1985 before the development of the second phase of Dublin Corporation's Civic Offices along Wood Quay. The first phase, designed by Sam Stephenson and finished in 1985, had at the time caused much public outrage and protest. The site contained one of the richest Viking archaeological finds in Europe yet construction was forced ahead before the site could be fully explored or preserved. It was a dark period for Dublin Corporation but the lessons were duly learned.

Top right: The second and final phase of the Civic Offices was officially opened on 29 January 1995. Constructed over a relatively short period of time and to within its budget of £14.3 million by Pierse Contracting, the building was described by the World Architecture Magazine as "arguably the most important public building to be built on the banks of the Liffey for 200 years". Architects for the Civic Offices were Scott Tallon Walker who were commended for their design in the Royal Institute of Architects of Ireland Triennial Medal Awards for 1992-94.

Middle right: The striking riverside structure of the Civic Offices is cleverly linked to the nearest of the original octagonal blocks by a glazed atrium section. The façade of granite and Portland stone and is set back at the eastern end to draw level with the line of Exchange Street Lower. This afforded an opportunity to create an entrance portico and a flight of steps of fitting civic proportions. The extended upper storey on the west end of the façade is supported by a single pillar to allow a view up Winetavern Street to Christ Church Cathedral. Wood Quay, virtually a derelict site since the buildings along it were demolished around 1967, has been elegantly reinstated.

Right: The atrium contains an appealing sub-tropical garden.

Far right: The public spaces incorporated into the development include a small park, an amphitheatre and a new pedestrian route along the line of the old city wall linking Essex Street West and Fishamble Street with Winetavern Street.

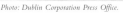
Photo: Dublin Corporation Press Office.

Above: Raheny Library represents the more modern faciltity which began to appear around the city in the 1970s.

Above: Children being introduced to the On-Line Service at Ballyfermot Library.

Above: Pembroke Library was designed by Kaye-Parry Ross and Hendy and opened in 1929 for the Pembroke Urban District Council on foot of a grant received from the Andrew Carnegie Trust. Carnegie was a hugely wealthy Scottish-American philanthropist who financed, among other things, the building of 2,500 libraries worldwide including 80 in Ireland. The famous Irish short story writer, Frank O'Connor, was appointed the first librarian of Pembroke.

Since opening its first two public libraries in 1884 in Capel Street and Thomas Street the Dublin Corporation Library Service has evolved in a dynamic way and has become a major gateway point for community learning, enabling people, for instance, to access global knowledge through computer programmes and internet applications. International co-operation is a fundamental key to library development and the Dublin Corporation service is involved in several European-wide research projects such as the Distance Education Provision and Facilitation Programme, the Shared Access to Cultural and Heritage Programme and the digitisation of photographic collections. There is now a city-wide network of community-based branch libraries in addition to a number of information services centres and specialist libraries which offer facilities including an Open Learning Centre, the Business Information Centre and the Music Library (all at the Central Library in the ILAC Centre), the Children's and Schools' Library Service, the Community and Youth Information Service, the Mobile Library Service and the Prison Library Service. Four other services, the Archives Collection, the Civic Museum, the Dublin and Irish Local Studies Collection and the International IMPAC Dublin Literary Award, are detailed on the next page.

Below left: Rathmines Library, another legacy from the Andrew Carnegie Trust, is a Baroque-style building dating from 1913 and was designed by Batchelor and Hicks. It was the first municipal library in Ireland to allow the public direct access to the book stacks.

Below right: The new facility at Cabra, on the Navan Road, is Dublin Corporation's latest state-of-the-art branch library. It contains the Library Service's Processing Centre and the Mobile Library Unit. The architect was Charles Donnelly of Dolan and Donnelly and construction was by William F. Rowley Ltd.

Above: The Civic Museum on William Street South was originally built for the Society of Artists who held their first exhibition here in 1766. It became the City Assembly House when Dublin Corporation transferred from the crumbling Tholsel to the house in 1791. The exhibition room was used for Council meetings until the members moved in 1852 to the Royal Exchange, now the City Hall on Cork Hill. Not as well known as it deserves, this building houses an important collection of exhibits associated with the history of Dublin. Old photographs, Malton prints (presented by President Sean T. O'Kelly for the opening of the Museum in 1953), maps and other documents record the various highlights in the development of the city. Nostalgic items of street furniture ranging from old bridge name tablets and pavement coal-hole covers to the pitted head of Horatio Nelson, salvaged from the bomb-blasted ruins of the Pillar, are prominently displayed. Exhibitions dealing with aspects of the city's history are regularly mounted. The Old Dublin Society meets here for lectures during the winter season.

Photo: Dublin Corporation Archives Collection.

Photo: Dublin Corporation Public Libraries.

Above left: This is an image, taken from the collection of the Dublin City Archives, of a Christmas card sent by Caitlín Bean Uí Chléirigh when she was Lord Mayor in 1939. As the widow of 1916 leader Tom Clarke, she chose an image of the GPO with an Irish inscription "Cuimhneachán" (meaning "In Commemoration"). The Dublin City Archives, which are open to the public, comprise the historic records of the municipal government of Dublin from the 12th century to the present. The municipal law in Ireland is based on the 102 charters granted by English monarchs since King Henry II issued the first one in 1172. All of these, as well as numerous other historic manuscripts, many written on parchment, are held in the Archives. Other material kept in the collection includes ancient maps and title deeds, drawings, charity petitions, Council minutes, lists of people who have received the Freedom of the City and documents belonging to the Wide Streets Commission (1757-1849).

Above right: Established in 1995, the International IMPAC Dublin Literary Award is the largest and most wide-ranging literary award for fiction in the world and carries an annual prize of £100,000. Selected libraries from all corners of the globe nominate books which are considered by an international panel of judges. The aim of the award is to recognise the contribution of great literature to society and to celebrate Dublin's famous literary traditions. Dublin Corporation's Public Library Service administers the award. The main sponsor, IMPAC, is the world's biggest productivity improvement company.

Below: The Dublin and Irish Local Studies Collection, situated at 138-142 Pearse Street, is a reference library containing an assembly of books, newspapers, periodicals, maps, photographs, prints and microfilms relating to the social, cultural and literary heritage of Dublin in particular and Ireland in general. Work to refurbish and extend the Pearse Street Library building (as shown below) commenced in May 2000. When finished there will be a 100 seat public reading room, modern database retrieval systems, exhibition and lecture areas and a cafeteria. The International IMPAC Dublin Literary Award Collection of nominated books and the Dublin Corporation Archives Collection will also be housed in the enlarged building as will the Headquarters of the Dublin Corporation Public Library Service.

Photo: Dublin Corporation Public Libaries.

Photo: courtesy of Hugh Lane Municipal Gallery of Modern Art.

Above: Set back from the street and flanked by curved screen walls the Hugh Lane Municipal Gallery of Modern Art was designed by Sir William Chambers and built between 1762 and 1765 as the townhouse for James Caulfeild (1728-1799), 1st Earl of Charlemont. The interior of the house is laid out on strict classical lines. The noble earl, a founder member of the Royal Irish Academy and a patron of the arts, would have heartily approved when Dublin Corporation purchased the house in 1927 and converted it for use as a picture gallery. Respecting the wonderful interior of the original house by hardly changing it all, the Corporation built the additional main exhibition rooms on the site of the former rear gardens. The new gallery opened in 1933.

The origins of the Lane Collection go back to Sir Hugh Lane (1875-1915), a successful Co. Cork-born art dealer who personally collected a large number of important European art works, including the eight outstanding paintings by the French Impressionists (see right margin). He also recognised the talents of contemporary Irish artists such as Nathaniel Hone and John Butler Yeats and believed that they should be shown alongside their European counterparts and so he began a campaign to establish a gallery of modern art in Dublin. A temporary gallery was opened in Harcourt Street in 1908 to house the Lane Collection but the inability of Dublin Corporation to settle quickly the question of a permanent home led Lane in 1913 to write a will bequeathing the pictures to London. A year later, following his appointment as director of the National Gallery of Ireland, he changed his mind and wrote an unwitnessed codicil to the will in which he once more left the paintings to Dublin. Tragically, Sir Hugh was lost with the sinking of the *Lusitania* in May 1915 and a long dispute over his will arose between the Irish and British Governments. A series of agreements, the last one concluded in 1993, resolved the issue by exhibiting most of the Collection in Dublin with the exception of the eight French Impressionists' works which must alternate between Dublin and London.

Apart from the Lane Bequest the gallery's collection comprises an extensive range of Irish and international paintings, drawings, sculpture and stained glass and it continues to grow through an active acquisition programme. The most recent donation has been the renowned studio of Francis Bacon.

Photo: courtesy of Hugh Lane Municipal Gallery.

Above: "Les Parapluies", an oil on canvas of a Paris street scene, was painted c.1881–1886 by Pierre-Auguste Renoir (1841–1919). This painting is one of eight exceptionally valuable French Impressionist works held jointly between the National Gallery in London and the Hugh Lane Municipal Gallery in Dublin. Every six years the four exhibited by each gallery are alternated. The current group in Dublin is composed of works by Manet, Renoir, Morisot, and Pissarro. Until 2005 London holds the canvasses of Degas, Vuillard, Monet and a second Manet.

Above: Stained glass entitled "The Eve of St. Agnes", executed in 1924 by Harry Clarke (1889 – 1931).

Above: The intriguing "Shark Lady in a Balldress" by Dorothy Cross (born 1956), was made in 1988 from cast and woven bronze.

Above: Completed in 1997, "Niall's Pony" by Basil Blackshaw (born 1932), is a fine example of this artist's richly painted figurative style.

Above: An interior view of the Hugh Lane Municipal Gallery of Modern Art. The Gallery hosts the Sundays at Noon concerts, a free-admission series of music programmes ranging from early music to premieres of contemporary works. These popular concerts were first inaugurated in 1976 and are grant-aided by the Arts Council.

Above: A photograph of the Francis Bacon studio at No. 7 Reece Mews in London, prior to its removal to the Hugh Lane Municipal Gallery of Modern Art. The remarkable donation of the complete studio contents by Bacon's heir, John Edwards, is the most important gift received by the gallery since it was founded by Sir Hugh Lane in 1908. Francis Bacon, an artist of international renown, was born in Dublin in 1909 and left for Berlin and Paris in 1925 before finally settling in London in 1929. His studio was located in the mews house where he lived from 1961 until his death in 1992. The studio is a virtual autobiography of this celebrated artist and provides valuable insights into his life. It contains some 10,000 items (now being catalogued by the gallery's Bacon Database team) including significant drawings and canvases, his paints and brushes, books and photographic material and his last unfinished self-portrait which was on the easel when he died.

All photos courtesy of Hugh Lane Municipal Gallery of Modern Art.

Above: A Dennis turntable ladder unit has a water cannon affixed to the top of the ladder. The turntable ladder on fire engines was invented at the Tara Street Station in the late 19th century.

Above: The new Fire Brigade Headquarters (designed by Henry J Lyons & Partners) opened in 1999 in Townsend Street. Formed in 1862, the Dublin Fire Brigade moved to Tara Street in 1907. The fire engines themselves then exited onto Pearse Street. The present building stands over the former yard at the rear of the old Tara Street Fire Station. The original station building has now been absorbed into a new hotel development. The balcony of the old Florentine-styled clock tower (designed by City Architect, Charles J McCarthy) was once used by lookouts in the days before people had access to telephones and alarm pillars (boxes placed on pillars which contained a telephone and alarm switch and were erected in the early part of the 20th century along many city centre streets). The tower was also used to hang hoses vertically to dry. The Dublin Fire Brigade serves both the city and county, an area of 922sq km (356sq miles). The 800 personnel answer in excess of 85,000 fire and accident emergency calls per year. There are fifteen fire stations in total although four are only retained (part-time) stations.

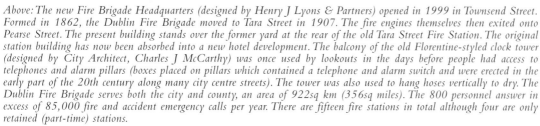

Above: In 1892 Dublin Corporation erected the Fruit and Vegetable Market (designed by Spencer Harty) at a cost of £100,000. In 1999 the Corporation refurbished the lovely red and yellow brick façade, decorated with terracotta floral panels, food motifs and ornamental iron grills, for around £1 million. It was built to replace the numerous individual markets operating unhygienically from various yards around the streets to the rear of the Four Courts.

Above: The Dublin Fire Brigade Training Centre occupies the former O'Brien Institute, an Irish Christian Brothers' boarding school for boys opened in 1888. W. T. Cosgrave, President of the Executive Council of the Irish Free State, was a notable past pupil of the school. The institution closed in 1972 and ten years later Dublin Corporation purchased the building. Originally designed in the French Gothic style by J.J. O'Callaghan, the building is now used to train Dublin Fire Brigade personnel and staff from other brigades around the country. Extensive ambulance courses are also held here in conjunction with the Northeastern University of Boston. The Brigade Historical Society and Museum are based in the Centre.

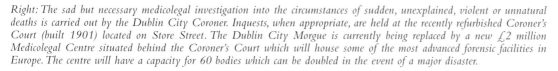

Right: The sad but necessary medicolegal investigation into the circumstances of sudden, unexplained, violent or unnatural deaths is carried out by the Dublin City Coroner. Inquests, when appropriate, are held at the recently refurbished Coroner's Court (built 1901) located on Store Street. The Dublin City Morgue is currently being replaced by a new £2 million Medicolegal Centre situated behind the Coroner's Court which will house some of the most advanced forensic facilities in Europe. The centre will have a capacity for 60 bodies which can be doubled in the event of a major disaster.

Top: An old brick-lined sewer under Westmorland Street contrasts with the giant tunnel (above) of the 4.8km (3 miles) long Greater Dublin Drainage Scheme (GDDS). The diameter of the tunnel is 3.66m (12ft). Completed in 1984 the GDDS was built to carry, in separated compartments, the storm and foul waters from the new towns of Blanchardstown, Lucan and Clondalkin and to relieve flood-prone areas such as Crumlin, Harold's Cross and Rathmines. The sewer network in Dublin totals 2,500km (1562 miles).

Above: A section of the Main Lift Pumping Station at Ringsend. There are also thirty area pumping stations around Dublin to assist the flow of waste water against contrary gradients.

Above: Picturesque Roundwood Reservoir is one of several reservoirs that collect water from the Wicklow and Dublin Mountains. The water is then sent to treatment works at Roundwood itself, Ballymore Eustace and Bohernabreena. On average, 1000 litres (1,760 pints) of water are delivered daily to every household in the Greater Dublin Area by Dublin Corporation.

Above: An artist's impression of the new Ringsend Waste Water Treatment Plant currently being built and due for completion in Spring 2002. This work is part of the Dublin Bay Project which is the largest waste water project being undertaken in Europe at this time. The £200 million capital cost (partly funded by the EU Cohesion Fund) will include the building of a modern pumping station at Sutton and the laying of a 11.5km (7 miles) long underwater pipeline from Sutton in a loop around Poolbeg Generating Station to the new treatment plant. This will end the discharge of untreated waste water off Howth Head, restore the water quality of Dublin Bay to high standards and facilitate the qualification of Dollymount Strand to Blue Flag status.

Above: One of nearly 500 Pay and Display machines which control the 9,000 on-street car parking spaces in the city. The machine's computer is solar powered.

Above: VMS signs, strategically located throughout the city, provide all-day parking and traffic conditions information.

From the early 1990s and with each succeeding year the traffic situation in the city has become progressively worse. As a result of the economic boom thousands of additional cars are annually pouring on to the roads. Gridlock occurred with increasing incidence. In 1997 the Office of the Director of Traffic was established to improve the co-ordination of traffic policy in Dublin city, to optimise the city's road network through the implementation of key traffic management and parking enforcement measures and to develop essential new road infrastructure projects. For instance, the introduction of Quality Bus Corridors has benefited public transport users and the enforcement of severe illegal-parking penalties has cleared road blockages and made finding on-street spaces easier for short-term parking.

The traditional cart and brush (top) is being replaced by the mechanised vacuum sweeper known as "the green machine" (above).

Photo: Dublin Corporation Press Office.

Above: The Traffic Control Centre, situated in the Civic Offices, allows Dublin Corporation traffic officials, the Gardaí, Dublin Bus and AA Roadwatch personnel to monitor traffic movements and illegal parking in the central area through the 53 CCTV cameras network. It is also used for other traffic management systems, such as computerised traffic signals and updating the VMS signs.

Below: a Scarab Sweeper attending to a suburban street. One failing of the Irish, it has to be said, is that they have not yet learned to keep public places litter-free. The collection of litter and refuse in the city is now carried out virtually on a 24-hour basis. Over 190,000 tons of refuse, including 15,000 tons of litter, are collected each year in the Dublin Corporation area.

The Electricity and Public Lighting Division, part of Dublin Corporation's Roads and Streets Department, is responsible for the planning, design, installation and maintenance of more than 45,000 public lighting units throughout the city. As well as designing contemporary street lamps the division also restores and maintains the city's large stock of period columns and fittings. There are hundreds of these decorative lamps all over the inner city and in the boroughs once controlled by the now-defunct Urban District Councils. Public lighting was first ordered for the streets of Dublin in 1616 when the Candlelight Law decreed that every fifth house should display a light for the convenience of passers-by. Fish blubber fuel replaced candles by the end of the 17th century. Gas lamps appeared by 1825 and the Corporation introduced electric street lamps in 1892.

1
2 3
4 5 6 7

Some examples of heritage or decorative lamp columns around the city are:

1 | The Five Lamps at the junction of Amiens Street and Portland Row were erected in 1870 in memory of General Henry Hall, a Co. Galway man who distinguished himself with the British Army in India.

2 | Baggot Street lamps (actually a modern re-creation).

3 | A common lamp standard found on many suburban streets.

4 | One of the three-branched lamps on O'Connell Bridge.

5 | Sea-horses decorate the lamps on Grattan (Capel Street) Bridge.

6 & 7 | Two examples of antique lamps now preserved in Merrion Square Park.

From the early 19th century the so-called nobility and gentry began to move residence from the city centre to the more desirable coastline or countryside on the outer fringes of the city. The advent from the middle of the century of scheduled public transport in the form of trains, omnibuses and trams encouraged the emerging professional, merchant and clerical middle classes to emigrate to the new suburbs. Left behind in the old inner city were the working classes and the unemployed who increasingly lived in deplorable conditions either in alleyways of crumbling houses or crowded into former Georgian mansions now decaying into unsanitary tenements. Many of the owners of these houses cared little about their tenants' welfare or the maintenance of their once grand buildings. As a result, by the turn of the 20th century Dublin possessed possibly the worst slums in Northern Europe. The most urgent concern facing Dublin Corporation on the formation of the Irish Free State in 1921 was the rehousing of tenement dwellers and the clearance of the slums. Despite the near impoverishment of the public coffers both of these tasks were undertaken with determination. Although it took several decades, tenement dwellers were eventually rehoused in decent accommodation.

Above: The beautifully refurbished Rates Office of Dublin Corporation is housed in the former Newcomen's Bank building in Castle Street. Designed by Thomas Ivory it was built in 1781 for the bank founded by Sir Thomas Newcomen. The building was taken over in 1831 by the Hibernian Bank, replacing Newcomen's Bank which had gone out of business six years earlier. Commercial rates represent 40% of the Corporation's total revenue.

Photo: courtesy The National Photographic Archives.

Above left: One of the many slum streets in the Dublin of over a century ago.

Above right: The layout of the new Marino Estate in the 1920s was designed to create variety and community interaction by the use of cul-de-sacs, short or curving roads, green spaces and a diversity of house design. Marino Mart, a complex of shops, schools, a library and other services was built simultaneously.

Below left: A corner view of the Marino Estate.

Below right: The high quality Corporation flats built 1994/95 along Bride Street and Golden Lane were designed by an architectural team comprising Conor O'Connor, Deputy Chief Housing Architect, Donal McCarthy and Eugene Gribben. The builders were Pierse Contracting.

Above: A secure and homely senior citizen development. Dublin Corporation is the largest housing authority in Ireland with approximately 24,500 rented dwellings (flats: 11,500, tenancy: 10,000, senior citizens: 3,000) and 14,500 tenant-purchase houses. The Housing and Community Development Services Department has the responsibility for managing and maintaining the Corporation's housing stock.

Within the area of its remit Dublin Corporation manages all of the public parks with the exception of St. Stephen's Green, Iveagh Park, Phoenix Park, the Irish National War Memorial, St Enda's Park, the Royal Hospital Kilmainham, and the National Botanic Gardens, all of which are under the care of Dúchas The Heritage Service, a division of the Department of Arts, Heritage, Gaeltacht and the Islands. Outside the central Dublin Corporation district but within the county limits the vast acreage of parks is looked after by the three County Councils. The Parks and Landscape Services Division of Dublin Corporation's Environment and Culture Department is responsible for 1416ha (3,500 acres) spread across 116 public parks and numerous open spaces which include such diverse areas as Georgian squares, heritage parks, suburban greens, neighbourhood parks, former cemeteries, nature parks, river valleys, coastal strips, motorway embankments, nature reserves, a wildlife sanctuary, sports grounds and children's playgrounds. The division also tends the city's 120,000 roadside trees and carries out 7,000 new plantings in this category every year. All these areas of activity require specialised skills which are provided by the division's 330 staff comprising general workers, craftsmen, park rangers, craft gardeners and horticultural and landscape professionals. The Parks and Landscape Services Division also runs the city's central nursery in St. Anne's Park and, at the same location, operates the enormous and highly successful Greenwaste Recycling Depot.

It is hard to believe that Dublin's public parks, now such a resplendent and much appreciated part of the city's fabric, are a relatively recent introduction. Most of the parks in the Georgian squares were excluded to the public until St. Stephen's Green was opened in 1880, followed by Merrion Square in 1974. The traditional tightly packed nature of Dublin's central core precluded any scope for parks until redevelopment in the 19th and 20th centuries provided the required spaces. The release into public ownership of large private estates gave further opportunity for park development.

Photo: courtesy of Jim O'Doherty.

Left: Herbert Park, Ballsbridge, was initially laid out to accommodate the Dublin International Exhibition in 1907. It was handed over in 1911 to the Pembroke Urban District Council by the Earl of Pembroke and was named in honour of his father, Lord Herbert of Lea. The park passed to Dublin Corporation in 1932.

Far left: A postcard view of the Canadian Pavilion's waterchute from the 1907 Exhibition. The water feature became today's duck pond.

Middle left: St Patrick's Park was developed on the site of cleared slums by Lord Iveagh, Edward Cecil Guinness, and presented by him to Dublin Corporation in the 1920s. With a cathedral on one side and Lord Iveagh's Play Centre (see page 68) on the other as its majestic backdrops the park displays colourful floral designs, classical ornaments, a fountain and an intriguing bricked arcade featuring a Literary Parade of notable Dublin writers (see page 256).

Below middle: Blessington Street Basin, a tiny park of under .75ha (2 acres), is one of the hidden treasures of the north inner city. Extensively refurbished in 1993/4 it was first built in 1803 as a reservoir for the city water supply.

Below: St Kevin's Park off Camden Row still evokes the reverent atmosphere of an old graveyard which it once was. Developed as a public park in the late 1960s it still deeply respects the remains of those buried there, several of whom were one-time prominent citizens. The ruined church originally goes back to at least 1226 and is believed to be the burial place of the martyred Archbishop Dermot O'Hurley who was hanged in 1584.

Above: A tablet in St Patrick's Park marks the reputed spot where St Patrick baptised his first Dublin converts in the 5th century.

Above: The refurbishment between 1996 and 1998 of Pearse Square had the effect of regenerating that end of Pearse Street as well as the terraces of houses surrounding the park on three sides. Its formal layout was based on the 1838 Ordnance Survey map of the park which was then known as Queen Square. The central bronze sculpture by Sandra Bell, commissioned by the Pearse Square Residents Association and the Parks and Landscape Services Division, is entitled "Harmony".

Top right: The Rose Garden in St Anne's Park. The park was first developed from 1835 as a private estate of nearly 202ha (500 acres) by the Guinness family. Lord Ardilaun (Sir Arthur Edward Guinness) was mainly responsible for all the plantations, the landscape features and the various buildings and follies. When the childless Lord and Lady Ardilaun passed away, the estate was inherited by their nephew Bishop Plunkett who in turn sold most of it to the Corporation for £55,000 in 1939. Over 81ha (200 acres) was set aside for housing and the remaining 113ha (279 acres) was retained as parkland.

Middle right: The Clock Tower in St Anne's Park overlooks the Miniature Rose Garden.

Bottle right: The magnificent Red Stables built by Lord Ardilaun which there are plans to turn into an arts centre.

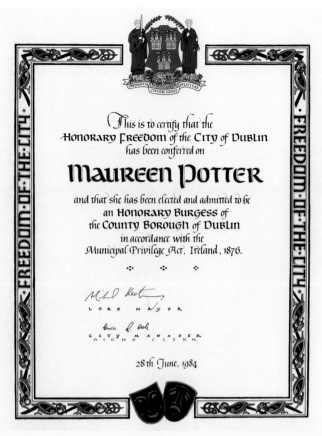

Above: The scroll of comedienne and actress Maureen Potter O'Leary, who was granted the Honorary Freedom of Dublin in 1984. This award, the highest in the city's gift, is awarded very rarely and in its long history of 124 years it has been conferred on only 70 people. The first person to receive the honour was Isaac Butt, founder of the Home Rule Party, on 4 September 1876. The recipient is chosen by a vote of the Dublin City Council and he or she signs the Roll of Honorary Freedom later, at a formal conferring ceremony. The Freedom is purely honorific with no financial or other benefits accruing to the recipients although on his or her death the flags of the city are flown at half-mast as a mark of respect.

Honorary Freedom of the City of Dublin

(some of the recipients down the years)

W. E. Gladstone (1877)	*Eamon de Valera (1975)*
Ulysses S. Grant (1878)	*Pope John Paul II (1979)*
Charles Stewart Parnell (1882)	*Crown Prince Akihito (1985)*
Sir Hugh Lane (1908)	*Stephen Roche (1987)*
John Count McCormack (1923)	*Nelson Mandela (1988)*
Major James Fitzmaurice (1928)	*Mother Teresa (1993)*
Sir John Lavery (1935)	*Jack Charlton (1994)*
George Bernard Shaw (1946)	*President William J. Clinton (1995)*
Sean T. Ó Ceallaigh (1953)	*Gabriel M. Byrne (1999)*
Sir Alfred Chester Beatty (1955)	*U2 (2000)*
John Fitzgerald Kennedy (1963)	*Aung Sin Suu Kyi (2000)*

On 1 January 1994 Dublin County Council and the Corporation of Dun Laoghaire were replaced by three new administrative counties; South Dublin, Fingal and Dun Laoghaire-Rathdown. The area covered by the Dun Laoghaire-Rathdown County Council is bounded on the north by Dublin City, to the south by Co. Wicklow, to the east by the Irish Sea and to the west by the foothills of the Dublin Mountains. A population of 189,999 (1996 census) resides within the council's jurisdiction of 127sq km (49sq miles), taking in districts of Ballybrack, Blackrock, Clonskeagh, Dundrum, Dun Laoghaire and Glencullen.

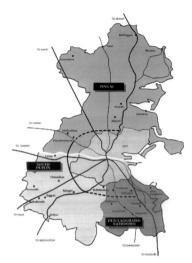

Above: Map of the Dublin Corporation and the three County Council areas.

Above: The motto on the crest of the Dun Laoghaire-Rathdown County Council, "O Chuan go Sliabh", means "From the Harbour to the Mountain" signifying the breadth of the county.

Above right: The County Hall of Dun Laoghaire-Rathdown on Marine Road is a successful amalgam of two periods and two modes of architecture. Designed in a Venetian style by J. L. Robinson the original Dun Loaghaire Town Hall was opened in 1880. The superb extension was added in 1998 and while it is uncompromisingly modern in design it is still sympathetic to the older adjoining building. Architects for the extension were McCullough Mulvin in association with Robinson Keefe and Devane.

Right: In 1977 the Maritime Institute of Ireland, a body devoted to the promotion of our seafaring heritage, opened the National Maritime Museum in the former Mariners' Church at Haigh Terrace, Dun Laoghaire. The church was built in 1837 for the benefit of visiting sailors and of those from the Royal Navy guardships permanently stationed in the harbour. Dominated by the revolving lighting optic, which shone from the Baily Lighthouse until 1972, the museum possesses one of the most significant maritime collections in these islands. A contender for pride of place must be the 11.6m (38ft) long French naval ship's boat normally used for ferrying senior officers. It was captured after the French invasion fleet, organised by Wolfe Tone, turned back from Bantry Bay in 1796. Still displaying its post-French Revolution colours of red, white and blue, the craft is believed to be the oldest surviving ship's boat in the world.

The county of Fingal covers an area of 450sq km (173sq miles) and stretches from the River Liffey up along the borders of Co. Meath to just north of Balbriggan. The county has a population of at least 167,433 (1996 census) who live in rural settings such as Lusk, Rush, Ballyboghill, Oldtown, Naul, Balrothery, Garristown and St Margarets and in the urban areas of Blanchardstown, Castleknock, Mulhuddart, Clonsilla, Balbriggan, Donabate, Swords, Skerries, Malahide, Portmarnock, Baldoyle, Sutton and Howth. Balbriggan still has its own Town Commissioners.

Fingal County Council

Above: The crest of the Fingal County Council is dominated by the raven and the longboat, both symbols of the Viking past. The motto: Flúirse Talaimh is Mara means "Rich in Land and Sea".

Above: The open competition to design the Fingal County Hall in Swords was won by Bucholz McEvoy Architects. Opened in 2000 the hall has a number of interesting design features not least being the 5-storey suspended glass façade. It was engineered by RFR of Paris (who were responsible for the Louvre Pyramid) and erected by Gruppo Bodino from Turin. The layout of the building was heavily influenced by the retention order on the existing trees. A mature Himalayan Cedar, projecting beyond the line of the other trees, especially suggested curving the front part of the Hall around it in a arc. Project architect was David O'Connor (County Architect) and BDP Ltd. worked in association with Merritt Bucholz & Karin McEvoy. The main contractor was P. J. Hegarty.

Left: Newbridge House was built in 1736 for Archbishop Charles Cobbe who had purchased lands at Donabate. The house stayed with the Cobbe family until Dublin County Council acquired it in 1985. As part of the agreement, the family generously granted, on loan to the Council, the original furniture, paintings and objets d'art so the house uniquely retains its own rich collection of contents. The Cobbe family still continues to reside from time to time at Newbridge. The Parks Department of Fingal County Council now maintains the house and the 145.7ha (360 acres) of the demesne which is preserved as a fine example of an 18th century landscape. Adjoining the house is a marvellous cobbled courtyard and around it are stone outhouses which have been restored and opened as a museum of late 18th century rural life in Ireland. An 8ha (20 acres) working farm is attached to the museum and contains the animals associated with traditional Irish farms such as cattle, sheep, chickens, horses, hens, pigs, goats and pheasants. The house, farm and regional park are open to the public.

South Dublin County Council administers, from its headquarters at Tallaght, an area of 223sq km (86sq miles) which stretches southwards from the River Liffey to the Wicklow border and from Dublin City westwards to Co Kildare. The main urban areas of the county, whose population is around 250,000, are Lucan, Clondalkin, Tallaght, Rathfarnham and Templeogue.

Above: The crest of South Dublin County Council carries the symbols of the essential characteristics of the administrative area. The Rivers Liffey and Dodder are represented by the blue, wavy bands. The linked series of inverted V shapes symbolises the border hills. St. Maelruan's monastery, as an early Christian seat of learning at Tallaght, is remembered by the open book bearing a Celtic cross. The interlaced pattern at the base of the shield conveys the notion of infrastructure such as the construction of roads, buildings and so forth.

Above: The contractor chosen to build the South Dublin County Council's Headquarters at Tallaght was John Paul Construction and the selected designer was Gilroy McMahon. The building was completed in the record time of one year and staff began to arrive in March 1994. At the same time a County Library was erected which, along with the new Civic Theatre, gave a sense of enclosure to a new urban space, the first in a series of interlinked plazas which will help to develop an urbanism so long missing in Tallaght. The sculpture "Interaction" is by Michael Bulfin and symbolises the complexities of life and human interactions at all levels.

Right: The Civic Theatre in Tallaght, opened in 1998, has been a major catalyst in creating the perception of Tallaght Town Centre as being just that: a town centre. Providing an eclectic range of performances the theatre has become a draw, not just to the local community, but to the whole county and city of Dublin. Designed by the Architectural Services Department of the South Dublin County Council (under Eddie Conroy and Brian Brennan), the Civic Theatre has a main auditorium seating 320 patrons and a more intimate studio space with 80 seats.

Chapter Seven

Stately Presence

No sooner was the ink dry on the 1921 Treaty between the new Irish Free State and Britain than former comrades-in-arms fell out with each other over the terms of the accord. The feud of words soon escalated into a full-blown Civil War which heaped further devastation onto a city barely recovered from the destruction of the 1916 Rebellion. When peace was finally restored in 1923 the job of rebuilding the ruined city centre was immediately begun. However, the emotional scars left behind by "brother fighting brother" would take longer to heal. Apart from the reinstatement of O'Connell Street and its neighbouring streets and the rebuilding of the Custom House and the Four Courts, Dublin Corporation and the Government had the awesome task of urgently rehousing the tens of thousands of people who were living cheek by jowl in appalling tenements. To say that the country lacked the economic wealth to carry out these basic tasks would be an understatement and yet, in a generation, huge inroads had been made to alleviate the miserable housing conditions. The Government itself owned a huge stock of buildings of architectural merit and of cultural importance but such were the demands on limited financial resources that many of these treasures were sadly neglected and some were even squandered or destroyed altogether. In the inglorious 1960s and 70s Government and public bodies even led the way in ruthlessly sweeping aside the legacies of centuries in favour of bland or downright ugly developments.

Above: The official emblem of Ireland is the Harp and it is used, for example, on the reverse side of Irish coins and on all Government stationery. The actual design is modelled on the so-called Brian Boru Harp held at Trinity College (see page 34).

Thankfully, attitudes have since changed for the better and the unprecedented strengthening of the Government's finances from the 1990s has led to a massive reinvestment in public properties which has, for the most part, successfully reinstated and revealed again the many remaining examples of Dublin's rich heritage. The state agency vested with the responsibility to oversee the design, building and maintenance of state-owned buildings is the Office of Public Works. Publicly-owned historic sites, monuments, visitor centres and parks are normally under the care of Dúchas The Heritage Service, part of the Department of Arts, Heritage, Gaeltacht and the Islands.

Above: Leinster House was built in 1745 for the Earl of Kildare (he was created Duke of Leinster in 1766). Richard Cassels (1690-1751) was the architect and he designed what was to become the largest mansion in the city. The Kildare family sold the house in 1815 to the Dublin Society (later the Royal Dublin Society). The Society built extensions to the main house, including the lecture theatre, and its various scholarly collections evolved into the adjoining National Library and National Museum. In 1922 the house was bought by the Government to serve as a Parliament House in which Dáil Éireann (the Lower House) and Seanad Éireann (the Senate or Upper House) would sit. The Project Management Services unit of the Office of Public Works are currently supervising a £25 million extension to Leinster House which will provide additional Government offices.

Right: The Dáil Chamber occupies the former RDS Lecture Theatre.

Photo: courtesy of Dúchas The Heritage Service.

In the late 1980s, Charles J. Haughey, then Taoiseach (Prime Minister), sought to provide a distinctive identity for the seat of Government and at the same time raise Dublin's status as a European capital. His vehicle to achieve this and at the same time provide much needed additional accommodation for Government offices was the rather imperial-looking complex of buildings on Merrion Street which was first opened in 1922. Designed by Sir Aston Webb in the expansive Edwardian Baroque style, it was to be the last major construction undertaken by the British Government in Dublin while the whole of Ireland was still part of the Empire. Government offices were allocated the wings next to the street and the Royal College of Science (later followed by the Engineering Department of the University College Dublin) was given the recessed central block. When the university's engineering facility re-located to Belfield the Government set about transforming the whole complex into what would be known as Government Buildings. A large part of the £17.6 million funding required for the conversion was largely defrayed by the sale of a row of state-owned Georgian houses on the opposite side of Merrion Street. These houses now form part of the Merrion Hotel. Externally, the buildings had become a dark grey colour from the build-up of years of grime and pollution. When the stonework was cleaned the resulting brightness of the façades and the new visibility of the architectural embellishments came almost as a shock to Dubliners who had simply not noticed the buildings before then. The floodlighting of the exterior and the courtyard fountain feature imparted an altogether new night-time character to this part of the city. Begun in Spring 1989, the conversion of the interior of Government Buildings was stunning. The halls, staircases, corridors and rooms, redecorated in a light and airy manner, are a showcase for Irish artists practising in the disciplines of painting, sculpture, glasswork, woodwork, tapestry making, carpet weaving and furniture making. Where possible, only Irish materials, including native woods, were used.

Government Buildings now house the offices of The Taoiseach and of the Department of The Taoiseach, the Government Secretariat, the Cabinet Suite (the Council Chamber and associated offices), the Press Conference Room, some Government departments and offices for TDs (Teachtaí Dála or Members of Parliament). Charles J. Haughey, moved into his new office in December 1990 and work was completed to the remainder of the accommodation within a year. The refurbishment was a supreme achievement by all concerned. The OPW architectural team included Klaus Unger, David Byers and Angela Rolfe, the same group who had just completed the restoration of Dublin Castle and the building of its new Conference Centre. The main contractor was McInerney Contracting (since acquired by Pierse Contracting).

Above: Government Buildings, Merrion Street, was begun in 1904 and completed in 1922. On top of the flanking wings and the columnar screen are fine sculptures by Charles W. Harrison.

Photo: courtesy of Department of The Taoiseach.

Above: The new ceremonial staircase with its Irish handmade carpet leads from the inner hall of Government Buildings to the first floor, passing Evie Hone's stained-glass window "My Four Green Fields" which was originally executed for the Irish Pavilion at the World Trade Fair held in New York in 1939.

Above: The Royal Military Infirmary, designed by James Gandon (except for the latertower and cupola), opened in 1788. It functioned as a military hospital until replaced by the new King George V Hospital (St. Bricin's) in 1913. The British Army then took over the building to use it as its Irish General Headquarters. In 1923, following the Anglo-Irish Treaty, it became the headquarters of the Irish Army, which purpose it still serves. It was completely refurbished in the early to mid-1990s.

Below: The headquarters of the Department of Education are located in the former town-house of Sir Marcus Beresford, Earl of Tyrone. Built in 1740, Tyrone House was designed by Richard Cassels, the architect of Leinster House. The Government bought the premises in 1835 for the then Board of National Education. George Bernard Shaw attended the Model School which was built in the grounds of Tyrone House.

Top & above: Dr. Robert Clayton, the Protestant Bishop of Cork and Ross, was an ambitious man, and eagerly sought the limelight of Dublin and its influential society. To this end he had a splendid town mansion built in 1736 on St Stephen's Green. The building was the first Dublin house to be designed by the German, Richard Cassels, the architect of Leinster House. Dr.Clayton fell into disgrace when he publicly disputed aspects of the doctrine of the Trinity and eventually he became mentally unhinged. He died in 1758 and is buried in an old graveyard in Donnybrook. The house was purchased from his widow by the Earl of Mountcashel. By 1793 the original portico had been removed because of persistent thefts of the lead from the flat roof. In 1809, John Philpott Curran, Master of the Rolls, became the new owner. After Curran's death the house passed through a succession of barrister-owners until Benjamin Lee Guinness (Lord Iveagh) bought it in 1856. The house next door, at number 81, was soon acquired, and in 1866 the two buildings were joined and refaced in Portland stone to present the view familiar today. The house was further decorated and in 1896 the lavish ballroom was added to the rear. Three generations of the Guinness family lived here until Rupert, second Earl of Iveagh (the title comes from Iveagh, Co. Down), presented the house to the Irish nation in 1939. Since then it has been the headquarters of the Department of Foreign Affairs. Iveagh House, as the building is now known, has one of the most sumptuous interiors in the country.

Above: A view of the General Post Office (GPO). The first Dublin postmaster, Nicholas Fitzsymon, was appointed in 1562 and in 1599 regular mail services were established between Dublin and London. A Letter Office (from where one could post or receive a letter) was operating in Castle Street by 1638. In 1668 the letter office moved to High Street, then Fishamble Street (1680) and Sycamore Alley (1709). Queen Anne passed a Bill in 1711 making the Letter Offices around the Empire subject to the Postmaster General in London. Fownes Court became the new location of the Letter Office, by then known as the General Post Office, and from there it moved to College Green (1771) before finally settling in 1818 into its first purpose-built home in Sackville (now O'Connell) Street. The National Penny Post was inaugurated in 1840 and the modern mail system was launched. The GPO, a striking building by any standard, was designed by Francis Johnston and cost £50,000 to build. Granite was used throughout except for the portico and its six Ionic columns where Portland stone was employed. Surmounting the scene are Edward Smyth's sculptures of Mercury, Hibernia and Fidelity. In March 1916 the public office was reopened after extensive modernisation. One month later it and the whole building except the façade lay in rubble. The GPO had been occupied as the virtual headquarters of the Rebels during the 1916 Rising and had been set ablaze by the British artillery. In 1929 a reconstructed GPO opened again for business. Advantage had been taken of the destruction in Henry Street to lengthen the building on that side from 36.5m (120ft) to 100.5m (330ft). A further extensive renovation was carried out in 1984 to mark the creation of An Post, a semi-state company which had been formed from the old Department of Posts and Telegraphs.

Above: The headquarters of the Office of Public Works (OPW) occupies the residence built in 1760 for the Monck family. It was purchased by the Government in 1848 and passed on to the OPW in 1913. The OPW is responsible for designing, building and maintaining Government properties including the overseas embassies.

Photo: courtesy of the National Photographic Archive.

Above: The ruined hulk of the GPO in the aftermath of the 1916 Rebellion.

Left: Architects for the Central Bank were Sam Stephenson and Associates. Built between 1972 and 1978 its method of construction was unique in Dublin for that time. Each floor was built separately on the ground and then hoisted into position to hang suspended from the central core. Work to upgrade the front plaza was completed in early 2000.

Above: The former Royal Irish Constabulary's (RIC) Officers' Club was attached to that organisation's training depot in the Phoenix Park. In 1922 the RIC was disbanded and the Garda Síochána (Guardians of the Peace) was formed. The old RIC training depot is now the national headquarters of the Garda, a force of over 11,000 men and women.

Middle right: The first Garda station in Store Street was erected in 1880 for the "C" Division of the Dublin Metropolitan Police (DMP). Originally founded in 1836 as an unarmed regional police force separate from the RIC, the DMP was amalgamated with the Garda Síochána in 1925. Responsible for the North Central City, the station was caught up in the disturbances of the 1913 General Strike. When the GPO was occupied by the rebels in 1916 it is said that the Station Sergeant dispatched a couple of constables to oust the insurgents! The new high-tech station replaced the original building in the late 1990s. It was designed by Campbell Conroy Hickey Architects and built by Christopher Bennet & Sons.

Right: To help identify Garda Stations a traditional-style lamp is usually fixed over the entrance.

Far right: "B" Division, one of the six divisions in the Dublin Metropolitan region, is based in the granite-faced Pearse Street Garda Station, built in 1910. On either side of the station's two entrances are a pair of carved busts. One set represents the rank of inspector of the old DMP and denoted the officers' entrance. The other one represents constables and was the intended door for the rank and file.

Photo: courtesy of An Garda Síochána

Photo: courtesy of The National Gallery of Ireland.

Above: Inside a temporary Crystal Palace type structure, erected on the lawn of Leinster House, the country's greatest art collection up to then was assembled for showing at the 1853 Great Industrial Exhibition. This event inspired the foundation of the Irish Institution to promote the idea of a National Gallery. Public interest was cultivated by holding annual loan exhibitions of Old Masters and, with subscriptions starting to come in, a number of paintings were acquired. At the same time a committee had been formed to commemorate in some permanent way the munificence of William Dargan, the outstanding inaugurator of many Irish railway companies, who had almost single-handedly financed the Great Exhibition. Agreeing that an Irish National Gallery would be a fitting testimonial for Dargan, the committee donated £5,000 to the Irish Institution. Built as a copy of the neighbouring Natural History Museum, the Gallery opened in 1864 – the same day that Dargan's statue in the front lawn, sculpted by Thomas Farrell, was unveiled. In 1903 the Gallery was enlarged and the present portico entrance was constructed. A further extension, the North Wing, was opened in 1968 and both these additions are very well matched with the original narrow South Wing. The success of the Gallery is in part due to the succession of gifted directors who arranged many shrewd acquisitions. Early directors such as George Mulvany, Henry Doyle (the uncle of Sir Arthur Conan Doyle), Walter Armstrong and Sir Hugh Lane established the international reputation of the Gallery by purchasing important works of famous artists, European and Irish. George Bernard Shaw spent many a youthful day appreciating the treasures and his bequests to the Gallery, principally the royalties from "Pygmalion" and "My Fair Lady", have helped to further enrich the collection and make the National Gallery one of the finest for its size in the world. The National Gallery of Ireland is a most welcoming institution and offers many facilities including touch-screen computers, lectures, family and open days, drawing studies, school programmes and guided tours.

Above: "Doña Antonia Zárate, Actress" by Francisco de Goya (1746 – 1828). The National Gallery possesses an extraordinary range of works and many world-famous names are represented including Rembrandt, Fra Angelico, Velázquez, Vermeer, Murillo, Hogarth, Reynolds, Turner, Gainsborough, Titian, Caravaggio, Brueghel, Van Dyck, El Greco and Picasso. The Irish School includes Osborne, O'Conor, Maclise, Hone, Orpen, Jack B. Yeats, John B. Yeats and Paul Henry.

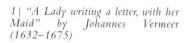

1 2 3
4 5
6

1| "A Lady writing a letter, with her Maid" by Johannes Vermeer (1632–1675)

2| "Farm at Lezaven" (the artist's estate) by Roderic O'Conor (1860–1940)

3| A view of the Baroque Room of the National Gallery of Ireland.

4 & 5| In the mid 1990s, at a cost of £9 million, the Gallery was upgraded to modern international standards and a comprehensive refurbishment was carried out to the 1968 North Wing (far right). An open courtyard was glazed in to provide a warm and attractively decorated atrium (right).

6| An artist's impression of the new 4,368sq m (44,000sq ft) extension which will link the Gallery to Clare Street by April 2001. The new wing will have suites of galleries, a centre for the study of Irish art, an audio-visual room, a Gallery shop, a Wintergarden Restaurant and other visitor amenities. Architects for the project are the Scottish firm, Benson & Forsyth and the main contractors are Michael McNamara & Co. Total cost will be around £20 million of which £7.5 million was granted from the European Regional Development Fund and £2 million was contributed from the Exchequer. The private sector, including significant individual corporate sponsorships, provided the balance.

Left: From its foundation in 1731 the Dublin (later to become the Royal Dublin) Society (RDS) built up a library for the use of members which was transferred to Leinster House when this building became the headquarters of the RDS in 1815. The library received a great boost in 1863 when it inherited the vast and varied collection of Dr Jasper Joly. Joly had intimated in his will that his life's work should be made accessible to the general public and accordingly, after the submission of a special commissioner's report, the Dublin Science and Art Museums Act of 1877 was passed. Under the terms of this Act the Library (except for certain books), the Museum, the School of Art, and the Botanic Gardens were transferred from the Society to the guardianship of the State. Some land on either side of Leinster House was purchased by the Government and plans were drawn up in 1884 for the magnificent buildings which today house the National Library of Ireland and the National Museum of Ireland. On the official opening day, 15 August 1890, the Lord Lieutenant, Earl Zetland, conferred the honour of knighthood on the senior architect, Thomas Newenham Deane. Reference material in the Library is mainly concerned with items of Irish origin or interest and consists of books, newspapers, periodicals, maps, prints, manuscripts, topographical drawings and Government reports. There are also collections of ballads and posters and copies of printed publications of Irish works where such originals are only held in foreign libraries. A free Genealogical Service is available for those researching their family history. The National Photographic Archive (see page 110) is located at Meeting House Square in Temple Bar and the Heraldic Office and Museum is housed in adjacent premises to the main library in Kildare Street.

Photo: courtesy of The National Library of Ireland.

Above: An artist's impression of the extension to the National Library of Ireland due for completion by the end of 2000. The National College of Art & Design (NCAD) building, the site of the new extension, was built in 1827 for the Drawing Schools of the (Royal) Dublin Society. The last of the NCAD staff and students left the building in 1998 (for their new premises in Thomas Street) and work began to adapt and extend it for integration into the National Library. The extension is located between the original library and Leinster House. It will provide extra space for public reading rooms, archive storage, seminar rooms, an Oireachtas Book Repository, a new Prints and Drawings Department and a vastly improved genealogical research and advisory facility.

Left: The interior of the main Reading Room of the National Library of Ireland.

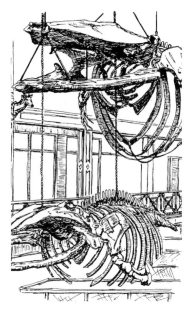

Above: In 1792 the Dublin Society purchased the Leskean Collection of minerals and insects and housed them in its Hawkins Street premises. From these humble beginnings the museum steadily grew and eventually moved to its present home on Merrion Street, designed by Frederick Clarendon, in 1857. The Natural History Museum now has one of the finest collections of insects in the world today. Ireland's varied wildlife is represented on the ground floor and the collection of animals from all over the world is displayed on the upper floor and galleries. From the ceiling are suspended the skeletons of two whales which has perished after becoming stranded along the Irish coast. Today the museum is an important research and identification centre in the study of insects and Ireland's wild fauna.

Above: The National Museum of Ireland was opened in 1890 at Kildare Street and was the result of merging together the collections of the Royal Dublin Society, The Royal Irish Academy and, later on, the Royal Society of Antiquaries of Ireland. The archaeological collections include; "Prehistoric Ireland", "Ireland's Gold" (the finest collection of prehistoric gold in Europe), "The Treasury" (Celtic and Medieval art), and "Viking Age Ireland". "Ancient Egypt" gives a glimpse of a fascinating civilisation. "The Road to Irish Independence" deals with the struggles for Irish freedom 1916-1921.

Below: When Collins Barracks was built in 1701 as The Barracks (later known as the Royal Barracks) it could accommodate 5,000 soldiers and was believed at that time to be the largest in the world. By 1992, when the Government declared its intention to close it down, Collins Barracks was already the world's oldest purpose-built barracks in continuous use in the world. On 18 September 1997 the National Museum of Ireland opened its additional new premises in the restored and revamped buildings of Collins Barracks. The Office of Public Works, architects Gilroy McMahon and contractors Pierse Contracting, carried out the sensitive conversion. Collins Barracks contains the National Museum's Decorative Arts collection as well as artefacts ranging from weaponry, furniture, folklife and costume to silver, ceramics and glassware.

Above: The National Museum of Ireland, Collins Barracks, is located in four-storey stone buildings around Clarke Square, one of the parade squares of the former barracks. Each tenth step of a measured 100 military paces is still marked out on the façades. It is hoped, at a later stage, to convert buildings around the other two squares for use by the Museum.

The Chester Beatty Library moved from secluded Shrewsbury Road and re-opened on 7 February 2000 in its new state-of-the-art home in and behind the Clock Tower building at Dublin Castle. Sir Alfred Chester Beatty (1875-1968), a New York-born mining millionaire, purchased over his lifetime a remarkable collection of precious material from the Middle and Far East. Living much of his later life in Dublin and becoming Ireland's first Honorary Citizen in 1957, he decided to leave the results of his life's work to the nation. The Collection, now arranged within themes through a series of excitingly laid-out exhibition rooms, is considered to be one of the most important of its kind in the world. Certainly the Library of Qur'ans (Korans), dating from the 9th century, is said to be second only to the Topkapi Collection in Istanbul. The outstanding exhibits also include Babylonian clay tablets from 2700BC, ancient Egyptian papyri, some of the earliest known Gospel texts from pre-200AD, Chinese jade books, miniature paintings from the courts of India's Mughal emperors, Chinese snuff boxes, illuminated Persian manuscripts, European medieval and renaissance manuscripts and other objets d'art from across Asia, the Middle East, North Africa and Europe. The Chester Beatty Library is a charitable trust supported by Government as a national institution.

Photo: courtesy of the Trustees of the Chester Beatty Library.

Above: "The Annunciation", a 15th century miniature from Ms. W82 of the Chester Beatty Library Collection.

Photo: courtesy of the Trustees of the Chester Beatty Library.

Above: "The Entrance to Enoshima", a Japanese print from "36 Views of Mount Fuji", Hiroshige, 1858

Photo: courtesy of the Trustees of the Chester Beatty Library.

Above: The impressive staircase in the Clock Tower building had suffered from extensive dry rot and had to be restored.

Photo: courtesy of the Trustees of the Chester Beatty Library.

Above: The Library and Reading Room contains original mahogany bookcases (made by Hicks of Dublin in 1950) and the marvellous Chinese-style lacquered ceiling transferred from Shrewsbury Road.

Above: This red-bricked contemporary building at the north entrance to Meeting House Square off Essex Street was designed by architects O'Donnell & Tuomey and completed in June 1996. It houses the National Photographic Archive in whose air-conditioned basement are stored, among other photographic records, up to a quarter of a million glass-plate negatives. The arched entrance from the forecourt to the Archive suggests a bridge linking Essex Street East to the square. The upper storeys of the building contain the offices, studios, darkrooms and teaching spaces for the Dublin Institute of Technology School of Photography. A projector room over the ground floor aims its projectors at the external wall of the Photographic Gallery on the opposite side of the square on the occasion of summertime outdoor film shows (see page 212).

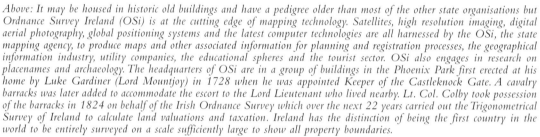

Above: It may be housed in historic old buildings and have a pedigree older than most of the other state organisations but Ordnance Survey Ireland (OSi) is at the cutting edge of mapping technology. Satellites, high resolution imaging, digital aerial photography, global positioning systems and the latest computer technologies are all harnessed by the OSi, the state mapping agency, to produce maps and other associated information for planning and registration processes, the geographical information industry, utility companies, the educational spheres and the tourist sector. OSi also engages in research on placenames and archaeology. The headquarters of OSi are in a group of buildings in the Phoenix Park first erected at his home by Luke Gardiner (Lord Mountjoy) in 1728 when he was appointed Keeper of the Castleknock Gate. A cavalry barracks was later added to accommodate the escort to the Lord Lieutenant who lived nearby. Lt. Col. Colby took possession of the barracks in 1824 on behalf of the Irish Ordnance Survey which over the next 22 years carried out the Trigonometrical Survey of Ireland to calculate land valuations and taxation. Ireland has the distinction of being the first country in the world to be entirely surveyed on a scale sufficiently large to show all property boundaries.

Right: The Waterways Visitor Centre rather appropriately rests on stilts over the waters of the Grand Canal Quay. Operated by Dúchas The Heritage Service, the centre explores Ireland's inland waterways, their historical background and their modern amenities.

Right: The Meteorological Centre, at Glasnevin, headquarters for Met Éireann, the Irish Meteorological Service, was built by John Sisk & Son in 1979 to a design by Liam McCormick. Its pyramid-shaped outline had as much to do with allowing light through to neighbouring houses as it had to do with any symbolic reference to the ancient astronomers of Egypt and Mexico.

Below: One of Dublin's finest yet least known parks is the Iveagh Gardens located between Earlsfort Terrace (behind the National Concert Hall) and Harcourt Street. Closing off the vista at the end of the central path is the Cascade, one of several distinctive features that grace this secluded oasis. The cascade itself is an immense rockery composed of limestone, sandstone and granite gathered from every corner of Ireland. 1364 litres (three hundred gallons) a second plunge over the rocks and into the pool below. The layout of the gardens varies from the formal to the free natural environment and includes a rustic grotto, rockeries, fountains, a maze, a rosarium, archery grounds, sweeping lawns, statuary, wilderness and woodlands, all contained within the 3.4ha (8 acres) site. In 1777 the Earl of Clonmel built his mansion on Harcourt Street and took in what is now the Iveagh Gardens as his own private demesne. After his death they became known as Coburg Gardens and in 1860 they were attached to a new mansion, Iveagh House, built on St. Stephen's Green. The new owner was Benjamin Lee Guinness (Lord Iveagh) who, three years later, leased the grounds to the Dublin Exhibition Palace and Winter Gardens Company. This organisation built a large exhibition centre on Earlsfort Terrace (later to be remodelled when University College Dublin occupied it from 1918) and an enormous glass structure to house the Winter Gardens. The park, as we know it today, was then laid out by the eminent landscape designer, Ninian Nivan. When the exhibitions had run their course the gardens reverted back to Lord Iveagh who sold them on to University College Dublin in 1939. The state bought the gardens in 1994 and, under Dúchas The Heritage Service, they have since been undergoing extensive refurbishment.

Top & above: One of the fountains and the Rosarium in the Iveagh Gardens.

Above: In 1956 the fountain of the "Three Fates" was presented by the German Federal Republic to the people of Ireland in recognition of the contributions made by them towards the relief of distress in post-war Germany. It was erected at the Leeson Street entrance to St Stephen's Green. The bronze monument was designed by the eminent Bavarian sculptor, Professor Joseph Wackerle, whose most famous work is the main city fountain in Munich. Called Norenbrunnen, the 2.7m (9ft) high figures on the limestone rockery, portray the legendary Fates from Nordic mythology as they spin and weave the thread of man's destiny.

Above: The origins of tranquil St Stephen's Green, set right in the middle of the south city centre, go back to medieval days when it was a marshy common used for public grazing. In 1663 Dublin Corporation decided to sell the perimeter lands of the common as building lots and maintain the inner core as a green open space. The Green was surrounded by a stone wall and laid out with formal pathways around the boundary. By 1814 the Green had deteriorated to such an extent that it was handed over to commissioners representing the local householders. They redesigned the park, demolished the walls and erected a railings. Admittance to the park was confined to the local residents which was deeply resented by other citizens accustomed to its accessibility. Lord Ardilaun (Sir Arthur Edward Guinness) resolved the problem when he secured, in 1877, the passing of an Act entrusting the maintenance of the Green to the Commissioners of Public Works, which allowed access to the public again from 1880. Ardilaun also paid off the accrued debts of the Green and funded the new landscaping, the results of which are evident today. St Stephen's Green is now under the care of Dúchas The Heritage Service.

Above: The first battle of the Second Boer War started at 2.30 p.m. on 20 October 1899 when the Royal Dublin Fusiliers clashed with Luke Meyer's scouts at Smith's Nek Pass, east of Dundee. In 1907 the Duke of Connaught opened the triumphal arch, erected at the Grafton Street end of St Stephen's Green, as a memorial to the 212 officers and men of the five battalions of the Royal Dublin Fusiliers who fell in that war. The names of some of the battlefields are carved around the granite blocks of the arch and those of the fallen are inscribed on limestone panels over the gates.

Left: Fountain, St Stephen's Green.

The turbulent history of Ireland has produced many an army that campaigned across Irish soil for one espoused cause or another. By the 17th century the last fighting native army was crushed at the Battle of Aughrim in 1691. The Protestant Ascendancy enrolled its own superbly equipped 100,000 strong Volunteer Army in 1778 but it was dissolved five years later. While the disastrous rebellion of 1798 did bring tens of thousands into the field to fight the British forces, they lacked the formal organisation and discipline of an army. Irish regiments and militia were formed in the 19th century but always as part of the British Army. The abortive Easter Rising of 1916 led to the formation two years later of the Irish Republican Army, a force that had grown to 114,000 combatants prior to the Treaty with Britain in December 1921. After the Treaty the new National Army of the Irish Free State took over the seven major barracks of the British Army in Dublin along with 41 other military installations. At the end of the Civil War in April 1923 the National Army had 55,000 soldiers which had decreased to 11,000 by 1927. The figure has reduced slightly since then but the emphasis today is on the quality of personnel, training and equipment rather than numbers.

Above: Marlborough Cavalry Barracks, at Blackhorse Avenue, completed in the early 1890s, was initially garrisoned by the 10th Hussars. The glamour and pomp of the cavalry were well matched by the magnificence and flamboyance of the architecture. In a composite of styles the buildings sprout a symphony of towers, turrets, spires, cupolas and tall chimneys. Handed over to the Irish Army in 1922, the barracks was subsequently renamed after Brigadier Richard McKee who was killed by the British Auxiliaries on Bloody Sunday, 1920.

Above: The Pearse Museum, at St Enda's Park, Rathfarnham, was a former school run by Patrick Pearse. From here he, his brother, two of the teachers and some pupils left to participate in the 1916 Rising.

Left: Cathal Brugha (formerly Portobello) Barracks was built between 1810 and 1815. One of the largest barracks in the country it served as GHQ for the National Army in 1922. It was from here that Michael Collins, the Commander-in-Chief, departed on that fateful trip in August 1922, during the Civil War, which ended in an ambush and his death at Béal na mBláth, Co. Cork.

Above: This DeHavilland Vampire Jet is one of several aircraft, the earliest dating from before the Second World War to those more recently decommissioned, which are parked in an informal outdoor museum at Baldonnel Aerodrome.

Photo: courtesy of the Air Corp.

Above: A Casa CN235 of the Air Corps.

Above: In 1917, Captain Sholto Douglas of the Royal Flying Corps (the precursor of the Royal Air Force) was sent to Ireland to survey permanent sites for military airfields. He selected Gormanstown, Tallaght, Aldergrove, Collinstown and Baldonnel. All have survived today as airfields except Tallaght - it is now under the concrete of the Cookstown Industrial Estate. In May 1922, the Irish Air Corps (initially called the Irish Air Service) took over Baldonnel, and later Gormanstown, from the RFC. Its first aircraft was a Martynside, which had been secretly bought in 1921 to fly Michael Collins home in case the Treaty negotiations with Britain failed. By the end of 1922 the Air Corps had 14 pilots, all Great War veterans, and as many planes. In 1928, the German plane "Bremen" began the first successful east-west non-stop Transatlantic service from Baldonnel with Col James Fitzmaurice, Commanding Officer of the Air Corps, as a member of the crew. In 1936 Aer Lingus commenced its regular scheduled services from the aerodrome until Dublin Airport (Collinstown) was made ready in 1940. Today's Air Corps is on the verge of gradually modernising its ageing fleet. Its role is not one of front-line defence but of support to the regular army and navy and to the civil powers. The fleet includes the all-important helicopter wing that provides vital land and air-sea rescue services. Naval support is in the form of two Casa CN235 aircraft which are equipped with the latest electronic detection devices. Ministerial transport is catered for by a Gulfstream IV twin-engined jet and a Beech King Air 200 twin turbo propeller aircraft.

Above: When the leaders of the 1916 Easter Rising were executed their bodies were buried in quicklime on a plot of land at Arbour Hill, directly to the rear of Collins Barracks. In 1956 a permanent memorial was erected to their memory. It consists of a paved terrace backed by a curving screen wall on which sculptor Michael Biggs carved the Proclamation of the Irish Republic in Irish and in English.

Right: The Croppies Acre Memorial Park was opened in 1998 and commemorates the scores of rebels (known as Croppies) who were captured after the 1798 Rebellion. They were subsequently hanged, shot or beheaded and then thrown in mass graves dug on this land when it was waste ground in front of Collins Barracks.

Above: The Irish National War Memorial, Islandbridge.

When the senseless carnage of the First World War finally halted and the Irish nation, among many other countries around the world, counted the tragic toll of its dead there was a groundswell of opinion that a suitable memorial should be erected to commemorate the known 49,400 Irish soldiers who lost their lives, mainly on the fields of France. A Memorial Committee was formed and after its first meeting in the Viceregal Lodge in 1919, a fund was launched which raised a staggering £45,000 (worth at least 100 times that amount today) within the first year. The memorial record of those officially listed as killed was compiled into four great volumes and a hundred copies of these Books of Remembrance were published in 1923. The committee searched for a suitable site and was offered the Longmeadows Estate along the banks of the Liffey at Islandbridge by the Government in 1929. The War Memorial was to occupy an area of about 8ha (20 acres) set into a linear park totalling 60ha (148 acres). Work commenced in late 1933 and, ironically, was completed in 1939, just before the outbreak of the Second World War. The Memorial and Gardens were designed by Sir Edwin Lutyens (1869-1944), a distinguished architect and landscape designer, famous for designing many stately gardens, war memorials and, not least, the layout of New Delhi including the Viceroy's Palace. The Gardens are laid out in symmetrical forms and the built features include the centrally placed War Stone of Irish granite which weighs 7 and a half tons. This "altar" is flanked on either side by two fountain basins with obelisks in their centres representing candles. South of the War Stone stands the Great Cross directly in line with the main avenue. Four pillar bookrooms, two at either end of the central lawn, contain the Books of Remembrance. On the far side of each pair of bookrooms, through the pergolas of granite columns and oak beams, are the outstanding sunken rose gardens. These have central lily ponds and are encircled by yew hedges. The Irish National War Memorial, the largest of its kind in these islands, is under the care of Dúchas The Heritage Service in conjunction with the National War Committee.

Above: The Seaman's Memorial on City Quay (unveiled in 1990) honours the 136 seamen lost while serving on Irish merchant ships during the Second World War. Even though Ireland remained neutral during the War and the ships had "Éire" (Ireland) brightly painted in huge letters on their sides, fourteen of them were still sunk. Eight fell prey to U-boats, three to mines, one to an unidentified aircraft and two disappeared without trace.

Right: Mountjoy Jail, built between 1847 and 1850, is named after Luke Gardiner, Lord Mountjoy, who was responsible for developing large parts of Dublin's northside (see also page 120) The jail's tall chimneys, so much part of the local topography, were designed to allow a complete change of air every eight minutes throughout the prison. Many executions took place on the prison's scaffold or in the execution chamber. The most famous was that of patriot Kevin Barry, in 1920. The last capital punishment was carried out in 1954. Made famous by Brendan Behan in "The Quare Fella", "The Ould Triangle" is still hanging on its strap but no longer goes "jingle jangle" to announce fall-in for work every morning and Mass on Sundays. The opening of Cloverhill Remand Prison and the Midland Prison in Portlaoise will eliminate previous overcrowding and allow the first comprehensive modernisation of Mountjoy since it was built. The vista as shown in the drawing has since been concealed from view from the North Circular by the building of the new Women's Prison.

Middle right: The inner courtyard of the Women's Prison. The new £13 million prison was completed in 1999 and is capable of holding 80 prisoners in comfortable and dignified surroundings. Called the Dóchas (Hope) Centre, it has no bars but large windows, no cells but airy rooms and well-behaved residents have the door key to their own rooms. The prison layout is composed of seven self-contained residential houses, a block containing a gym and facilities for further education and work training.

Above: A view of the Women's Prison from the North Circular Road.

10-14th June 1768. | **Freeman's Journal** | *Issue No. 7891*

At Night a numerous Mob perambulated the Town all Night and the succeeding Day, in which short Period they sacked about 40 Houses. The Devastation committed upon this occasion not withstanding the remarkable industry of our Magistrates, consisting of twenty eight, to prevent it, cannot be equalled by any one similar Circumstance in the Memory of Man. Forty of the Rioters were apprehended by the Lord Mayor and Sheriffs (most of whom were found fatigued after their Day's Hard Labour, intoxicated by Liquor) at Ringsend, where they finished their Work, by destroying two other Houses, as they were conducted to Newgate, where they now remain - miserable Objects indeed. Who would not wish to live in the Free City! Sensible and spirited Magistrates.

Chapter Eight

Institutional Heritage

THERE WAS little concern among the populations of Viking and Medieval Dublin for the establishment of fine seats of learning, for research academies or for foundations to look after the general welfare of people. Energies were sapped with the daily grind to stay alive and to sustain one's family in the face of poor living conditions, pestilence, famines and high mortality rates. Only the privileged could afford the finer things of life yet, even for them, their own concerns with the constant struggle to maintain privilege in the face of enemies from within and without coupled with everyone's relatively short life span left little room to create the very institutions that would have been to the advantage of all. Besides, the economy of the town, especially from the 14th century, was more often than not in tatters.

There was, of course, the Government and the Church. Both of these bodies have left an enormous institutional legacy as indeed has the municipal authority, Dublin Corporation. Attempts were made in the 14th century to set up a university based at St. Patrick's Cathedral but it eventually foundered. It would be 1592 before a properly constituted university, Trinity College, was established. The great priories and abbeys at one time provided some semblance of care to the wretched poor and the sick, a service which all but disappeared with the dissolution of the monasteries in the mid 16th century. It would be the early 18th century before concerned citizens began the process of building general and specialised hospitals.

The middle years of that century also ushered in the Age of Enlightenment when many institutions across a wide spectrum of learning, including the sciences, agriculture, medicine, art and the classics, were founded. This process accelerated over the following centuries and laid the foundation for the richness and vibrancy in the life, culture and economy of Ireland today.

Left: The Royal Irish Academy is one of the country's principal learned societies and was founded in 1785 to promote the "advancement of science, polite literature and antiquities". In 1852 it moved to its present abode in Dawson Street, Northland House, built in 1770 for the Knox Family of Dungannon. Treasures of the Academy include the Ardagh Chalice, the Tara Brooch and the Cross of Cong (all on display in the National Museum, Kildare Street) as well as many rare books and manuscripts. An important function of the Academy today is the publication of major works of Irish interest.

Above: Part of the Royal Dublin Society (RDS) Showgrounds.

Above: The main building of the RDS in Ballsbridge which houses its headquarters, members' rooms, libraries and exhibition halls. On 14 June 1731, 14 men met to form the Dublin Society (the "Royal" prefix was only added in 1821) to promote "husbandry, manufactures and other useful arts and sciences". The venue for their first few meetings was a room belonging to the Philosophical Society of Trinity College. For the next 200 years the society was to lead a rather nomadic existence. From October 1731 the meetings were accommodated in the Lords' Common Room at the Irish Parliament House in College Green. Thence to Shaw's Court in 1757 and to Grafton Street ten years later. After a further span of 29 years Hawkins Street became the headquarters until the penultimate move to Leinster House in 1814. When the Dublin Science and Art Museums Act of 1877 transferred control of the Library, Museum, Botanical Gardens and School of Art from the Society to the Government the compensation money was used to lease 15 acres in Ballsbridge. From 1881 the Spring and Horse Shows were held there. That first site roughly corresponds to today's Jumping Enclosure. The Agricultural Hall was removed from Kildare Street and re-erected in Ballsbridge to become the South Hall. Further building and land acquisition took place which reached a peak following the arrival of all the RDS departments after the Free State Government commandeered Leinster House in 1923. Compensation offered this time was £68,000. The 1950s saw much needed expansion across the Simmonscourt Road which culminated in 1972 with the purchase of the Masonic Girls' Orphanage and its adjoining land. Daithi P. Hanly's gigantic 1.4ha (3 acre) Simmonscourt Pavilion was begun in 1974. This structure is surmounted by a weathervane representing the legendary Arkle ridden by Pat Taffe. The Showgrounds are still the home to the fashionable International Horse Show every August. In 2000 the RDS developed the luxury Four Seasons Hotel on its grounds at the corner of Merrion and Simmonscourt Roads, having earlier sold off the Masonic Girls' Orphanage to Bewleys to build their hotel (see pages 176 and 179).

Right: John Stearne, Professor of Physic and Laws in Trinity, founded the Fraternity of Physicians and was granted a Royal Charter from Charles II in 1667. Sir Patrick Dun, personal physician to the Duke of Ormond, became president of the Fraternity in 1681 and eleven years later he widened the powers of the institution by gaining a new Charter and a new name – the King and Queen's College of Physicians in Ireland. In the same year the college abandoned Trinity Hall, its first home, and met in Dun's house. After his death in 1713 it had to wait a further 90 years before finding another permanent headquarters, this time in the new Sir Patrick Dun's Hospital. A disastrous fire in the original Kildare Street Club in 1860 gave the college an opportunity to build its own premises next door. Designed by William Murray, the classically-fronted building, which has some quite beautiful interiors, is far larger that one would expect from the outside. Renamed in 1890 as the Royal College of Physicians of Ireland, the college possesses possibly the finest medical library in Ireland. Some renowned past Presidents include physicians such as Robert Graves, William Stokes and Dominic Corrigan.

King George III granted a group of petitioning surgeons a charter in 1784 releasing them from their "preposterous union with the company of barbers". This was a reference to the medieval guild system wherein barbers extended their tonsorial expertise to include bodily surgery, often with dire consequences. The Royal College of Surgeons in Ireland (see Appendix D) first met in the boardroom of the Rotunda Hospital, and soon after inaugurated the School of Anatomy and Surgery in the Surgeons' Hall, a previously disused premises in Mercer Street. Early success prompted the need for more space, so the college purchased an old Quaker cemetery at the corner of St Stephen's Green and York Street and a new building, designed by Edward Parke, was opened there in 1810. By 1827 expansion was again considered necessary and the architect William Murray Senior (his son later designed the new College of Physicians on Kildare Street in 1860) more than doubled the original width of the façade but retained Parke's design adding three Greek deities over the pediment. During the Easter Rising a small group of rebels under Commandant Michael Mallin and Countess Markiewicz occupied the building for a week and a dent from a bullet can still be seen in the boardroom door. Built to accommodate lecture and conference halls, laboratories and offices, the modern wing to the rear was opened in 1977.

Although the College is primarily a surgical institution it has the country's largest medical school with more than 1,000 students from 45 different countries in attendance. This was brought about in 1886 when the undergraduate training of surgeons and physicians was merged. The majority of students are from overseas, many from developing countries, a fact that allows the College to make an important contribution to Third-World development. Some famous graduates of the College of Surgeons include Sir Philip Crampton (1777-1858), Abraham Colles (1773-1843) who is internationally known for his description of the common wrist fracture still called the "Colles Fracture" and Oliver St John Gogarty (1878 – 1957), an ear, nose and throat surgeon but more remembered as a wit and a poet. He lived with James Joyce in the Martello Tower in Sandycove and the character Buck Mulligan in Ulysses is based on him.

Above: Lord Ardilaun (Sir Arthur Edward Guinness), who personally bore the cost of landscaping St Stephen's Green before it was opened to the public in 1880. His bronze effigy, sculptured in 1892 by James Farrell, gazes with mild curiosity on the comings and goings around the Royal College of Surgeons in Ireland.

Above: Mary Mercer built a house for the care of poor girls in 1724 and ten years later it was converted into a 50 bed hospital. The oldest part of what became Mercer's Hospital dates from 1757 but the bulk of the building is late Victorian. Mercer's was closed in 1983 but its splendid medical tradition was, in a way, continued when the Royal College of Surgeons in Ireland bought it and an adjoining property to extend the college's campus. The former hospital is now a Community and an International Travel Health Centre run by the College. A new wing attached to Mercer's, Mercer Court, provides modern accommodation for students.

Above: The sculpture outside a convent on Baggot Street is that of Catherine McAuley, the foundress of the Sisters of Mercy. Her life-long concern was to alleviate the sufferings of the sick, especially those in reduced circumstances, and her vision was shared by many other women who joined her order. She died in 1841 but her work still lives on in the institutions founded by her sisters. In 1854 a group of sisters from Dublin, Carlow and Liverpool travelled to the Crimea and tirelessly worked alongside Florence Nightingale tending to the sick and wounded during that terrible war.

Above: Eccles Street was to have been part of a great convergence of streets ending at a magnificent circus of grand mansions. Lord Mountjoy's dream to develop this part of Dublin was shattered, as was his skull at the Battle of New Ross in the 1798 Rebellion. However, Eccles Street itself was built in the Georgian manner and one of its houses , no. 7, entered literary fame as the home of Leopold Bloom in James Joyce's "Ulysses". The sisters of Mercy bought the north-west end of the street and commenced to build, in 1851, a hospital intended for the sick poor of the city's northside. The Mater Misericordiae (Mother of Mercy) Hospital opened its doors in 1861 (the architect was John Bourke)and gradually it grew to take in virtually the whole block between Eccles Street and the North Circular Road. The original hospital building fitted in well with the Georgian streetscape but unfortunately the lower end of the street's northside was demolished (including No. 7) to make way for welcome but less visually pleasing hospital extensions. The main extension was built in 1989 and The Mater is now the only large general hospital in the inner city following the relocation of Jervis Street, the Adelaide and the Meath.

Right: The new Tallaght Hospital (officially called the Adelaide & Meath Hospital incorporating the National Children's Hospital) accepted its first patients on Sunday 21 June 1998. Planning began in 1981 to amalgamate three inner city hospitals; the Adelaide (founded 1839), the Meath (1753) and the National Children's Hospital (1821) and in 1985, following an architectural competition the firm of Robinson Keefe Devane was appointed to design the complex. Building on the 14ha (35 acre) site commenced in October 1993 under the main contractor, Laing Paul Construction, and was completed in 1998. At a cost of £140 million it was the largest capital investment in healthcare ever undertaken by the State. The hospital has 589 beds, a staggering 2,408 rooms and the main corridor is almost a quarter of a mile long (353.1m). It is a teaching centre for the medical faculty of Trinity College.

Above: The Coombe Hospital Memorial is in fact the former portico to the first Coombe Lying-in (Maternity) Hospital which was founded in 1826 for the relief of poor women in childbirth. A new and larger hospital was opened off Cork Street in 1967 and the old building, save for the portico, was demolished to make way for a housing development. On the steps at the rear of the memorial are inscribed the wondrous nicknames of the locality's legendary street characters such as "Stab the Rasher", "Johnny Forty Coats" and "Shell Shock Joe".

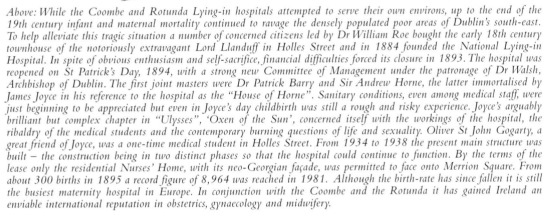

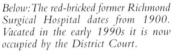

Above: While the Coombe and Rotunda Lying-in hospitals attempted to serve their own environs, up to the end of the 19th century infant and maternal mortality continued to ravage the densely populated poor areas of Dublin's south-east. To help alleviate this tragic situation a number of concerned citizens led by Dr William Roe bought the early 18th century townhouse of the notoriously extravagant Lord Llanduff in Holles Street and in 1884 founded the National Lying-in Hospital. In spite of obvious enthusiasm and self-sacrifice, financial difficulties forced its closure in 1893. The hospital was reopened on St Patrick's Day, 1894, with a strong new Committee of Management under the patronage of Dr Walsh, Archbishop of Dublin. The first joint masters were Dr Patrick Barry and Sir Andrew Horne, the latter immortalised by James Joyce in his reference to the hospital as the "House of Horne". Sanitary conditions, even among medical staff, were just beginning to be appreciated but even in Joyce's day childbirth was still a rough and risky experience. Joyce's arguably brilliant but complex chapter in "Ulysses", 'Oxen of the Sun', concerned itself with the workings of the hospital, the ribaldry of the medical students and the contemporary burning questions of life and sexuality. Oliver St John Gogarty, a great friend of Joyce, was a one-time medical student in Holles Street. From 1934 to 1938 the present main structure was built – the construction being in two distinct phases so that the hospital could continue to function. By the terms of the lease only the residential Nurses' Home, with its neo-Georgian façade, was permitted to face onto Merrion Square. From about 300 births in 1895 a record figure of 8,964 was reached in 1981. Although the birth-rate has since fallen it is still the busiest maternity hospital in Europe. In conjunction with the Coombe and the Rotunda it has gained Ireland an enviable international reputation in obstetrics, gynaecology and midwifery.

Below: The red-bricked former Richmond Surgical Hospital dates from 1900. Vacated in the early 1990s it is now occupied by the District Court.

University College Dublin (UCD) is the largest university in Ireland with approximately 17,400 undergraduate and post-graduate students. UCD owes its origins to the foundation in 1851 of the Catholic University of Ireland. Lectures first started in 1854 at No. 86 St. Stephen's Green (see page 52). The College received its Royal Charter in 1908 and was incorporated with the former Queen's Colleges at Cork and Galway (Belfast remained a Queen's College) into the new National University of Ireland. By 1960 the campus at Earlsfort Terrace had become overcrowded and the Government approved the transfer of the University to Belfield, 5km (3 miles) south of Dublin, where land had been quietly accumulated since 1934. Not everybody left Earlsfort Terrace and the building still houses the Medical Faculty and sections of the Engineering Faculty. The Great Hall has been transformed into the National Concert Hall. The campus at Belfield (named after Belfield House, the first property bought in 1934) measures 141ha (350 acres) and, as a matter of policy, is heavily landscaped and wooded.

Above: In 1963 an international competition was held in which architects were invited to submit designs for the layout of University College Dublin's new campus at Bellfield and specifically for the Arts and Commerce and Administration Buildings. Architects from over twenty countries participated and the winning design was that of a Polish architect who settled in Dublin as a result and went on to enrich the city with many more of his designs. The architect was Andrzej Wejchert who went on with with his wife, Danuta, to form A & D Wejchert Architects. The Administration Building (above) was designed by Wejchert in association with Robinson Keefe & Devane. The building contractor was John Sisk & Son. It received the Triennial Gold Medal 1971-73 from the Royal Institute of Architects of Ireland.

Right: Roebuck House, Belfield.

Far Right: This 60m (197ft) tower was built in 1972 to provide constant water pressure to all the buildings in UCD. Made of reinforced concrete the stem is pentagonal and the tank is in the form of a duodecahedron. Architects for the project were A & D Wejchert. John Paul Construction erected this geometrically precise and awkward-to-manoeuvre juggernaut, assisted by structural engineers, Thomas Garland & Partners.

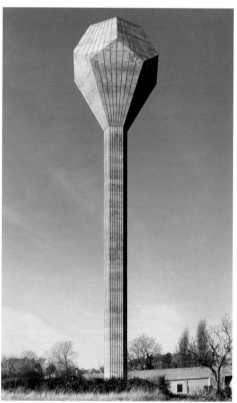

1   2
3   4
   5

1 | *The Library Building.*

2 | *Students on Campus.*

3 | *Belgrove Student Residences*

4 | *The coat-of-arms of UCD.*

5 | *The Daedalus Building, UCD, is the university's most recent building (1997) and houses the microcomputer and language centres.*

All photos: courtesy of University College Dublin.

Above: The Pro-Cathedral, dedicated to St Mary, was begun in 1816 under Archbishop Troy and finished in 1825 under Archbishop Murray. Dr Troy had hoped to build on the site now occupied by the GPO on O'Connell Street but fear of Protestant opposition persuaded him to pick the more secluded ground of the recently vacated house of Lord Annesley on Marlborough Street. The extensive vaults of the Church run under the street to the Department of Education complex and contain nearly one thousand remains including an archbishop or two. The title "Pro-Cathedral" is applied because no Roman Catholic Archbishop of Dublin has requested the Pope to revoke, from a Roman Catholic standpoint, the cathedral status granted to Christ Church (now Church of Ireland) in the 12th century.

Right: St Stephen's (fondly nicknamed the "Pepper Canister" on account of the tower's shape) was consecrated in 1824. Designed by John Bowden it cost £5,169 to build, of which £3,784 was donated by the Board of First Fruits, an organisation which taxed the first year's income of newly ordained clergymen. Situated on Mount Street Upper the church has a wonderful Victorian Renaissance interior which lends well to religious services and concerts, both of which are frequently held here.

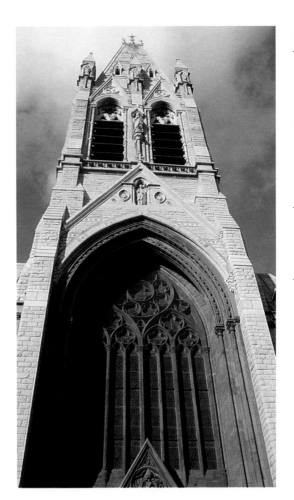

Above: St Andrew's Church beautifully refurbished, under architects Ashlin Coleman Heelan, as the headquarters of Dublin Tourism in 1996, was first opened for worship in 1866. Designed by Charles Lanyon, the church replaced an earlier one destroyed by fire in 1860 which in turn had succeeded a medieval St Andrew's which had stood nearer to Dublin Castle. The site of the present-day St Andrew's was opposite the Thingmount, or Thingmote, a huge earthen mound 12m (40ft) in height and 73m (240ft) in circumference raised by the Vikings as a ceremonial and law-making venue. It was levelled in 1685 and the clay was used to heighten Nassau Street to protect it from flooding (the old level of the street can be guaged by looking over the wall into the grounds of Trinity College).

Left: The soaring tower and spire of John's Lane Church on Thomas Street is one of the great landmarks of Dublin and is unusual in that the tower is rectangular rather than square in shape. Officially known as St John the Baptist and St Augustine the church's popular name comes from the time when it was proscribed to practice Roman Catholicism and parishioners had to use a clandestine chapel in the adjoining John's Lane. It was built for the Augustinians between 1862 and 1911. James Pearse, Patrick Pearse's father, was the sculptor of the twelve apostles in the niches around the tower. The architect was Edward Welby Pugin who was assisted by George Coppinger Ashlin. The church stands on the site of Dublin's first hospital, St. John's, founded by the Norseman, Ailred the Palmer (after whom Palmerstown is named).

Above: In 1860 Father Père Jules Leman bought Castledawson, a house built in 1790 at Blackrock on behalf of the French Holy Ghost Fathers. The congregation of the Holy Spirit (CSSp), as the order is officially known, was founded in Paris in 1703. Over the following years Blackrock College grew in size and influence. For a period after 1874, in the newly-purchased adjoining property, Williamstown Castle, it ran an innovative post-secondary Civil Service College to prepare pupils for civil service examinations. From 1881 until the early 1900s Blackrock College ran a third level institution called Blackrock University College which functioned as an affiliated college to the Royal University to allow pupils to sit degree courses. Initially founded principally to offer a high level of educational opportunities to Roman Catholic boys and to encourage vocations for the missions, Blackrock College is still one of the primary first and second level schools in the country. In its distinguished history it has produced many leading figures in Irish and international society including no less than twenty three bishops. Illustrious past pupils include Eamon de Valera (1882-1975), Archbishop John Charles McQuaid (1895-1973), writer Myles na gCopaleen (Brian O'Nolan, 1911-1966), poet Pádraic Ó Conaire (1882-1928), rock singer Bob Geldof and Labour Party Leader Ruairí Quinn.

Above: The Freemasons' Hall, Molesworth Street, was erected in 1865 on the site of the townhouse of the first Grand Master in Ireland, Richard Parsons, 1st Earl of Rosse. It was designed by a Birmingham architect, Edward Holmes. Freemasonary, a non-sectarian and non-political fraternal and charitable organisation, was first formed in Ireland in 1725.

Above: The Masonic symbol is based on the stone mason's square and compass.

Above: In 1768 Gustavus Hume, a surgeon from Mercer's Hospital and a property speculator, laid out both Hume Street and a short cul-de-sac crossing at its eastern end, which he proposed to name Hume Row. When his relation by marriage, Henry Loftus, Earl of Ely, decided to build a house in the cul-de-sac Hume changed the name to Ely Place. The Earl raised a magnificent 36-roomed mansion which, in the intervening years, has changed very little. Henry Loftus was an extravagant and somewhat eccentric man who lived well and enjoyed the social whirl to the full. He lavished much of his wealth on his main home at Rathfarnham Castle, but spared nothing in the embellishment of Ely House. Several of the grand rooms are still resplendent with their stucco walls and ceilings, marble fireplaces and other fine ornamentations. One of the outstanding interior elements is the striking staircase. It consists of three flights of Portland stone stairs with a life-size statue of Hercules at the base. The carved mahogany handrail sweeps over the gilt figures representing some of the Twelve Labours of Hercules. They include the Erymanthian boar, Stymphalian birds, the Nemean lion, the Cretan bull, the Arcadian stag and Cerberus, the three headed dog, guardian of the nether regions. In 1922 Ely House came into the possession of the Knights of St. Columbanus, a Roman Catholic lay order founded seven years earlier in Belfast by Canon James O'Neill. Some of the achievements of the order include the endowment of a Chair of Catholic Sociology at St. Patrick's College, Maynooth, the establishment of the Catholic Communications Institute and the playing of a pivotal role in the foundation of the Credit Union Movement in Ireland.

Left: The casket containing the body of the 3rd century Roman Martyr, St. Valentine, lies under a side altar in the Church of Our Lady of Mount Carmel, Aungier Street. It was donated by Pope Gregory XVI in 1835 to the visiting head of the Carmelite order in Dublin, Fr. John Spratt. St. Valentine is the patron saint of lovers and his feast day, 14 February, is connected to the old belief that birds started mating on that date. The church, commonly referred to as Whitefriar Street Church, is a direct link to medieval Dublin. The Carmelites had a monastery on the same site from at least 1279 until 1539 when it was suppressed. They then held on in "safe" houses during times of religious persecution until they re-established their monastery in 1825. Another tangible connection to early Dublin, this time the late 15th century, is the black wooden statue of Our Lady now venerated on an altar dedicated to Our Lady of Dublin. The statue once belonged to St. Mary's Abbey. When that Abbey was dissolved it is believed the statue was used as a pig trough (it has a hollowed-out back). The statue turned up again in a chapel in Mary's Lane around 1749 and vanished again when the chapel closed in 1816. Amazingly, Fr. John Spratt found the statue in a second-hand shop in 1824 and it has been honoured in Our Lady of Mount Carmel ever since.

Photo: courtesy of David Park 20-20 VisionDesign.

Above: Poolbeg Generating Station seen from the Great South Wall. The huge twin chimneys are each 207m (680ft) high and it can take maintenance personnel an hour to climb to the top. The emissions from the chimneys are mostly steam vapour and not polluting smoke.

Dublin Corporation obtained an order from the Board of Trade in 1888 to begin a system to supply electricity to Dublin. Within three years, work had commenced on the new power station in Fleet Street and on the laying of underground cables. The huge dynamos, engines and fly-wheels were installed by Messrs. Hammond & Company. Work was completed and the plant handed over to the Electric Lighting Committee of Dublin Corporation on 23 September 1892. The Metropole and Shelbourne Hotels were the first commercial units to be supplied with the new incandescent lights and street lighting was installed along College Green, Grafton Street, College Street, Dame Street, Parliament Street, Capel Street, Mary Street, Henry Street, Sackville (O'Connell) Street, D'Olier Street and Westmoreland Street using 78 lamp posts. The 900 kilowatts were produced by a staff of one manager, one electrician, one switchroom attendant, three drivers, three dynamo men, two cleaners, one fitter, three lamp trimmers and two boilermen. The new venture was so successful that in the space of a year an extention was built and by 1903 the power station was relocated to Pigeon House Fort on the River Liffey estuary. The Electricity Supply Board (ESB) was established in 1927 to provide electricity on a national basis and it took over control of the Pigeon House Generating Station two years later. In 1965 the ESB decided to build a new station beside the ageing Pigeon House, the first stage of which was commissioned in early 1971. Up to 1994 the station utilised three turbines producing a total of 511 megawatts (Mw) and since that date an two more turbines have been installed in the adjoining new Combined Cycle Plant. These additional turbines, fuelled by natural gas, with diesel oil as back-up, produce 150Mw of power each. Their exhaust gases are recycled to make steam, thus producing overall another 160Mw of extra power for no additional fuel input.

Above: Three Armstorng-Frederick Long Barrell cannons which now stand at the entrance to Poolbeg Generating Station were once part of the 18th century ordnance belonging to the Pigeon House Fort. That bastion was constructed by the British to defend Pigeon House Harbour and it also served as a last-ditch resort in the event of a successful Irish rebellion.

Above: in 1904 the newly founded Irish National Theatre Company bought the old city morgue building at Marlborough Street and had it fitted out as the Abbey Theatre. The plays for the opening night were written by W. B. Yeats and Lady Gregory. Following a fire in 1951 a new building to house the Abbey and Peacock Theatres was designed by Michael Scott and opened in 1966. In 1990 the Abbey was refurbished and extended, work that included a new portico and bar. The night of the launch of the new facilities also saw the premiere of the phenomenally successful play by Brian Friel, "Dancing at Lughnasa". In June 2000 it was announced by the Abbey Theatre that a figure of £40 million will be requested from an already sympathetic Government to totally rebuild the interior of the Abbey and the Peacock.

Below left: The contemporary appearance of the American Embassy actually dates back to 1964 when Dublin had precious little modern architecture and what it did have, apart from an occasional exception, was of poor quality. The designers, American John McL. Johansen and Irishman Michael Scott, drew their inspiration from ancient Celtic motifs.

Below right: In 1927 the American Ambassador took up residence in the former Phoenix Park home of the British Government's Chief Secretary to Ireland. The house was built by Sir John Blaquiere, Secretary to the Lord Lieutenant in 1776, and was used by the Chief Secretary from 1782 until 1921.

Chapter Nine
Cathedrals (and Chapels) of Commerce

Above: A descendant of the medieval markets, the Moore Street outdoor fish, vegetable and fruit market, is still going strong. Ownership of each stall was and still is usually handed down from generation to generation.

COMMERCIAL ACTIVITY among the Celts in Ireland was modest and was rarely concerned beyond the immediate needs of the community. The barter system was widely used as they had no coinage. Their unit of currency was the cow and a family's wealth was judged on the number of cows it possessed. The Vikings changed all that. They introduced the use of money for the first time (the Romans never occupied Ireland and thus their monetary system was only used for sporadic trading with Roman Britain). Under the Vikings, Dublin became an important frontier port and was always busy with the import and export of merchandise. Stalls and markets were set up along the streets to handle the selling of produce, goods and services. This practice was continued and expanded by the Anglo-Normans and their English overlords although small shops did begin to appear in medieval Dublin. Many of the streets in the older parts of Dublin still bear the names associated with the trades carried on there a millennium ago; Fishamble Street, Cook Street, Cornmarket, Haymarket, Winetavern Street and so on.

The narrow and crowded streets of Elizabethan Dublin rang to the cries of vendors who operated from their tiny shops and kerbside stalls, and hygiene was not uppermost in people's minds. Commodities, of course, would not be mass-produced until at least the 19th century so choice and standards varied widely. The Georgian period ushered in a more organised form of retailing. Commodious shops opened along streets designated for the purpose. After all, the tone of the great residential streets could not be lowered by the trappings of commercialism and retailing. At least that was the plan. Two of the primary residential streets soon succumbed to mere shopkeepers and have since become the principal shopping thoroughfares - Grafton Street and O'Connell Street. Even into the mid 19th century specialised shops were still the dominant form of retailing and up to the turn of the next century the wealthy usually had their purchases selected for them by the store's floorwalker (assistant manager) and delivered straight to their houses.

Above: The Saturday market in Meeting House Square in Temple Bar is a recent but welcome innovation. Organically grown food is one of the features of this market.

Towards the latter half of the 19th century mass production, the spread of department stores and greater freedom for women led to a boom in retailing and to some extent created the consumer society that is now so familiar. The viability of any city centre today depends on a number of factors, not least the success and strength of its retail core. Dublin city centre answered the threat of suburban shopping centres by enlarging and upgrading the existing department stores, by encouraging the opening of speciality shops, restaurants and entertainment venues and by improving the environment of the streets to attract shoppers. The suburban shopping centres for their part have become larger, made access easier, attracted the big retailing names and now provide more spacious and pleasant surroundings than heretofore. There is a place for both systems in a properly balanced city.

Right and below right: Replacing the grimy old Castle Market on South Great George's Street, the monumental Gothic-embellished structure of the South City Markets was opened as the city's first major shopping centre in 1881. A year later Dublin's biggest fire to date consumed the building and devastated the livelihood of the stallholders. There was an outpouring of public sympathy for their plight and a subscription fund was opened. The centre was restored minus its four great pyramid towers and reopened in 1894. Today the central Market Arcade, whose stalls function in a Victorian ambience beautifully restored by its owners, the Don-Lay Group, is a browser's delight. South Great George's Street, which descended into the commercial doldrums in the 1970s, is beginning to return to the prominence it once held as a shopping precinct.

Above: Dublin is renowned for the style of its wooden shopfronts. This fine example, dating from 1898, is in Anglesea Street in Temple Bar.

Above & top left: At the corner of Parliament Street and Essex Quay stands one of Dublin's most unusual and best-loved buildings. Sunlight Chambers was built in 1901 as the base for the Irish operations of Lever Brothers, the English soap and detergent manufacturers. "Sunlight" was the company's brand name for their soap product, hence the name of their Irish headquarters. The architect of the Italianate-styled building was Liverpudlian Edward Ould. Conrad Dressler, a sculptor and potter of some reputation at that time, was engaged to design and craft the remarkable series of four roundels and twelve panels around the three faces of the building. The glazed ceramic faiences or friezes, in the manner of the famous 15th century artist, Luca della Robbia, were made in Dressler's own Medmenham Pottery in Buckinghamshire. They depict the toils of man, the extraction of raw materials to manufacture soap, the bargaining of merchants buying oils and scents and women scrubbing and washing clothes. In 1999, the owners of Sunlight Chambers, Michael E. Hanahoe Solicitors, commissioned a complete restoration of the building. Under architect, Gilroy McMahon, and project manager John McNamara, various experts set to work including historic buildings consultant, David Slattery, stone conservator, John Kelly and ceramic conservator, Eileen O'Leary of Leinster Studios. The result is an outstanding restoration of great public appeal.

Above: photo courtesy of Anne Reeves-Smyth.

Above: The four "before" and "after" photographs graphically reveal the results of the painstaking work of pottery conservator, Eileen O'Leary, assisted by Anne Reeves-Smyth. They had to carefully remove a century of pollution and ingrained dirt particles, using brushes, a tiny steam cleaner, scalpels and non-ionic detergents. Damaged parts were remodelled or filled, then repainted and a fresh hard-wearing glaze applied. The result is a work-of-art in itself and a breathtaking enhancement to the streetscape.

In a move that preceded the recent spate of European bank mergers by thirty years, three Irish banks came together to see if closer co-operation between them could not collectively serve them better in a growing and increasingly competitive market. Munster & Leinster Bank, the Provincial Bank of Ireland and the Royal Bank of Ireland formally merged in 1966 as Allied Irish Banks Ltd. Each bank still maintained its own identity but it soon became clear that the continuing inter-competition of the three banks and their own mutual presence on the same streets was wasteful of resources. Consequently it was decided in 1969 to fully integrate the three banks under Allied Irish Banks. The new headquarters operated from Lansdowne House, Ballsbridge until the Bankcentre was built in 1979 on Merrion Road.

Above and left: In 1973 the Royal Dublin Society sold its 5.5ha (13 and a half acres) bloodstock sales paddocks to Allied Irish Banks. Within six years the bank's new head office, Bankcentre, was completed by the contractors, G & T Crampton, and occupied by 1,200 headquarters staff. Architects for the project were Robinson Keefe and Devane. The eight interconnecting blocks gradually rise from three stories in the front to five storeys at the rear with the intention of lessening the impact of their bulk on Merrion Road. The squared look of the blocks is softened by reflecting pools and intensive planting and complemented by the sculpted lines of trees. The latter are trimmed and pleached (by Southern Tree Surgeons) to form an interwined rectangular effect rather like a hedge on stilts. This effect also affords a certain privacy, especially to the residents along Serpentine Avenue, without cutting off the view at ground level. The stainless steel sculpture (left) entitled "Freedom", is by Alexandra Wejchert.

Above: AIB in College Street was opened in 1868 as the head office of the Provincial Bank of Ireland, designed by William George Murray and built by one John Nolan. The Irish Builder commented that the bank had moved "from their backward and unsuitable premises in William Street to a more convenient and circumstanced establishment". Its rich and impressive interior is equally matched by the decorative exterior. The sculptures in the pediment by Samuel Lynn depict the Genius of Banking flanked on the right by a merchant representing the Spirit of Commerce and Manufacture and on the left by a female representing Agriculture.

Above: Designed by the firm Deane, Son & Woodward, this bank was built in 1874 at the corner of Dame Street and Palace Street for the Munster and Leinster Bank.

Above: When the Royal Bank of Ireland was formed in 1836 it acquired the building in Foster Place belonging to Shaw's Bank, an institution which traced its origins back to 1797. The present building, whose relatively plain façade belies the grandiose interior, was built in 1859. AIB is due to transfer the operation of this bank to the refurbished branch in College Street but until such time as this happens Foster Place will remain the oldest continuously operating bank location in Ireland.

Above: The AIB Drive-in Bank at Stillorgan, Co Dublin. Opened in 1990, it was then believed to be Europe's first bank of this kind.

Bank of Ireland Group

Above: The chevron-styled Bank of Ireland logotype symbolises branches from the "Tree of Life". Like a tree, the bank has grown from small beginnings to reach great heights with an ever-spreading canopy.

Above: The Bank Of Ireland at 28 Lower O'Connell Street carries the motto over the door "Bona Fides Reipublicae Stabilitas". While the literal translation is "Good Faith is the Cornerstone of the State", the intended meaning is that you can rely on the bank to safeguard your money.

Photo: courtsey of Bank of Ireland.

Above: The headquarters of the Bank of Ireland on Baggot Street was designed by Scott Tallon Walker and was opened in 1972. The Bank of Ireland was first incorporated in 1783 and the 19 staff greeted their first customers at the Mary's Abbey offices on the 25th June of that year. The capital of the bank, authorised by an Act of the Irish Parliament, was £660,000 – the market capitalisation in March 1999 was almost £8 billion. David La Touche, the grandson of the Huguenot founder of a successful private bank, was elected first Governor of the Bank. Until 1825, when seven branches around Ireland were opened, the bank's business was centred around Dublin. By 1920 there were 75 full branches nationwide. In 1958 Bank of Ireland acquired the Hibernian Bank Ltd and followed seven years later with a takeover of the Irish interests of the National Bank Ltd (Daniel O'Connell had been its first chairman). These acquisitions led to the formation of the Bank of Ireland Group.

Left: An interior photograph of La Touche House, the Bank of Ireland's Group Treasury Building in the International Financial Services Centre. As well as the Group Treasury Department the premises also houses other international trading divisions of the bank.

Above: The entrance to the Dublin Stock Exchange on Anglesea Street. The building was designed by Miller & Symes of Great Brunswick (Pearse) Street.

Above: Sailing from Ringsend in 1695, the armed merchant vessel, the "Ouzel" (old English name for a blackbird), set course for the Middle East. After three years without news of the ship it was presumed lost and the owners, Ferris, Twigg & Cash, claimed on the underwriters. Then, remarkably, in 1700 a battered "Ouzel" limped back into Dublin. The crew explained that they had been attacked and imprisoned by Algerian pirates but had recently succeeded in repossessing their ship while their captors were drunk. Their welcome return soon caused consternation as to the rightful ownership of the pirate booty which then filled the holds. Ferris, Twigg & Cash had already been paid in full and the insurers had claim only to the ship itself and the original cargo. The courts of law haggled interminably for 5 years so the matter was submitted to and quickly settled by the arbitration of a group of merchants and traders who instructed that the pirate treasure was to be sold to alleviate poverty among the merchants of Dublin. From this achievement arose the Ouzel Galley Society, a permanent arbitration body which lingered on until 1888. A committee of merchants had evolved from the Society in 1761 which in its turn established the Chamber of Commerce in 1783. Thus the Dublin Chamber shares with two other chambers in the UK the distinction of being the oldest in these islands. Number 7 Clare Street became the present headquarters of the Chamber in 1964.

Far left: The impressive Victorian trading floor of The Dublin Stock Exchange on Angelsea Street. Originally founded in 1799, the Dublin Stock Exchange first met in the Coffee House of the Royal Exchange (now the City Hall) before moving to the Commercial Buildings in Dame Street. It relocated to its present building in 1878. The Floor of the Exchange saw its role somewhat diminished from 1986 when much of the trading activity switched to the computerised dealing rooms of brokers. It finally closed on the 6th of June 2000 and the venerable room, now a listed interior, awaits a new use.

Left: The Northern Bank purchased the former Hibernian Bank at the corner of Church Lane and College Green in 1979 and then carried out an extensive refurbishment which revealed the bank's ornate exterior as well as the exquisite plastered ceiling of the Banking Hall. The building had originally belonged to a private bank, Ball and Company, from whom it was bought in 1888. National Australia Bank Group acquired the Northern Bank in 1987 and operates as National Irish Bank in the Republic.

Above: The new Ulster Bank Group Centre at George's Quay. It was developed by Irish Life as a speculative high-specification office block and was ready for occupation by early 1993. The modern aspect of the building is finely set off by the insertion of a Georgian limestone portico at the entrance to the front plaza. This was rescued from Richmond House, near Nenagh, Co. Tipperary, before it was demolished. Architects for the scheme were Keane Murphy Duff (Ian Duff was the project architect) and construction was by John Sisk & Son. The development was seen by Irish Life as far back as the 1970s as part of the process to return Dublin's main business core to the city centre. Evidence of others following that vision can now be seen all along the quaysides. The George's Quay building was designed to be a low energy user and was one of the first developments in Ireland (the Treasury Building on Grand Canal Street was another) to receive the British Research Establishment Certificate for being environmentally sensitive.

Above: Ulster Bank first came to Dublin in 1862 and opened its College Green branch in 1891. The building was designed by Thomas Drew, the winner of an architectural competition. However, the interior was left to the second-place prize-winner, George C. Ashlin, a Belfast man who had earlier distinguished himself by the restoration of Dublin's two cathedrals, St Patrick's and Christ Church.

Photo: courtesy of Ulster Bank.

Above: The scene at George's Quay before redevelopment. Irish Life had been assembling the site since 1973 and had completed the acquisitions by 1985 but had to wait for an improvement in the economic climate and the granting of Designated Area Status (for tax reliefs) before proceeding with the building.

Above: The honour of opening the world's first purpose-built department store goes to Dublin. Peter Paul McSwiney and George Delaney opened the doors of their Palatial Mart on Sackville (O'Connell) Street in 1853. Today the store is known as Clery & Company. Successive owners of the Palatial Mart were M. J. Clery (1883), Denis Guiney (1940) and Mary Guiney (1967). The present building, designed by Ashlin and Coleman, was opened in 1922 to replace the one burnt down in the Rising of 1916.

Above: The Irish Yeast Company on College Green has a fine carved wooden shop front. The style and layout of this magical shop has not been changed for several decades.

Above: When the St Stephen's Green Centre opened in October 1988 it was then the country's largest shopping centre. Its style was intended to reflect a conservatory on the side facing the Green and to mirror the brickwork design of the opposing Gaiety Theatre on The South King Street elevation. It was developed jointly by Power Securities and British Land. The architect was Jim Toomey.

The ability to mass produce clothing, advanced by the invention of the sewing machine in 1846 by Elias Howe, ensured an increasing supply and variety of garments from about the fourth decade of the 18th century. With the introduction from the 1850s of practical waterproof clothing and the humble umbrella, people could, at last, be comfortable walking around in wet weather. In addition, the improvements in public transport made it safe, convenient and respectable, even for women, to travel on their own into town. Newspapers were being more widely read and advertising was creating a demand for goods. The age of fashion consciousness, consumerism and the department store had arrived.

Top: The 19th century façade on Henry Street. As well as the Henry Street store, Arnotts has branches on Grafton Street, in the Stillorgan Shopping Centre and on North Earl Street (operating as Boyers).

In 1845 Sir John Arnott injected capital into the firm of Cannock, White & Co. which had been established two years earlier at numbers 11, 13, 14, 15 Henry Street (No.12 was a police station and was not acquired until 1870). In 1865 George Cannock returned to Limerick and the store's name was changed to John Arnott & Co. Sir John Arnott was born in Fifeshire in 1814 and died in 1898 after a distinguished career which included several directorships, the Lord Mayoralty of Cork (1859-61), election to Parliament (1859-64), ownership of *The Irish Times* (1874), a ship building yard, bakery shops, mills, factories and even a brewery. A disastrous fire in 1894 destroyed the hotchpotch group of Georgian-styled buildings and George Beater was employed to design the present Victorian edifice fronting Henry Street. Arnotts is now the oldest department store in Ireland and as a result of the recent extension and redevelopment it is also the country's largest department store with a selling area of around 27,870sq m (300,000sq ft). Only four stores in Britain, including Harrods and Selfridges, are bigger.

Above: The modernised frontage on Liffey Street. The architectural aspects of the rebuilding have blended with and greatly enhanced the neighbouring buildings.

Right: The rebuilt and extended façade of Arnotts Department Store on Abbey Street.

Above left & right: Two views of the refurbished interior of Arnotts. In the original Henry Street section of the extended store many of the Victorian features such as cast-iron pillars and railings have been preserved. A striking glass dome overlooks the five retail floors and the 22 separate departments as well as several concessions. The recent massive extension, which almost doubled the floor space to some 27,870sq m (300,000sq ft), was completed in 1999 at a cost of £45 million. Keane Murphy Duff were the architects. The redevelopment has not only protected existing jobs and indeed created hundreds more but has also made a significant contribution to the revitalisation of the city centre. Around half a million people visit Arnotts during a peak week.

Far left: After Richard Wingfield sold Powerscourt House (see page 52) in 1807 to the Government, the architect Francis Johnston was appointed to add three groups of buildings around the courtyard of the mansion for use as a Stamp Office and to erect the clock tower and bell situated on Clarendon Street.

Left: A view of the Powerscourt House courtyard before being enclosed and roofed over in 1981 as the Powerscourt Townhouse Centre. The architect on this occasion was Jim Toomey, acting for the developers, Power Corporation.

Left: A view today of the magnificent interior of the Powerscourt Centre which was again upgraded in 1999 by the current owners, Clarendon Properties, still using the services of Jim Toomey.

Photo: courtesy of Marks & Spencer.

Top: During the reconstruction for the new Marks & Spencer Store, No. 5 Duke Street, an early Georgian house wih original timber panelling and fireplaces, was retained from the first floor upwards. The upper levels of the building were stitched and tied to prevent movement of the shell while a steel tower was erected to the underside of the first floor which was then flat-jacked to take the load. The ground floor and basement could then be safely demolished.

Above: The completed No. 5 Duke Street.

Above: Marks & Spencer first traded in Grafton Street in 1987 and seven years later the company agreed terms with Brown Thomas to buy their prestigious store further down the street. Brown Thomas moved across the road to relocate in Switzers, another famous department store by then in the ownership of Galen Weston, also the proprietor of Brown Thomas. Part of the deal included the transfer of the old Marks & Spencer shop to a subsidiary of Brown Thomas, a real case of corporate musical chairs. The old Brown Thomas store, first founded in 1849 by James Thomas and John Brown, was completely gutted on the inside but the unique and much-loved façade on Grafton Street was retained. The façades on Duke Street are replicas based on the appearance of the block in the mid-19th century. One building, however, No. 5 Duke Street, was completely retained from the first floor upwards. G. & T. Crampton, the main contractor, completed the rebuilding on schedule and the new Marks & Spencer store opened its doors in September 1996. Several of the original internal features were retained including Corinthian pillars, fireplaces, the magnificent marble staircase, cornices and friezes. Architects for the redevelopment were Scott Tallon Walker who were advised on the historic aspects of the building's architecture by David Slattery.

Below left: The sweeping marble staircase in Marks & Spencer now leads from the ground floor to the upper levels. In the days of Brown Thomas it led to the basement.

Below right: Brown Thomas moved into the former Switzers Department Store, which it had owned since 1991, in early 1995. This followed a £30 million expenditure on upgrading the store that was first founded by a Swiss immigrant in 1838.

Photo: courtesy of Marks & Spencer.

Supermarkets were first introduced to Dublin, on a small scale at first, in the late 1950s. They changed the pattern of food shopping from being a daily chore to a weekly one. In the 1960s the arrival of suburban shopping centres allowed access in one's own neighbourhood to a wide range of consumer goods. The huge increase in car ownership from the 1990s persuaded developers to open even larger and more sophisticated shopping centres. Super-centres have had to move even further away from the central core of the city in order to attract wider catchment areas and also to find the vast tracts of land needed for such development. The city centre, for its part, continues to assert itself and the area around Henry Street and Mary Street now has about 209,000sq m (2 and a quarter million sq ft) of retail space.

Above left: Costing £50 million to build (the same again was spent by the tenants to fit it out), the Jervis Shopping Centre was opened on 1 November 1996. It comprises 30,657sq m (330,000sq ft) of retail space and an overhead car park for 750 cars. Wide and double-height malls, giving an air of spaciousness within, converge to a central rotunda 20.5m (67 ft) high. The developers retained four Georgian merchant houses on the Abbey Street side and, in assocation with the Dublin Civic Trust, fully restored two that had original interiors. Developed by Jervis Shopping Centre Ltd, the centre was designed by Joseph Doyle and built by Pierse Contracting.

Above right: The façade of the former Jervis Street Hospital was retained on the west side of the Jervis Shopping Centre. Behind it, on the upper levels, are 16 duplex apartments.

Left: Tallaght, on the south-west fringes of Dublin, was designated as one of the capital's satellite towns. As a result, its population grew from 352 in 1951 to over 70,000 by 1990. With little or no local shopping facilities for such a large number of residents Monarch Properties and Guardian Royal Exchange Properties came together to develop The Square Towncentre at Tallaght. The new shopping centre, with its distinctive glass pyramid, was opened on 23 October 1990. A second phase extension was added on in 1996 giving a total retail area of 53,417sq m (575,000sq ft). By the time of the second phase the original developers had sold most of their stake to other developers and financial institutions. Architects for The Square were Burke-Kennedy Doyle and the main contractor was John Sisk & Son.

Photo: courtesy of the Blancherstown Centre.

Above: The high curved and glazed roofs admit natural light into all of the six broad malls and the 60,385sq m (650,000sq ft) of retail space in the Blanchardstown Centre, imparting a feeling of spaciousness throughout. The interior is further enhanced by the use of polished stainless steel, ceramic tiles and pillars of Japanese reconstituted white glass. The architects, A & D Wejchert, cleverly used the site's natural fall to provide, as it were, two ground floors, each with its own direct opening to a car park. Travelators connect these two floors with each other. There are presently 151 retail outlets in the centre. Contractors for the main complex were John Sisk & Son.

Above: On 16 October 1996 the £60 million first phase of Blanchardstown Centre, the largest of its kind in the Republic, was opened. It represented the new generation of shopping centres that, while still predominantly trading as retail malls, are more community-based offering a whole range of additional services including health, leisure, entertainment, cultural and residential facilities. A full-time chapel was built and handed over to the Dublin Diocese by the developers, Green Properties plc. All this development accords to and follows from the designation of the Blanchardstown complex as a Town Centre. Over 3,000 people are now directly employed at the Blanchardstown Centre, a figure that will grow with the future development of the adjacent office parks. The early uncertainties in 1993 of developing a site at all were dispelled when the two main anchor tenants, Dunnes Stores and Roches Stores, signed agreements. Initially the centre was a little smaller than that designed in 1991 but due to its immediate success an additional 12.5 ha (31 acres) were acquired and it has since grown beyond any earlier envisaged plans.

Above: The central retail core at the Blancherstown Centre is encircled not only by the customary car parks but also by three retail parks, restaurants, a large themed pub, blocks of apartments, an arts centre and a public library. High-technology offices, an hotel and a multi-storey car park will, when built, reinforce the development's status as an actual town centre.

Chapter Ten
Waterways, Railways, Highways and Skyways

SHANK'S MARE was mankind's earliest form of conveyance and walking has become fashionable again if only for exercise, for enjoyment of the scenery or to bypass traffic gridlock. The first improvement on shank's mare in heavily forested pre-historic Ireland was a rudimentary boat fashioned either by hollowing out tree trunks or by stretching animal hides over a wickerwork frame. In time, the horse was introduced and the Celts, who carved a network of roads across the country, used chariots for hunting and war-making. The coastal kingdoms of pre-Christian Ireland developed fleets of small ships and harassed the western seaboard of Britain and often carried away slaves. A superior form of clinker-built ship arrived with the Vikings and a steady evolution in shipbuilding went forward from there. The building of canals in the late 18th century allowed for comfortable, secure (from highwaymen) and leisurely travel for large numbers of people on boats operated to a strict timetable. On land there was little progress until the arrival of scheduled mail coaches in the 1790s although, even then, passengers experienced extreme discomfort until the surface of the highways improved. By the end of the 19th century a vast labyrinth of roads traversed the country.

The real breakthrough in mass transportation came with the building of the railways which commenced in Ireland from 1834. Railway companies vied with each other to lay down tracks even to remote areas where there would be little hope of an economic return. The explosion in car ownership from the mid-20th century was to the detriment of the railways and serious decline set in. By the end of the 1990s it was clear that that the continuing boom in car sales was clogging up the roads and decisions were made by the Government to invest hundreds of millions of pounds in public transport. The wheel had turned the full circle. Meanwhile air transport in Ireland grew at a phenomenal rate spurred on by razor-sharp competition between the carriers. By the end of the 20th century the Dublin-London route was the busiest in Europe.

Above: Leading up from Blackhall Place is a road simply called "Stoneybatter". The name is a corruption of Stony Bóthar (bóthar is the Irish word for road). Bóthar na gCloch, the road of the stones, is possibly a direct descendant of the old Celtic Slí Chualann (see page 11) and so Stoneybatter can claim unique antiquity in the city. A bóthar had to be the width of two cows, one lengthways, one crossways. A slighe had to allow two chariots to pass each other.

Above: Slí na Sláinte (The Way of Health), a system of colourfully signposted walks located all over Ireland, designed by the Irish Heart Foundation. The idea has been so successful that it has been patented internationally and adopted by 16 other countries including Sweden.

Above: Islandbridge, situated beyond any tidal influence, provides a serene setting for leisure boating on the River Liffey. Several rowing clubs are positioned along this stretch of the river.

Above: The Grand Canal at Mespil Road provides an almost idyllic setting as it curves its way through the south inner city. A link between Dublin and the River Shannon was first mooted in 1715 but it did not become a reality until the Grand Canal, begun in 1755, reached the Shannon in 1805. Unlike its English counterparts, the canal failed to encourage the growth of industry along its route and the barges mainly carried bulky but low revenue-yielding agricultural produce. There was a limited but excellent passenger service. However, even this was terminated in 1852 when the canal proved uncompetitive with the railways. The operating company failed to meet costs and ultimately CIE, Ireland's national transport company, took over the Grand Canal in 1950. It is now in the hands of Waterways Ireland, a joint Republic of Ireland and Northern Ireland statuory body committed to the restoration of Ireland's canals and inland waterways. The canal remains navigable from the River Liffey to the Shannon and now, within the city limits, the water is of sufficient quality to support a variety of fish.

Above: A date plaque on (John) McCarthy Bridge over the Grand Canal at Baggot Street.

Right: (Joseph) Huband Bridge (1791) is a lovely old stone bridge at the end of Mount Street Upper. All the bridges over the Grand Canal in Dublin were named after the then directors of the Company of Undertakers of the Grand Canal.

Photo: courtesy of The National Gallery of Ireland.

Above: A complex series of lock gates, still in perfect working order, controls entry from the River Liffey, via the Camden, Westmoreland and Buckingham Locks onto the sheltered waters of the Grand Canal Docks.

Top left: The opening of the Ringsend Docks on St. George's Day, 23rd April 1796, by the Lord Lieutenant, Earl of Camden, who was first to sail his yacht "Dorset" through the locks. The docks were designed to hold 600 ships but rarely more than a few dozen availed of the facilities. From a painting by William Ashford (1746-1824) in the National Gallery of Ireland.

At their peaks, the Grand Canal carried an annual load of 110,000 passengers and 310,000 tons of freight (in 1845) and the Royal Canal carried 46,000 passengers and 134,000 tons of cargo (in 1833) per annum. The faster railways and improved roads killed the commercial viability of the two canals. The Royal Canal closed in 1955 and the Grand Canal followed in 1960. An absurd suggestion to turn them into roadways was thankfully rejected and now the canals are being rejuvenated. Their through-navigation has already been restored and their other natural qualities are being enhanced. Amenities are being improved for walking, cycling and fishing, opportunities for wildlife conservation and study are being provided and many wonderful examples of canal engineering and waterside industrial architecture are being refurbished.

Left: A partial view of the 10ha (25 acres) of water in the Grand Canal Docks. After decades of neglect, the land surrounding the docks will form a vital part of a vast renewal scheme being spearheaded by the Dublin Docklands Development Authority. The water area will be developed as a varied leisure amenity girdled by new commercial and apartment blocks.

Above left: The Royal Canal, scything through Dublin's northside, was built to rival the Grand Canal. Led by a former director of the Grand Canal, Mr John Binns, work commenced in 1790. Starting at Spencer Dock (built by the Railway Board in 1783), just below the Custom House and joined initially by a spur from Broadstone Harbour in Phibsborough (this spur is now a fine linear park), the canal did not finally reach the Shannon until 1817. The total construction cost was £1,421,954 which included the construction of 80 bridges and 47 locks. By this time the Grand Canal was well established and business on its rival never really took off. The Royal Canal was sold in 1845 to the Midland Great Western Railway who wished to build a rail line along its banks. The canal became the responsibility of Coras Iompair Eireann (CIE), the state national transport company formed in 1944 from the amalgamation of the Dublin United Tramway Company and the Great Southern Railway, the then owners of the Midland Great Western. Waterways Ireland is now in charge of the Royal Canal.

Above right: A flower-bedecked Royal Canal lock-keeper's cottage situated at Newcomen Bridge near the North Strand.

Below: On March 24 1997 the granite-stone Baily Lighthouse on Howth's Dungriffin promontory was the last of the 82 lighthouses provided by the Commissioners of Irish Lights to be fully automated. Baily's powerful light (of 1,217,690 candelas intensity and turning one full revolution every 15 seconds, which can be seen 27 nautical miles away) and its other modern navigational aids are now controlled and monitored from the Irish Lights facility at Dun Laoghaire. The first Baily Lighthouse was built in 1667, higher up on Howth Summit. It consisted of a small cottage and a square stone tower on top of which coals burned in a brazier. In 1790 an improved tower was re-equipped with recently invented but still relatively crude lenses. The location of this beacon had never been wise as, ironically, when it was needed most, it was itself shrouded in mist or cloud. The current lighthouse was built in 1814. The Commissioners of Irish Lights owe their ancestry to the letters patent granted to Sir Robert Reading in 1665 by King Charles II to build six lighthouses around Ireland. From this beginning a series of organisations held responsibility until 1867 when the Commissioners of Irish Lights were established following the re-orginisation of the former Port Authority, the Corporation for Preserving and Improving the Port of Dublin.

Photo: courtesy of Peter Barrow Photographers.

Dublin Port is managed under the Harbours Act, 1996 by Dublin Port Company (see Appendix D). The area consists of the waters of the River Liffey below the Matt Talbot Bridge and the sea, westward of a line drawn from the Baily Lighthouse to the North Burford Bank Buoy, through to the South Burford Bank Buoy to Sorrento Point including all bays, creeks, harbours and tidal docks excluding Dun Laoghaire Harbour. The land area under the control of Dublin Port amounts to 270ha (667 acres).

From the time the Vikings built their tiny harbour near Dublin Castle, acute shortage of docking space and the increasing size of ships have constantly pushed the location of the port further downriver. Over the centuries the wharves, cranes and warehouses leapfrogged each other and when they ran out of land more had to be reclaimed from the waters of the Liffey and its estuary. Ireland's current buoyant economic activity has placed enormous pressure on the port and on the infrastructure leading to and within it. Facilities have been upgraded in an attempt to cope but the port's future success may depend on the vexed question of reclaiming yet more land from the sea. Dublin Port is the busiest port in Ireland with an annual throughput of 20 million tons of cargo and approximately 1.4 million passengers.

Above: An aerial view of Dublin Port looking in a north-easterly direction.

Below: A Merchant Ferries Ro/Ro ship berthed at one of the deep-water terminals in Dublin Port. The cargo terminal on the other side was linked in 1998 with a direct rail connection to the national mainline network.

Above: In 1998 Dublin Port Company spent £15 million upgrading the ferryport facility. The enhancement included this very modern multi-user passenger ferry terminal, opened by An Taoiseach, Mr Bertie Ahern, in January 1998. Architect for the terminal was Brian Traynor of Traynor O'Toole Partnership and the contractor was John Paul Construction. Around 1.4 million passengers travel through the Port annually, a figure that is constantly rising with the regular introduction of bigger and faster ships by the ferry operators.

Bottom left: The latest ship to use the ferryport is the high-speed catamaran, the M. V. Dublin Swift, which entered service on behalf of Irish Ferries in June 1999. Built in Australia, the ferry can carry 200 cars and 800 passengers and cruises at 39 knots per hour. Average sailing time from Dublin to Holyhead is 1 hour 49 minutes. Irish Ferries, a division of Irish Continental Group plc, is Ireland's largest passenger and roll-on-roll-off ferry company. In 2001 the company will take delivery of the world's largest cruise ferry, the M. V. Ulysses. Built in Finland, it will carry 1,300 cars and 2,000 passengers and crew.

Bottom right: Leisure boats including a traditional Galway Hooker riding at anchor on the Liffey just north of the Pigeon House Road.

Left: The modern Stena Line Ferry Terminal in Dun Laoghaire. The Swedish ferry company, the largest in the world, commenced its operations from Ireland in 1990 when it bought Sealink British Ferries. The company is named after Stena Allan Ollsson who started a service in 1962 between Sweden and Denmark.

Above: "Hibernia" operated Ireland's first steam passenger train from Dublin to Kingstown (Dun Laoghaire) on 17 December 1834. What has been described as "Railway Mania" took hold of the country so that by the end of 1860 there were no fewer than 30 companies operating 1,364 route miles using 324 locomotives. William Dargan, the enterprising builder of the first line, had laid 600 of those miles by 1853. Mileage had reached the 3,000 mark by 1924, the peak of independent operation before the onset of amalgamations which led ultimately to the formation in 1944 of a single operator in the Republic: Córas Iompair Éireann (lit. the transport system of Ireland).

Photo: courtesy of Chris Ferris.

Left: No. 461 at Connolly Station, a 2-6-0 locomotive, was built by Beyer Peacock & Co., Manchester, in 1922, for the Dublin South Eastern Railway Company. Withdrawn from service in 1965, it still pulls regular excursions on behalf of the Railway Preservation Society of Ireland.

Below: A DART (Dublin Area Rapid Transit) train hugging the coastline near Killiney, Co. Dublin.

Above: In 1986 Córas Iompair Éireann became the parent company of its three operating divisions; Bus Átha Cliath (Dublin Bus), Iarnród Éireann (Irish Rail) and Bus Éireann. Busáras (it literally means bus building) was Dublin's first purpose-built modern office block and it included accommodation on the ground floor for the bus station operated by Bus Éireann. Designed by Michael Scott, it was opened in 1953 and has stood the test of time with aplomb although an increasing level of bus activity places the facilities, especially coach parking space, under severe pressure. Total number of passengers using the station in a year is estimated at about four million. The busiest day of the week is Friday. On the Friday of the October Bank Holiday in 1999 there were 215 departures and 115 arrivals on Expressway services alone, carrying 13,200 passengers. On top of that there are local services, tour buses and the frequent Airlink coaches (operated by Dublin Bus) from Dublin Airport. Bus Éireann's fleet comprises about 670 vehicles (120 are based in Dublin) including the long-distance Volvos and Scanias of the Expressway service. Busáras will see the development of more high frequency services and will grow as a major interchange hub between DART, LUAS (the new light rail system), the upgraded suburban rail service and Intercity Rail.

Above: Electrification work on the Howth to Bray line started in 1980 and the first electric trains ran in 1984. Although considered by many at its inauguration to be a white elephant, the DART (Dublin Area Rapid Transit) service has been an outstanding success. Carrying up to 80,000 passengers on 85 round trips a day (the pre-DART diesel system was carrying as few as 9,000 per day), by the late 1990s it had reached its total capacity at peak hours. Twenty-six new carriages joined the fleet in 2000 allowing the operation of 8-carriage trains during the peaks. Additionally, the service was extended to Greystones and Malahide. The original DART carriages were built by Linke-Hoffmann-Busch in Germany while the new vehicles (costing around £1.5 million per two-car set) were made by Alstom in Barcelona (above) and the Tokyu Car Corporation & Mitsui in Japan. Another suburban line, the Maynooth Line, is also being upgraded and will be operated by additional Mitsui diesel-powered carriages in 2001.

Above: By the late 1980s and early 1990s Bus Átha Cliath was struggling to maintain customer share. A falling standard of service and reduced frequency (often due to traffic congestion) pushed more people into their cars. Since then a radical overhaul of route planning and the introduction of cleaner, brighter and more environmentally-friendly buses, of small high frequency mini-buses and of the QBCS (Quality Bus Corridors) have won back the public. With nearly a thousand vehicles in a relatively young fleet (average age was only 5 and a half years in 1999) Bus Átha Cliath now carries the equivalent of 190 million passengers per annum. Over the next five years, under the National Development Plan, £250 million will be spent on bus development including the purchase of 350 additional buses, most with low floor access for the mobility impaired, extended garaging facilities and real-time passenger information displays at bus stops (advising when the next bus is due etc.). Bus Átha Cliath plans to remain the premier carrier in the emerging transport solutions for a traffic beleaguered city.

At the end of 1999 Iarnród Éireann commenced "On Track 2000", the country's most ambitious transport investment programme to date, funded by the Irish Government and the European Union. Over a five-year period £1 billion will be spent on track renewal, new trains and carriages, refurbishment of stations and updating of the signalling systems. The long decline of the railways has not only been halted but their future critical role in the transport and economic infrastructure of the country has at last been recognised.

Above: Pearse Station was the Dublin terminus for Ireland's first railway in 1834. It was linked by the so-called Loop Line (officially the City of Dublin Junction Railway) to Connolly Station in 1891. A hole was punched into the facade to receive the tracks crossing Westland Row. The station was refurbished in 1996 under architects, Murray O'Laoire. Pearse Station is due for a considerable redesign if and when a major development around the station is granted the clearance to go ahead.

Above: The passenger concourse and train hall of Connolly Station had suffered from lack of investment until the 1990s. In 1996, as a start to a £4 million investment, the train hall was refurbished to include a completely restored roof. This view is taken from the cut-limestone ramp and shows the dramatic ship's bow-like canopy over the main entrance. Inside there is a compatible mixing of the old Victorian iron roof trusses, pillars and red brick arches with contemporary designs and material used for the new extensions and refurbishments. The departures and arrivals board reminds the traveller that Connolly is the Republic's only international terminus in that it receives the cross-border express from Belfast.

Right: Initially proposing to site their new terminus opposite the GPO on Sackville (now O'Connell) Street, the Dublin and Drogheda Railway finally decided on Amiens Street. William Deane Butler designed the Italianate-styled building and chose Wicklow granite for the façade. The vehicle ramp was added in 1875 and the Loop Line connected Connolly Station to the Wexford line in 1891. Considered until recently to have been located on the periphery of the city centre, the development of the IFSC and the North Docklands has placed Connolly right at the heart of Dublin's fastest growing commercial and residential district. The airspace over the station was exploited to provide offices for the Deutsche Bank in the expanding International Financial Services Centre (IFSC). Utilising some old vaults, new entrances from Amiens Street and from the IFSC were opened in early 2000. Further developments in the future will include a LUAS light rail and a Metro interchange. The architects for the refurbishment were B.D.P. Architecture Ltd in association with the Architects' Department of Ianród Éireann. The main contractor was Graham Construction.

Left: The first O'Connell Bridge (then called Carlisle Bridge) was completed in 1795 to the designs of James Gandon. As it was found to be too steep and narrow for the increased traffic of the 1870s, Bindon B Stoney, the Chief Engineer of the Port and Docks Board, was commissioned to redesign Carlisle Bridge. Copying Gandon's architectural details Stoney created a bridge that was flat and as wide as Sackville (O'Connell) Street. The bridge is unique in that its width is nearly the same as its length. Named in honour of Daniel O'Connell, the new bridge was opened in 1880.

Left: William Rowan Hamilton (1805-1865), arguably Ireland's greatest mathematical mind, and Broombridge, an elegant twin-arched bridge over the Royal Canal and the railway at Cabra, are inextricably linked. While walking along the banks of the canal in 1843 he suddenly solved a nagging problem he had had in developing an algebraic technique for dealing with three-dimensional space. In his excitement Hamilton picked up a stone and scratched the formula of quaternions, $I^2 = J^2 = K^2 = IJK = -1$, on the stonework of the bridge.

Left: The last train to run across the nine arches of the Milltown Viaduct did so in December 1958. Now the city's most famous railway bridge is to vibrate again to the passage of trains, this time to LUAS, the new light rail transit system.

The number of vehicles on the roads of Ireland has risen beyond all original estimates. In 1923 there were only 9,000 licensed vehicles. By 1938 the figure had risen to 49,000, an average increase of 2,600 per annum. By early 1990 the numbers exceeded one million for the first time and at the end of 1999 they stood at nearly 1.7 million, with annual sales of new cars now reaching around 250,000 per annum. For decades development of the road infrastructure around Dublin had not kept pace with the increase in cars and commercial transport and lagged far behind comparable European cities. However, there has been a dramatic improvement in recent years. Leading out from the city, radial motorways are replacing the National Trunk Roads and a circular motorway or C Ring connects through each radial route in turn. The C Ring is composed of the Northern Cross Motorway (starting near Dublin Airport), the Western Parkway (skirting west of Palmerstown) and the Southern Cross Motorway (ending at Sandyford). The latter is due for completion in 2004 and collectively these roads are known as the M50, now the busiest road in Ireland with over 150,000 journeys a day recorded in 1999. The authority with overall responsibility for planning and supervising the construction and improvement of the country's main network of roads is the National Roads Authority, established by the Minister for the Environment on 1 January 1994. Over £5 billion will be spent on the road network under the National Development Plan between 2000 and 2006.

Above: A Liffey Valley-eye's view of the West Link Bridge built by National Toll Roads to a design by Ove Arup and Partners and opened in 1989. It is 385m (1,263ft) long and and at its highest point 41m (134ft) above the Strawberry Beds and the River Liffey. It is now proposed to build a second bridge alongside the West Link to double the crossing capacity.

Below: The East Link Bridge is the most easterly crossing of the River Liffey and was the first modern toll bridge in Dublin. The main contractor on behalf of National Toll Roads was Irishenco Ltd., and the bridge, which has a lifting centre section, was formally opened 21 October 1984.

Photo: courtesy of Peter Barrow Photographers.

Above: The complexity of the Navan Road Interchange is obvious from this aerial photograph. Opened 6 December 1996, the M50 motorway is crossed by a sweeping roundabout, a canal, a railway line and a large main-sewer pipe. Construction work was by P. J. Walls (Civil) Ltd. and engineering works were in charge of Jons Civil Engineering Co. Ltd.

Ireland's earliest civil airport was opened in 1931 at Kildonan, near Finglas in north County Dublin, by Hugh Cahill, the founder of Iona Airways. In June 1935 the Lord Mayor of Dublin, Alfie Byrne, suggested building an airport at Collinstown (the present site of Dublin Airport) as an urgently needed relief scheme to alleviate the widespread unemployment brought on by the Economic War with Britain. His idea found little favour and in May 1936 Aer Lingus, the new national airline, commenced operations from Baldonnel Military Aerodrome. On that inaugural flight Captain O.E. Armstrong flew to Bristol with five passengers (the airline's first ever ticket was issued to the wife of the company's future chairman, Seán Ó hUadhaigh) and a cargo payload consisting of one parcel of *The Irish Times* bound for London.

The Government appointed Major Gerry Carroll of the Army Aer Corps and R. W. Sullivan, assistant aeronautical engineer at Baldonnel, to search out a more suitable site for a new civil airport. Their findings vindicated Alfie Byrne's earlier suggestion and work started at Collinstown in the spring of 1937. In April of the same year Aer Rianta (see Appendix D), the current owner of Dublin Airport, was established as a state company charged with the management of the airport and the development of aviation in Ireland. It was then closely bound to Aer Lingus and both companies shared the same directors. The new airport's main grass runway, 1.6km (1 mile) in length, was completed in October 1939. A few years later the passenger terminal was ready and on Thursday 19 January 1940 the first Aer Lingus plane to depart Collinstown, a Lockheed 14, took off for Liverpool at 0900 hours. Dublin Airport was a reality.

Above: An aerial view of Dublin Airport shows the extent of the facilities and the land-holding. The total property comprises 1093ha (2,700 acres) but as Dublin is one of the fastest growing airports in Europe more land will be required. A second parallel runway is planned to meet expected market demand. Access to the airport will be markedly improved by the widening of the surrounding motorways and the insertion of two additional approach roads into the airport itself by the end of 2000. The future opening of dedicated main rail, light rail (LUAS) and Metro connections from the city will further enhance airport access.

Photo: courtesy of Aer Rianta.

Above: The seemingly incongruous presence of a Georgian house in the middle of a busy international airport never fails to surprise visitors. Considering that the airport land is an amalgam of many former farms it is not surprising that at least one stately home did survive especially if it had its uses. Corballis House, once the home in the 18th century of a Lord Mayor of Dublin, Thomas Wilkinson, has served as a training centre for many years and latterly as an office complex.

The terrible years of the Second World War hindered further progress or expansion at Dublin Airport, but after the cessation of hostilities development was rapid. The grass strip was replaced by three concrete runways and Aer Lingus, the main carrier using the airport in the 1940s, began increasing its fleet to meet the surge in demand. British European Airways led the influx of overseas airlines in 1957 and a year later Aer Lingus commenced Transatlantic operations. Sharp traffic increases dictated the construction of additional passenger facilities between 1959 and 1963 including the North Terminal and the airport's first two piers. Perhaps reflecting the optimism of the 60s, plans were drawn up for the ultimate development of the overall site to enable it to handle up to 40 million passengers per annum. These farseeing blueprints still drive the airport's growth and are the foundation for the continuing success now enjoyed by Dublin Airport. Aer Rianta set about implementing these plans and the first phase of a new terminal, to replace the original 1940s one, opened in 1972 in time for the introduction of wide-bodied aircraft such as the Boeing 747 Jumbo. However, worldwide energy crises and the resultant recessions along with the troubles in Northern Ireland severely restricted growth in traffic and in further construction during the rest of the 1970s and the first half of the 1980s.

Right: Pier C-Terminal West is a recent addition to terminal facilities. Designed by Henry J. Lyons & Partners and built by P. J. Walls Ltd., it was completed in 1999 at a cost of £50 million.

Photo: courtesy of Aer Rianta.

Above: The interior of Pier C before it was opened to receive its first passengers.

Above: New shopping concourse opened in 1998.

In the late 1980s, construction of the first of the two new runways envisaged in the aforementioned plans and the installation of additional facilities in the new terminal facilitated the doubling of traffic from 2 and a half to 5 million passengers between 1986 and 1989. Despite another downturn in traffic, Aer Rianta decided in 1992 to determinedly implement the full scope of the original plan– christened *The Airport 1 Plan* – by starting a next phase to bring the airport capacity up to 20 million passengers per annum during the following decade. Year by year dramatic expansion of aprons, taxiways, check-in and boarding areas, car parks and runways was undertaken. Provision of this extra capacity, combined with the very vibrant Irish economy, the liberalisation of air services, low cost international access and increased competition led to the current boom in air travel. Traffic again doubled from 1994 to 1999, reaching almost 14 million by the year 2000, of whom 3 million were tourists attracted to Dublin, one of Europe's most popular visitor destinations. Indeed, the Dublin-London route is the busiest scheduled international route in Europe. Thirty scheduled airlines travelling to 73 destinations now use the airport. Until the new work could be brought on-stream, the sudden and unprecedented growth in air travel placed enormous strain on the existing airport's passenger and aircraft handling facilities with demand at times exceeding capacity. However, the hundreds of millions of pounds invested by Aer Rianta on extensions and improvements have again resulted in the excess capacity necessary to promote further growth. Terminal space and boarding areas have been doubled in the last couple of years alone and airfield system capacity has grown by 30%. Without a rail alternative to the airport and a greater level of taxi availability, car parking will continue to present a need for more and more space. Already there are 20,000 car spaces including a short-term multi-storey car park, the largest in Ireland. Significant public transport improvements have been achieved in the last two years with a major increase in the number of bus operators serving the airport, a wider network of direct links and major increases in seat capacity. Early completion of the planned rail and LUAS (light rail) links is also a priority. So far the company has been able to fund its own capital programmes but such are the amounts involved for the future that floating a percentage of the company to raise the required cash injections is being considered.

Below: Airports, by their very nature, should be extremely efficient and functional places. This can leave them rather bland and soulless. To relieve this anonymity and at the same time give passengers a distinctly Irish experience Aer Rianta devised the Christmas Lights Festival, the Arts Festival and the Heritage Programme. The Aer Rianta Arts Festival is an annual event celebrated throughout the terminals involving the performing and the visual arts. In the Heritage Programme an impressive array of displays featuring Ireland's rich culture and heritage have been strategically placed in clusters around the airport. The five main themes are Irish-American Emigration, Irish Literary Nobel Laureates, Discovery (below left: one of the boards explaining some of the treasures held by the National Cultural Institutions), Historic Irish Towns and Dublinisation (below right: the 19th century drawings by Bartlett and Petrie). Additionally, the grounds of the airport have been pleasantly landscaped by Aer Rianta.

Photo: courtesy of Aer Rianta.

Above: The passenger terminal, buttressed by twin spiral car ramps, dates from the early 1970s.

Above right: A line-up of fire appliances at the ready in front of the airport's fire station.

Below left: Interior view of the new terminal extension opened in 2000.

Below right: Artist's impression of the new terminal extension. Architects were Henry J. Lyons & Partners.

It is to the great credit of Aer Rianta and the Department of Public Enterprise (formerly the Department of Transport and Power) that in the 1960s they had enough vision to develop long-range plans, procure and then carefully husband sufficient land and space for continuous growth. It is hard to imagine that 40 years ago provision was first made to safeguard the land-holding so that Dublin airport would eventually be able to handle up to 40 million passengers per annum, yet that was the effect of those early decisions. Other airports abroad, such as those in Oslo, Munich and Hong Kong, were unable to further expand with the result that they have had to relocate to new sites. Additionaly land banks at Dublin have also been reserved over the years to allow the future laying of tracks for rail and LUAS systems.

While Aer Rianta's attention has obviously been on the planned development of the airport itself, it has had a vital role in the creation of a virtual new town around the airfield's periphery. Dublin Airport with its surrounding linked facilities and developments is one of the most complex and fastest growing commercial zones in Europe and is the single biggest economic unit in Ireland. Already there are over 100 companies engaging an on-site workforce of 13,000 staff and supporting an estimated 50,000 additional jobs in Dublin. This represents around 10% of the Dublin region's workforce. The airport is also seeing the creation of industrial, business and retail parks around its environs. This is acting as a further magnet for more business, much of which will be channelled as passengers and cargo through the airport which will in turn create more employment opportunities. It is certainly all a far cry from the days of grass runways and wooden huts.

Photo: courtesy of Aer Rianta.

Photo: courtesy of Aer Rianta.

Photo: courtesy of Aer Lingus.

Above: The first Aer Lingus aircraft, the deHavilland Dragon DH-84. It was registered EI-AB1 and named "Iolar" (Eagle). The usual seating configuration was for five passengers. Aer Lingus has preserved, in full flying serviceability, a sister aircraft of the "Iolar" which was restored for the company's 50th anniversary in 1986.

Photo: courtesy of Aer Lingus.

Above: Aer Lingus commenced transatlantic operations in April 1958 with Lockheed LI049 Super Constellations on lease from Seaboard and Western Airlines. They were disposed of in December 1960 in favour of the Boeing 720, which at 864kph (540mph), was twice as fast.

The first person to lift off Irish soil in a man-made apparatus was Richard Crosbie who sailed his balloon from Dublin's Ranelagh Gardens to the North Strand in 1785. A Belfast garage mechanic, Harry Ferguson, was the first to fly a heavier-than-air machine in Ireland. In his own self-built plane he flew a mere 130m (425ft) in 1909. First across the Irish Sea (at least for most of it; he ditched and had to swim the final 50m) was Robert Lorraine in 1910 who had set off from Holyhead. Denys Corbett Wilson kept his feet dry when he successfully flew from Britain to Ireland in 1912. In 1919 Alcock and Brown were first to conquer the Atlantic when they crash-landed at Clifden, Co. Galway. The much more difficult East to West crossing was achieved in 1928 by the German aircraft "Bremen" which had set off from Baldonnel. The three-man crew included Col. James Fitzmaurice of the Irish Army Air Corps. By 1930 Ireland's first airline, Iona National Airways, was operating.

Photo: courtesy of Aer Lingus.

Above: Aer Lingus bought its first Douglas DC-3 in 1940 and by the mid-1950s the airline had thirteen of these reliable workhorses. The last DC-3 was taken out of service in April 1964.

On the same day the giant liner, the Queen Mary, was launched, 27 May 1936, the inaugural Aer Lingus flight took off from Baldonnel Military Aerodrome for Bristol in England. Set up by the Irish Government a month earlier, the fledgling airline soon supplemented that little twin-engined deHavilland DH-84 with two of her bigger sisters, the four engined DH-86. A Douglas DC-3 followed in 1940. Aer Lingus (from the Irish, Aer Loingeas, meaning Air Fleet) continued to operate a limited service to the UK during World War ll and after 1945, with the acquisition of six more DC-3s, the network was expanded to include Paris, Amsterdam and Lourdes. From then on additional routes were constantly added and transatlantic services commenced in 1958. In a notoriously cyclical business of progression and downturns and despite intense competition Aer Lingus has maintained its reputation as a quality, first choice airline with a strong business and leisure customer loyalty base. The fleet of around 40 aircraft is one of the most modern of any European airline. On 1 June 2000 Aer Lingus joined the OneWorld Alliance, a strategic and marketing consortium consisting of major airlines such as British Airways, American Airlines, Qantas, Cathay Pacific and Iberia.

Below: The sleek lines of the powerful Airbus A330, one of six which now operate the transatlantic routes from Dublin, Shannon and Belfast to New York, Newark, Boston, Chicago, Los Angeles and Washington.

Photo: courtesy of Aer Lingus.

Above: Hangar 6 at Dublin Airport is the flagship facility of FLS Aerospace (Ireland). This mammoth grey and blue hangar can simultaneously handle two Boeing 747-type aircraft in addition to five Boeing 737s. Constructed between November 1989 and early 1991, the hangar is 158m (520ft) wide and over 22.5m (65ft) tall, had the longest steel span in Ireland at the time of building and cost £35 million to construct. The floor area exceeds that of Croke Park. The main contractor was John Sisk & Son. The structural engineer was Muir Associates in association with Sir Frederick Snow & Partners. Conscious of the massive size of the hangar the architects, Henry J. Lyons & Partners, softened its impact on the environment by painting the exterior blue and grey, the predominant colours of the Irish skyline. There are five other hangars and related workshops in a complex that stretches from the old terminal to the Swords Road. At any one time the hangars can, in total, accommodate four jumbos and nine shorthaul aircraft such as the Airbus 321 and Boeing 737. FLS Aerospace (Irl) has the capacity to employ up to 2,000 staff (there are currently 1,600 employees) and to support this huge activity a spare parts store stocks up to 75,000 individual parts. In addition to aircraft the facility also provides maintenance for the fleets of ground vehicles at the airport numbering 1,000 units, for the hangars themselves and for plant, workshops and assorted other buildings around the airport.

FLS Aerospace, a Danish multinational company (see Appendix D), acquired TEAM Aer Lingus, the airline's maintenance subsidiary, in December 1998. Aer Lingus had developed its own maintenance base from its foundation in 1936 and the company encouraged the expansion of the maintenance and engineering departments to additionally take in work from other airlines. If the maintenance division, which had long outgrown the needs of the parent airline's fleet, was to succeed internationally it became clear that it must find another owner who could capitalise on the enormous and highly respected skills of the then 1,500 strong workforce. The purchase of TEAM by FLS Aerospace proved in effect to be less of an acquisition and more of a partnership. Customers of FLS Aerospace (Irl) include Aer Lingus, Trans Aer, Virgin, UPS, SAS, Delta, Cityjet, Aer Turas and Corsair.

Below: An internal view of Hangar 6. There are varying degrees of maintenance and checks required to be carried out on aircraft, depending on hours flown. A "D" check involves practically dismantling the complete aircraft from tail to wing tip and can take from 40,000 to 70,000 man-hours to complete.

Photo: courtesy of FLS Aerospace.

Chapter Eleven

Enriched by Diversity

IN IRELAND'S long history there have been many occasions when the country received large numbers of immigrants. The early settlers of prehistoric times were joined by nomadic tribes who crossed over from Britain or directly from Europe. Foremost among the latter were the Celts who arrived in separate waves from about the 5th century BC. Sometimes new arrivals came bearing arms in a spirit of conquest, at other times they were fleeing brutality in their own homelands. Some came to stop over on their way to the New World and went no further. Others, including craftsmen and artists, were invited to ennoble the country with their architecture, sculpture, stucco work and painting. Medieval Irish monks brought back many new ideas to their home country from their international missions, as did the priests of the 16th to 18th centuries who were obliged to obtain their clerical training in the Irish colleges of Salamanca, Louvain and Rome because of anti-Catholic laws.

Only in recent years have economic immigrants arrived in search of employment as, previously, Ireland's own sons and daughters had once to emigrate to find work. Now a labour shortage in Ireland is attracting workers from both inside and outside the European Community. The relatively generous Irish social welfare system is also enticing people from countries with low standards of living. Refugees and asylum seekers have recently begun to arrive to Ireland in relatively large numbers, but nothing, it must be said, compared to the country's own emigration figures of less than a generation ago. Only now are the Government agencies being sufficiently resourced to handle the applications from immigrants and provide the services required by individuals and families. For whatever reason people come, they bring with them their own distinct culture which should be both preserved for them and infused into that of the host country to everyone's enrichment.

Within a country's own population there are also groups who appear not to "fit in". Ireland's own minority are the Travellers who have their own unique society and culture but have become somewhat lost and disgruntled in a world that no longer values the services they once offered. Their lives are harsh to say the least, especially for those who live in caravans parked along the side of the road or in muddy fields. The settled community will have to create the conditions that will allow the Travellers themselves to fashion their own future, a future that might not be full integration but rather a dignified and fruitful independence with full rights.

Above: Dating from around the 1st century A.D. this bronze object, known as the Petrie Crown, is decorated in the La Tène style. This was a form of Celtic art imported into Ireland which originated around Lake Neuchatel (a region of Switzerland).

Above: Entrance gate and railings of the Huguenot Graveyard on Merrion Row. The cemetery, opened in 1693 by non-conformist Huguenots, was restored in 1988 by the French Ministry of Foreign Affairs in association with FAS, the State Training Agency. It is cared for by Dublin Corporation.

Right: An internal view of the Huguenot Graveyard, a quiet oasis amid the flurry of the busy city centre streets.

Right: D'Olier Chambers, an 1890s ornate office block, stands at the corner of D'Olier and Hawkins streets. It commemorates Jeremiah D'Olier (1745-1817), a Huguenot goldsmith, who became a City Sheriff, a founder of the Bank of Ireland and a member of the Wide Streets Commission. When D'Olier Street was laid out at the start of the 19th century by the Commission it was named in his honour. D'Olier's family originally came from Toulouse. Jeremiah D'Olier fashioned the current Deputy Mayor's chain in 1796. Other famous people of Huguenot extraction associated with Dublin were David laTouche (banker), Elias Bouhéreau (librarian, Marsh's Library), John Rocque (cartographer), James Gandon and Richard Cassels (architects), Joseph Sheridan leFanu and Charles Robert Maturin (novelists) and William Dargan (railway pioneer).

Huguenots were French Calvinist Protestants who constantly bickered with the Catholic majority in France from the mid-16th century. They endured the murder of 20,000 of their followers during the infamous St Bartholomew's Day Massacre in 1572. Wars broke out between the two religious groups until Henry IV (a Huguenot himself) signed the Edict of Nantes in 1598. This did not end the persecutions which gathered momentum in the next century. A trickle of Huguenot refugees began to arrive in Ireland from about 1630 onwards. The trickle became a flood when Louis XIV revoked the Edict of Nantes in 1685. More than 50,000 Huguenots fled from France with several thousand of these arriving into Ireland. In Dublin they settled mostly around the Coombe district and immediately enriched the commercial and artistic life of the city with their masterly skills in weaving, textile making, goldsmithing and silversmithing.

Left: Tapestry entitled "The Glorious Battle of the Boyne" which hangs in the House of Lords, Bank of Ireland, College Green. The centrepiece figure on a rearing horse is King William III of Orange urging his troops on to eventual victory over James II of England. Such works as this tapestry were carried out by immigrant Dutch craftsmen who were encouraged to settle in Dublin after William had secured the English throne (see also page 59).

Below: Architecture in Dublin from the 17th century to the early 18th century was strongly influenced by Huguenot and Dutch settlers. A common form of building was the gable-fronted house reminiscent of a Dutch urban streetscape. These houses were called Dutch Billies (after the Dutchman, King William III) and although they once proliferated around Dublin only a few examples still remain. Some survivors include (from the left) Kevin Street, Molesworth Street, Duke Street (The Bailey, bar and restaurant) and Leeson Street (The Institute of Education). The last two were recently reconstructed.

Above left: The Religious Society of Friends (Quakers), who first arrived to Ireland in 1654, built a Meeting House in Temple Bar's Sycamore Alley in 1692. From here they expanded onto Eustace Street where they constructed an impressive new house in 1728. The Quakers have remained there ever since, although part of their premises, at number 6 Eustace Street, has been given over to the Irish Film Centre since 1992. Once prominent in the commercial and philanthropic life of Ireland, they contributed household names to the manufacturing and retail businesses such as Pim, Jacob, Bewley, Walpole, Webb and Haughton. The Quakers also provided much of the voluntary relief work carried out during the Great Famine of the 1840s.

Above right: The earliest surviving Presbyterian Church building in Dublin is the former Meeting House and School in Eustace Street, Temple Bar, which was first opened in 1728. In the mid 1990s it was restored and adapted for use as a children's cultural and theatrical centre known as The Ark. Basically, only the façade has survived years of depredation and under the direction of David Slattery the cement rendering was stripped back to reveal the brickwork and more than twenty layers of paint were removed from the Portland stone window surrounds. Architects for the project were Shane O'Toole and Michael Kelly in association with Group 91. The Presbyterian congregation (mainly of Scottish extraction), especially in the 19th century, contributed many prominent business families to Dublin. Familiar names in this context include: John Jameson, Distiller; Thomas Heiton, Coal Merchant; John Boyd Dunlop, inventor of the first useable pneumatic tyre; John Arnott, Department Store; Adam Millar, Wine Merchant; James Mackey, Seed Merchant; Alex Thom, Printer of Irish Almanacs & Directories; Thomas Weir, Jeweller; John Johnston (of Johnston, Mooney & O'Brien), Miller & Baker; Alex Findlater, Grocer & Wine Merchant; Gilbert Burns & William Todd, Department Store.

Below left: The small but gradual influx of Eastern Europeans and Middle Easterners into Ireland brought about the organisation, in 1981, of a Greek Orthodox community. It would take thirteen years of moving from one temporary building to another before a permanent church was founded in a former British Army School behind Collins Barracks on Arbour Hill. The Church of the Annunciation was consecrated by Archbishop Gregorios of Thyateira on 6 November 1994. The interior of the building was reconstructed into a proper Byzantine style using the plan of the 7th century church of Holy Dormition at Tessaly, in the North of Greece. The Irish foundation embraces all the different ethnic groupings in one sharing community.

Below right: The interior of a typical Greek Orthodox church is well represented at Arbour Hill. The Nathex (vestibule) leads into the three-aisled Naos (nave) which is marked out by columns and arches. The Sanctuary is divided from the Naos by the Icon Screen which displays four Royal Icons and twelve Feast Icons which were specially commissioned and hand-painted in Athens. The candelabras represent the column of fire by which God guided Moses at night to the promised land. The Irish Parish belongs to the Archdiocese of Thyateira, Great Britain, Ireland and Malta.

Left: In the early 18th century the Jewish community living around Dublin's northside opened a small graveyard in Ballybough near Fairview. The last burial took place here in 1958. The house which today stands in front of the cemetery bears the inscription "built in the year 5618". This Jewish calendar year corresponds to 1857 in the Gregorian calendar.

Some Jewish merchants would have visited Ireland down the centuries but the first community to settle here arrived over 300 years ago and they soon opened a synagogue in Crane Lane off Dublin's Dame Street. This group was mostly of Spanish and Portuguese origin and they appeared to have died out or dispersed by 1790. A few hundred Jewish immigrants arrived some thirty years later, opening synagogues in Wolfe Tone Street and Mary's Abbey. Finally, in the 1880s, several thousand Jews, fleeing from pogroms in Russia, arrived in Ireland on their way to America. Many stayed on, and in Dublin they generally settled around the South Circular Road in an area that became known as "Little Jerusalem". By the mid-1940s the number of Jews in Ireland exceeded 4,000 but, sadly, with the younger generations leaving for America and Israel, the numbers have since fallen to around 1,500.

Top and above: Two former Lord Mayors of Dublin were both Jewish and related. Robert Briscoe held office from 1956 to 1957 and again from 1961 to 1962. His son Ben wore the mayoral chain of office from 1988 to 1989. Between the pair they maintained a unique unbroken service for a father and son team as city councillors. Their combined terms stretch from 1930 to the present day.

Left: A pair of adjoining houses on Walworth Road was converted in 1918 to serve as a synagogue for the local Jewish community. It closed in the mid 1970s and was re-opened a decade later as a Jewish museum. The opening cermony was performed by the then President of Israel, Chaim Herzog, who once lived in nearby Bloomfield Avenue.

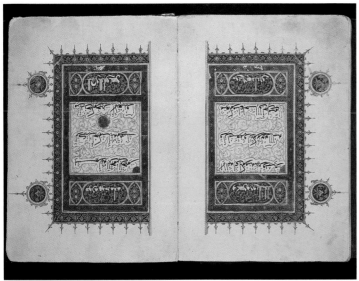

Above: These pages from a Persian Qur'an (Koran) dated 1467-68 are part of the collection held at the Chester Beatty Library and Galleries, Dublin Castle. The Qur'an is the last revealed Word of Allah and is the basic source of Islamic teachings and laws. The Word was revealed to the Prophet Muhammad (570-632) when he was forty years old. He was born in Makkah (Mecca), Saudi Arabia, but persecution drove him and his followers to Al Madinah (Medina) where he now lies buried. The specific acts of worship, known as the Four Pillars of Islam, are; 1) The declaration of faith and imitation of Muhammad's exemplary life, 2) Prayers that are prescribed five times a day, 3) Fasting days in the month of Ramadan, 4) Zakaat-an annual payment of 2 and a half percent of one's net savings to aid the poor, 5) Pilgrimage (Hajj) to Makkah once in a lifetime.

Above: The Finglas Road Chapel of the Latter-Day Saints (Mormons) was built in 1979. The Church also has two other centres, one at Bushy Park Road in Terenure and another in Clondalkin. The Church of Jesus Christ of the Latter Day Saints was founded on 6 April 1830 in Fayette, New York by Joseph Smith Jr. Following persecutions in 1844, in which Smith was killed by a mob, the church moved under its new President, Brigham Young, to an uninhabited part of the USA near Salt Lake. There they established a community which has since grown into Salt Lake City. The first branch in Ireland was established by Mormon missionaries in 1840 in Hillsborough, Co. Down. There are now approximately 5,000 members on the island of Ireland. The preservation of and support for the family as a basic unit of society is a main tenet of Mormon practice. In this context research into family history is encouraged. The church has a large genealogical centre in Salt Lake City (web site: www.familysearch.org) and a family history library at Finglas. Both services are free of charge.

Above: The famous Beshoff fish and chip restaurant was founded by Ivan Iylanovich Beshoff, a seaman in the navy of the Russian Tsar Nicholas II. He fled Russia after he took part in an ill-fated mutiny on the battleship Potemkin at Odessa in 1905 and arrived in Ireland in 1912 with the intention of travelling on to Canada. He missed his boat connection and decided to stay.

Above: Muslim families enjoying a day out at Newbridge Demesne, Co Dublin. From a tiny representation a generation ago the number of Muslims in Ireland has now grown to nearly 12,000, two-thirds of whom live in Dublin. Unfortunate refugees from Eastern Europe and parts of Africa are constantly adding to the figure but many Muslims reside here as doctors, business people, teachers, students, lecturers, administrators, restaurateurs and specialised workers.

Above: Opened on 14 November 1996 by President Mary Robinson, the Islamic Cultural Centre, off Roebuck Road, is, in its relatively simple lines, a stunning building and an enrichment to the civil architecture of Dublin. The four graceful corner blocks contain a school, a shop and restaurant, administration offices, a multi-purpose sports hall, apartments, small prayer and meeting rooms and an exquisite library. Airy courtyards and lobbies connect the corner blocks to the main Prayer Hall. A traditional dome surmounted by a copper crescent (representing the Lunar Calendar) and a flanking minaret inform the observer of the religious significance of the centre. The building was sponsored by the Al Maktoum family of Dubai on behalf of the Islamic Foundation of Ireland. Architects for the project were Michael Collins Associates and the main contractors were Duggan Brother (Contractors) Ltd. Structural engineering was carried out by Ove Arup & Partners and Brady Shipman Martin were the landscape architects.

Left: The main Prayer Hall, under the dome of the Mosque, is orientated towards the Kaaba, the Holy of Holies, at Makkah. The direction to face is marked on one wall by a niche called the Mihrab. To the right of the Mihrab, a Minbar (pulpit) is provided for the Imam who leads the congregation in prayer.

Photo: courtesy of Gerry O'Dea.

Above: A Travellers' camp in the early 1980s. It may have looked "romantic" to the casual observer but living conditions were usually miserable, especially during the Irish winter. Mortality was high and even today with improving standards only 1 percent of Travellers live over 60 years.

Right: The Pavee Point Travellers Centre moved into the sensitively converted Free Church on North Great Charles Street in 1990. Built in 1800 by the Methodists it was taken over by the Church of Ireland in 1828. It was called the Free Church because parishioners didn't have to pay for a pew. The Travellers' Centre was founded by John O'Connell who campaigned tirelessly for the rights of Travellers and to bring about a more caring society in which they could live, thrive, engage and appreciate their own culture. He died in November 1999 but his ideals live on in the work of Pavee Point which is helping to empower Travellers to secure for themselves a better future and to involve the majority population in processes to bring about equal rights for Travellers.

Above: Bridgeview, Clondalkin, is a scheme of twelve houses provided by Dublin Corporation to Traveller families.

Right: St Oliver's Park, Clondalkin, is a fourteen-bay site for Travellers and their caravans and is under the care of Dublin Corporation.

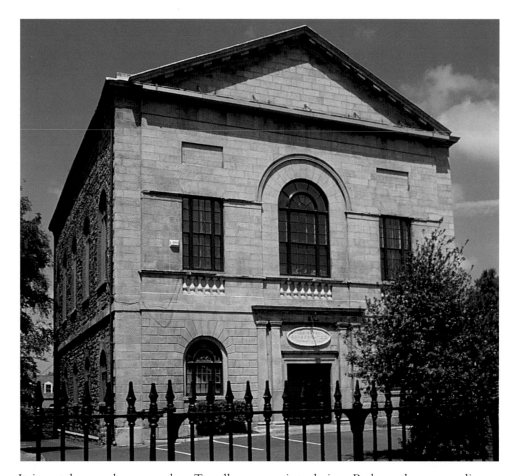

It is not known how or when Travellers came into being. Perhaps they were dispossessed farm labourers from the time of the Cromwellian Plantation but whatever their genesis they evolved their own culture and language (called Cant or Gammon). They fulfilled a useful role throughout the countryside by offering various services including the mending of tin containers (which earned them the name "Tinkers"). The widespread use of plastic, the emergence of the "throw-away" society and the decline in the rural population robbed the Travellers of their traditional way of life and many started to settle around cities and larger towns. Their population has doubled in a single generation and over 1,200 families still live on the side of the road or in illegal camps where basic services are denied to them. Education is one way through which Travellers may gain confidence and create opportunities to help themselves. Most Traveller children now attend primary school and a growing number, 750 at present, attend second level. Only 12 so far have attained third level diplomas or degrees but the success of a few may positively impact on the majority, given time and the support of the settled community.

At the time of publication refugees were arriving in Ireland at the rate of over one thousand per month. This is a small overall number by European standards but it puts Ireland into second place in the EU in terms of asylum applications received as a proportion of the total population. The categories of refugees fall into three main groupings, asylum seekers, economic refugees and so-called illegal immigrants. Many asylum seekers examined by a doctor in Dublin's main refugee medical unit had been tortured to some extent in their home countries. Currently, refugees come, in the main, from countries such as Sudan, Congo, Rwanda, Somalia, Iraq, Romania, Nigeria, Algeria, Eastern Europe and the Balkans. All these people, should they be allowed to stay in Ireland, have a valuable contribution to make to their host country and support services are beginning to effectively facilitate them to achieve this.

IRISH REFUGEE COUNCIL

Above: There are over 50 non-Governmental organisations working on behalf of refugees in Ireland. The national body that brings together all these groups is the Irish Refugee Council (IRC) which was established in 1992.

The aims of the IRC are:

(a) to promote the cause of refugees and asylum seekers,
(b) to ensure that Ireland's asylum policy and practice accord fully with international law and respect human rights,
(c) to heighten public awareness of refugee situations and their causes.

Photo: courtesy of Gerry O'Dea.

Left: Kosovan children enjoying a party at the Islamic Cultural Centre.

1 2 3
4 5
6 7 8

The increasing number of ethnic restaurants and shops is a welcome sign of the growing cosmopolitanism of the city.

1 | Indian

2 | Italian

3 | Thai

4 | Japanese

5 | Mexican

6 | Mongolian

7 | Chinese

8 | Creole

Chapter Twelve
Reviving the Spirits

THE DAMP and often chilly climate in Ireland has restricted al fresco entertaining to the warmer and sunnier days of the summer. It must be said, however, that it has come as a pleasant surprise to see the success of the recently introduced pavement cafés in Dublin. If asked a few years ago one would have dismissed this notion as being entirely impracticable but grateful patrons have since found them comfortable on many of the days of spring, summer and autumn. Optimistic restaurateurs often leave out the tables and chairs during the winter months and not without result on the balmier days. Café society has arrived! Yet it still might be argued that the customary Irish welcome is at its best in the warm and intimate atmosphere of the pub. After all, whiskey is said to have been invented in Ireland and Dublin is certainly the home of the "black brew". But even here change is rapidly taking place. Younger people are tending towards the larger pub which may also offer a complete change in style from the traditional interior. The theme pub has arrived! The Dubliner has also discovered the pleasures of eating out and in the current buoyant economic climate new restaurants have blossomed all over the city with many of them presenting international and ethnic cuisine. Coffee shops, many offering specialist fare, are burgeoning along every city street. Never before in the city's history have so many new hotels been opened over a short few years. It is the general perception that somewhere in Dublin a new hotel opens every week and this may not be too far off the mark. Dublin has arrived!

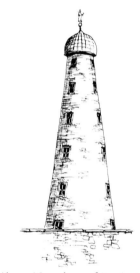

Above: Now shorn of its giant sails, the tapering tower of the former distillery windmill of George Roe can easily be seen from as far away as O'Connell Bridge. Now on Guinness property, the old windmill was once the tallest in these islands.

Above: The James's Street entrance into the world-famous brewery of Arthur Guinness (the Irish branch of the multi-national Diageo organisation is known as Guinness Ireland Group). The year showing the foundation of the brewery on one side of the gateway is complemented on the other side by the current date.

Above: Al fresco in Temple Bar.

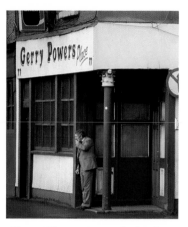

Photo: courtesy of Guinness Ireland Group.

Above: Countless wooden barrels stand in the yard of Guinness's St James's Gate Brewery in this late 19th century view.

Richard Guinness passed on his brewing expertise to his son Arthur, who bought, in 1759, an old disused brewery on a plot of land opposite to the site of St James's Gate, once part of the city's western defences. Arthur proved to be a dab hand at both brewing and business and his new firm prospered. In the early years Guinness only produced ale but in the 1770s a new drink came to his attention. London brewers had begun to export a dark coloured brew to Dublin called porter, so named because it was popular with the porters of Covent Garden and Billingsgate. Arthur dropped the brewing of ale in favour of the new porter (its dark colour came from the use of roasted barley). He later refined and strengthened the porter and called it extra stout porter which became popularly and famously known the world over as stout. Arthur Guinness, who died at his home in Gardiner Street in 1803, laid the foundations for a company whose name is now synonymous with Ireland. The brewery itself was at one time the largest in the world. Today St James's Gate is only part of the international brewing network of Guinness (there are now 50 breweries literally all over the planet) yet it exports more beer than any other single brewery in the world (400 million pints per year).

Left: The Guinness Storehouse, completed in 1904 to house the fermentation process, is one of Dublin's most remarkable industrial buildings reminiscent of the late 19th century buildings of the Chicago Architectural School. It is a massive structure rising to a height of eight storeys. Although the outer walls are of brick the structural framing is of steel. The designer was A. H. Hignett, an engineer employed by Guinness. The contractor was McLaughlin and Harvey. The Guinness Storehouse is being redeveloped at a cost of £30 million to provide a new world-class visitors' complex, state-of-the-art training facilities, a company archive, a hospitality suite, a panoramic bar and an exhibition gallery. It is scheduled to open in the latter half of 2000.

Right: For almost a century the Dublin Corporation Weights and Measures Department operated from this brick building on Harry Street, off Grafton Street. With the relocation of Weights and Measures the property was sold in 1998 to developer Ciaran Fahy who, in consultation with the Dublin Civic Trust, promptly set a superb renovation in train. A year later the premises were leased by Berry Brothers and Rudd, one of the oldest wine merchants in the world (established in London in 1698).

It is said that the distillation process which led to the invention of whiskey was perfected by Irish monks in the Early Christian period. Their Uisce Beatha (Water of Life) certainly seems to have helped sustain the holy men through all the travails of those unsettled times. A certain John Jameson thought that a wider circle of ordinary souls would also appreciate the refined spirit and in execution of this fine ideal he bought, in 1780, an interest in a small distillery at Bow Street. He, his son, his grandson and great grandson, all named John, steered the firm of John Jameson & Son into a prominent position both at home and abroad. The distillery's large stone buildings were erected between Smithfield and Bow Street in the late 1880s. Jameson united with the Powers and Paddy labels to form the Irish Distillers Group in 1966 and all distilling moved to Midleton, Co. Cork. The Bow Street premises, vacant since 1971, were incorporated into the modern Smithfield Village development in the late 1990s. Part of this re-development, carried out by Heritage Properties, included the 3,716sq m (40,000sq ft) Old Jameson Distillery, a £7 million investment by Irish Distillers to create a fascinating replica of a working distillery where visitors can follow each step of the process and afterwards indulge in a complimentary glass of Uisce Beatha. The centre was fitted out by London-based Robin Wade and Partners and the overall architectural design was handled by A & D Wejchert.

Above: The Bow Street entrance to the Old Jameson Distillery Visitor Centre.

Above left: Revealed in the foyer are many of the former distillery's 19th century structural elements.

Below left: The old Spirit Store in Smithfield was converted in 1980 to serve as the headquarters of Irish Distillers Group plc. It thus could be said that the company led the way in the extraordinary renewal that has since taken place in this part of Dublin.

Below right: The one-hour guided tour brings visitors past the full-sized copper pot stills.

Above left: Although renamed several times in its long history the same business has been purveyed in the premises of the Palace Bar since the 1840s. The walls and shelves of the pub are lined with a cornucopia of antiques, paintings and framed cartoons.

Above right: The owners of Mulligans Pub in Poolbeg Street have resolutely refused to "modernise" this much-loved establishment. Many public houses have had to be extended and updated to attract business but there is always room for the dignified old stalwarts who elect to maintain their traditions. Mulligans was originally founded in 1782. In fact, since 1 January 2000, under the Local Government Planning and Development Act, older pub interiors will be protected by law. Also, under the new Dublin Development Plan a number of pubs including Mulligans and The Palace Bar are especially listed for preservation.

Below left: Doheny & Nesbitts has been traditionally popular with politicians, civil servants, journalists and economists-hence the facetious sobriquet "The Doheny and Nesbitt School of Economics". Ned Doheny and Thomas Nesbitt sold their business in 1990 after 30 years at the helm. The new owners, Tom and Paul Mangan, have restored the premises and extended it to the rear using the same design features.

Below right: The interior of Ryans still remains much as it was when it was remodelled in 1896. Its fittings include intricately carved mahogany cases, decorative counter dividers and a number of snugs (partitioned-off corners).

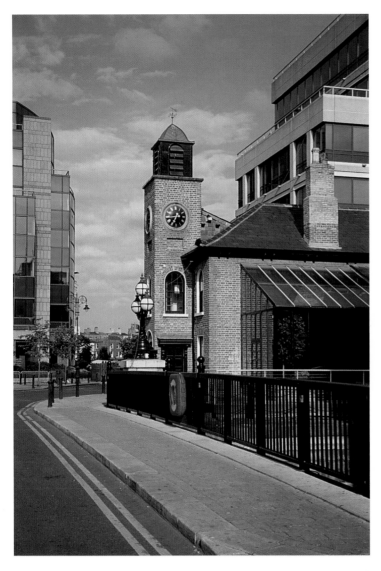

Above: The Harbourmaster Bar and Restaurant is housed in a very unusual building in the International Financial Services Centre. It was the former offices of the Master of the Custom House Docks and the interior has been redecorated to what it might have looked like in the 19th century. The high shelves are crowded with samples of goods which passed through the harbour in bygone days. It was developed in the early 1990s by the owners, the Thomas Read Group.

Above: The Mercantile Bar in the Adams Trinity Hotel off Dame Street is one of Dublin's latest bars bearing no relation to the traditional pub. Based in a sumptuous former banking hall the bars and restaurant are spread over three floors. The recurring theme, reinforced by the use of statuary, decoration and pictures, is of Ancient Greece.

Left: The cellars of Alex Findlater Wine Merchants are ideally situated in the extensive series of vaults which run under the former Harcourt Street Railway Station. The present company is a descendant of the famous but now defunct firm of Alex Findlater & Co. which had grocery and wine shops all over Dublin until their closure in 1969. Their drays (above) were a familiar sight around the city. The Findlater Museum, also housed in the vaults, traces both the history of this remarkable merchant family and 19th century Dublin in its collection of photographs, labels, packaging, accoutrements of the trade, advertisements, memorabilia and trophies.

Above: Bewleys of Grafton Street dates from 1927 and was the last venture of Ernest Bewley, the second son of the founder of the firm, Joshua Bewley. Sadly he did not see the success of this famous café as Ernest died in 1932, apparently from bad health brought on from financial troubles associated with the purchase and operation of Grafton Street. In 1990 a no less august body than the Council of Europe described Bewleys of Grafton Street as "one of the great cafes of Europe". In 1998 the café was extensively remodelled.

Below: Bewleys of Westmoreland Street was first opened at No 10 in 1896. It was later extended several times. A devastating fire in 1977 extensively damaged the exotic interior of the restaurant but the old atmosphere was subsequently restored. It underwent further refurbishment in early 2000.

Above: Bewleys Hotel on the Merrion Road at Ballsbridge includes and wraps around the former Masonic Girls Orphanage, a High Victorian-styled building dating from 1882 and designed by McCurdy and Mitchell. The 308-bedroom hotel is necessarily a large structure but in its design and selection of bricks it strongly echoes the original building and complements it. The character of the extensive lawns has been preserved and the existing fountain, whose origins have been traced back to the Dublin Exhibition of 1872, has been restored. Opened in 1999 the hotel was designed by Tony Hickie Architects and built by Ellen Construction.

In 1840 Joshua Bewley opened a small teashop in Sycamore Alley, beside the Olympia Theatre. Five years earlier his father Samuel had speculatively imported 3,000 chests of tea directly from China and started a new drinking fashion in Dublin. The first high street shop was opened at No.13 South Great George's Street in the mid 1870s. Tea was still the dominant drink so Joshua's son Ernest, in 1893, demonstrated the art of coffee making while his wife prepared freshly baked scones at the back of the shop. The idea was eminently successful and thus began the famous cafés and the bakery. Additional cafés followed on Westmoreland Street (1896), and Grafton Street (1927). Matters then settled down for over half a century and the three cafés became part of Dublin's folklore and the haunt of the literati. Generations of people flocked to the marble-topped tables and crimson-backed seating compartments of Bewleys to wash down sticky buns and delicious cakes with Jersey milk or, of course, with the legendary coffee. A financial crisis almost closed down the firm in 1986 but it was saved at the eleventh hour when Campbell Catering took it over in November of that year (although, thankfully, the Bewley family is still involved in the business). Since then many more Bewley Cafés as well as a couple of hotels have been opened in Ireland and outlets have been extended to the UK, the USA and Japan.

14th December 1793   **Freeman's Journal**   *Issue No.6,789.*

Shakespeare Tavern, Fowne's Street, Corner of Cope Street, Is opened for the Accommodation of the Public - The Larder is constantly supplied with every article in season. The Wines are of the first Quality and Flavour, which, with good Attendance and an unremitting attention to please, it is hoped will recommend to Patronage.

Large parties accommodated with Dinner in suitable stile, provided Notice be given on the Preceding Day. Soup every Day.

Above: The Gresham Hotel was founded in 1817 by Londoner, Thomas Gresham, in a pair of Georgian houses at No. 21 and No. 22 Upper Sackville (O'Connell) Street. His arrangement of town house comfort allied to first class service found favour with the gentry and he soon had to lease next door, at No. 20, as well. Gresham sold the hotel as a going concern to a group of Cork businessmen in 1865 who continued to expand the trade. A concert and dining hall was added in 1906 which became a hub of social activity in the city. Two hundred guests were trapped for a week in the hotel during the rebellion of 1916 but the building remained undamaged. It was, however, destroyed in the Civil War in 1922. Designed by Robert Atkinson, the present structure was opened in 1927. The recently rebuilt canopy and the restoration of the façade won the Royal Institute of Architects in Ireland Regional Award in 1999. The Gresham Hotel is part of the Ryan Hotel Group.

Below: The Clarence Hotel on Wellington Quay first opened for business in 1856 and built up a strong clientele base composed mostly of clergy, lawyers and businessmen from the provinces. By the 1990s it had become somewhat jaded and out-dated. It was then bought by Harry Crosbie, a well-known Dublin haulier, and by Bono and The Edge, two members of the famous Irish rock band U2, who restored it to its former glory but in a simpler and more contemporaneous style. The architects for the refurbishment (which included the addition of a luxury penthouse) were Costello Murray Beaumont, and Keith Hobbs of London-based United Designers handled the interior design. The Clarence Hotel was re-opened in June 1996 and has carved its own niche in attracting the stars of stage and screen.

Above: No 22 St Stephen's Green, with its unusual wrought-iron balcony, was built in 1790 for Sir Thomas Leighton who demolished a late 17th century house to make way for it. From 1884 until 1995 it was occupied by The Ancient and Most Benevolent Order of the Friendly Brothers of St Patrick, a social and charitable organisation founded in the early 17th century. The house was tastefully converted by its new owner, Mr Barry Canny, in 1999, into Browne's Brasserie and Townhouse.

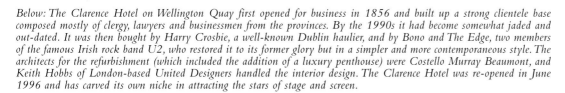

Left: The Morrison Hotel on Lower Ormond Quay, a 95 bedroom hotel in the contemporary idiom but highly individually designed, was opened in 1999. It replaced an ugly 1960s building. Like the Clarence Hotel on the opposite side of the river Morrison's has proved to be a mecca for the celebrities of the show business world. Its interior was designed by the Irish fashion designer John Rocha. The hotel is owned by the Thomas Read Group (see appendix D). The architects were Douglas Wallace Architects.

Above: Jurys Hotel, Ballsbridge, in a building since extended and modernised, was originally constructed in the 1960s as the home of the Intercontinental Hotel. The grounds at one time belonged to the Botanical Gardens of Trinity College and some specimen trees from that period are still growing in the grounds. Adjacent to the main Jurys Hotel, with an exclusive entrance on Lansdowne Road, is the Towers Hotel (built 1989), the luxury wing of the hotel.

William Jury opened a commercial boarding house at No. 7 College Green in 1839. Such was its success that adjoining properties were soon acquired. The hotel was rebuilt and expanded in 1859 and again in 1882. The Jury family sold the hotel in 1915 and over the next fifty years more improvements were carried out including the addition of the ballroom that became the birthplace of the famous Jury's Cabaret. The hotel was relocated to Ballsbridge in 1973 and the College Green premises were demolished. The renowned Jury's Bar was dismantled and shipped to Zurich where it was reassembled in one of the buildings owned by the UBS Bank. Through the 1980s and 1990s the Jurys Group opened new hotels and budget-style inns in Ireland, Britain and the USA and in May 1999 it acquired the Doyle Hotel Group. The Jurys Doyle Hotel Group now owns 30 hotels making it the largest Irish hotel conglomerate.

Above: Jurys Inn, Christchurch Place and opposite Christ Church Cathedral, was opened in April 1993 and it marked a new direction for the Jurys Group who had seen a need to open a string of high quality budget hotels. Built by Pierse Contracting to the design of Burke-Kennedy Doyle and Partners, the presence of the hotel helped to spark the amazing rejuvenation of what had been a rather run-down part of Dublin.

Above: The 100 bedroom Ripley Court Hotel, built across a long-abandoned derelict site, was opened in 1999. Developed by Hollybrook Construction and designed by Michael Lyons, the hotel presented a significant uplift to the lower end of Talbot Street which had become quite run-down over recent years. It also complements the upgrading of the street, the pavements and roadside furniture which was carried out by Dublin Corporation in 1999. The public room of the hotel and the adjoining Ripley Inn display some excellent examples of wood craftmanship. A new pedestrian route to Foley Street is being opened to the right of the hotel.

Photo: courtesy of the Radisson SAS Hotel.

Photo: courtesy of the Radisson SAS Hotel.

Above: The former ballroom of St Helen's is now used as a lounge for the Radisson SAS Hotel.

Above: The central portion of the Radisson SAS St Helen's Hotel occupies a mansion first built in 1750 for Thomas Cooley, a barrister and Member of Parliament from Duleek, Co Meath. Various other people came into ownership until, in 1851, Field Marshal Hugh Viscount Gough purchased the house and renamed it from "Seamount" to "St Helen's," most likely after St Helena, Napoleon's island of exile. Gough had distinguished himself while fighting in the Peninsular War under the Duke of Wellington. The Gough family remodelled St Helen's in the Victorian style and embellished the interior with copious amounts of Carrera marble. The exquisite gardens to the rear of the hotel were laid out at this time and are still named after the head gardener, a Mr. Webley. The next owner was John Nutting who bought the house in 1899 and reclad the red brick exterior with cut limestone and added other architectural features including balustrades and cornices. The house and lands were sold to the Christian Brothers in 1925 to use as a novitiate. In 1988 St Helen's was acquired by a building company and is today owned by the Cosgrave Property Group who restored it to its former splendour. It is managed by Radisson SAS Hotels Worldwide.

Below: Built on the exclusive grounds of the Royal Dublin Society, the Four Seasons Hotel is part of a world-wide luxury hotel chain founded by Isadore Sharp in Toronto, Canada in 1960. The Four Seasons Hotels Group is the largest luxury hotel management company in the world. Opened in mid-2000 the 259 bedroom hotel was designed by Michael Collins Associates. It was constructed by G&T Crampton for developers Simmonscourt Holdings.

Above: The new St Stephen's Green Hotel at the corner of Harcourt Street and Cuffe Street. The development, by O'Callaghan Hotels, incorporates two Georgian houses on Harcourt Street, of which No. 4 was the birthplace in 1912 of Edward Henry Carson, the founder of the Ulster Volunteers and leading politician in Northern Ireland until his death in 1935. Opened in 1999 the 77-bedroom hotel, with its bold corner glass atrium, was designed by James O'Connor of Arthur Gibney and Partners.

1   2

3   4

5

      6

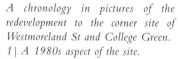

A chronology in pictures of the redevelopment to the corner site of Westmoreland St and College Green.

1| A 1980s aspect of the site.

2| An 1850 view of the site taken from Shaw's Dublin Pictorial Guide and Directory.

3/5| Work in progress.

4| Digging the foundations while retaining the more important facades.

6| The almost finished 164 bedroom, 5 star, Westin Hotel (owned by Starwood Hotels and Resorts Worldwide Inc). It was designed by Henry J Lyons and Partners and built by P. J. Walls. Structural engineers were McArdle McSweeney Associates. The developers were Treasury Holdings.

Chapter Thirteen
Twixt Sea and Mountains

SOME WORLD capitals are situated in spectacular coastal settings or at the edges of scenic hinterlands but few of them enjoy Dublin's enviable accessibility to both of these resources. Ireland's capital nestles at the mouth of several rivers and two canals which empty into a sweeping U-shaped bay. The northern arm of the bay terminates at the steep-cliffed head of the Howth Peninsula. Fingal, to the north of this arm, is an area of sheltered inlets and flat agricultural land imbued with a history of great antiquity. The River Liffey winds its way to the bay from the western side of Dublin, passing through valleys and plains speckled with charming townships, enchanting beauty spots and prehistoric monuments. The southern reaches of the city straggle into the foothills of the Dublin and Wicklow Mountains or along a coast dotted with atmospheric harbours and villages. A single chapter, even a complete book, is wholly inadequate to totally encompass such a vast canvas. This chapter can only offer a representative selection of some of the historic sites or places of natural interest and beauty that abound in the region.

Above and below: Two views of the quaint wooden bridge connecting the mainland with Bull Island at Dollymount. The bridge dates from 1907 but it in turn replaced two other structures, the earliest was erected in 1809 to convey workers and material during the building of the North Bull Wall.

Left: A view of the strand on Bull Island.

Above: Opened by Dublin Corporation in 1986, the Bull Island Interpretative Centre assists in the understanding of the unique flora and fauna and specialised habitats of the surrounding sand dunes and salt marshes. Declared a UNESCO Biosphere in 1981 and a National Nature Reserve in 1988, the island supports a huge variety of wading birds, many of them migratory. The birds include little terns, curlews, oystercatchers, herring gulls, lapwings, dunlins, redshanks and wintering Brent geese all the way from Arctic Canada. Thousands of ducks, including widgeon, shelduck and mallard enjoy the rich tidal feeding grounds.

Above: Houses overlooking the sea on Strand Road, Sutton.

Right: Location map of Bull Island.

Below: Taking to the wing on Bull Island.

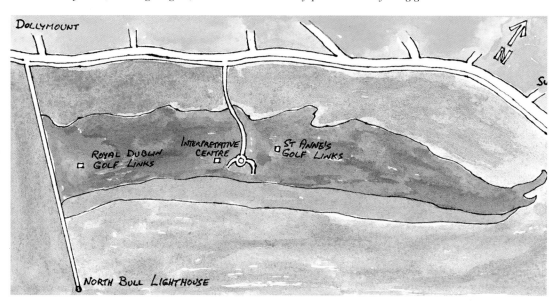

Above: A mile off the coast, directly north of Howth Harbour, lies the extraordinary little island of Ireland's Eye. It is a small island, easily reached by regular tourist boats. The ruins of a Martello Tower and an 8th century church are the only signs of previous habitation. In Celtic times the island was called Eria's Island. Eria was a woman's name and this became confused with Erin, the Irish name for Ireland. The Vikings substituted the word Island with Ey, their Norse equivalent, and so it became known as Erin's Ey and ultimately Ireland's Eye. Its most spectacular feature is the huge freestanding stack or rock called Thulla. During the spring and summer breeding seasons it simply seethes with the fluttering of thousands of guillemots, terns, gannets, razorbills and gulls. Around its waters and outcrops, cormorants, puffins and grey seals are in abundance.

Above: Red Rock is a prominent landmark on the Cliff Walk around the Howth Peninsula. An itinerary taking in some of the cliff paths as well as climbing Shielmartin Hill and Howth Summit offers breathtaking views of the bay, the city, Fingal and the semi-wilderness central basin of the Peninsula.

Above: Howth Castle was first built when Sir Almeric Tristram came into possession of the land in 1177. He adopted the name St Lawrence and his direct line lived here until 1909. The last earl passed the castle to his nephew Julian Gaisford and his descendants still reside at Howth. The present castle buildings were erected no earlier than 1564.

Above: Howth Harbour was built between 1807 and 1812 to serve as the official mail packet station on the Dublin to Holyhead route. All efforts to control the constant silting proved fruitless and Howth was barely completed when the hard decision was made to relocate the station to Dun Laoghaire. Since then Howth Harbour has evolved into a pleasant port offering facilities to the main east coast fishing fleet and to the prestigious Howth Yacht Club. The Yacht Club was founded in 1968 from the amalgamation of the Howth Sailing Club and the Howth Motor Yacht Club.

Below: The restored ramparts of Swords Castle illustrate the sensitive restoration being carried out by the owners, Fingal County Council, in association with FÁS. The castle was first built in the 1190s as the chief residence of the Archbishop of Dublin. Dutch refugees were settled here in 1583 and they repaired and extended the castle before it was more or less finally abandoned. Swords Castle, one of the largest of Ireland's medieval castles, is a key feature along the Ward River Valley Linear Park.

Below: The present castle at Rathfarnham was built in 1585 by Adam Loftus, Archbishop of Dublin. There had previously been a Norman castle on the site and before that a Celtic fort. There is a very fine 18th century interior by William Chambers and James Stuart. Sold by the Jesuits in 1985 to the Office of Public Works, Rathfarnham Castle has been thoroughly restored and is now under the care of Dúchas The Heritage Service.

Above: St MacCulin, a contemporary of St Patrick, founded his church at Lusk, in north Co. Dublin in the late 5th century. The round tower is all that remains today from the abbey that followed MacCulin's foundation. The square battlemented tower was part of the Anglo-Norman church. Located beside the towers is the Lusk Heritage Centre.

Above: Malahide Castle was built as a large fortress in 1185 by Sir Richard Talbot, a knight of King Henry II. It was adapted down the centuries to suit the times and remained in the hands of the Talbots until 1973. To save the castle and its collection of furniture for posterity, Dublin County Council bought the property and the 108ha (268 acres) demesne in 1975. Consequently the public now has access to one of the finest period interiors in the country as well as to the grounds and the castle's Botanical Gardens.

Below: Built as a large country manor house in 1738, Ardgillan Castle remained home to the Taylour family until 1962. As a concession for allowing the railway through their lands in the 19th century the Taylours were allowed to stop trains at Ardgillan Castle whenever they needed to travel. The house, now under the care of Fingal County Council, is situated on 80ha (198 acres) of rolling parkland with sweeping views of the sea coast between Balbriggan and Skerries. On display is the park itself, the rose garden, the walled garden and the restored Jameson glasshouse, a wonderful example of a Victorian conservatory. On permanent exhibition are the Down Survey Maps of Ireland drawn up between 1654-1658.

Below: Once a quaint country village, Clondalkin is now a key centre in the ever-growing conurbation of Dublin. The 26m (85ft) 9th century round tower is well preserved and still possesses its conical stone roof.

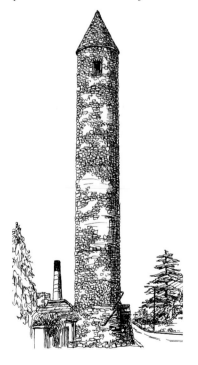

Above: The advanced technology of a bygone age is evident in the engineering complexities of the huge sails of the larger of the two Skerries windmills.

Below: The gentle turning of the waterwheel belies the vast power generated by its motion.

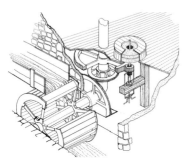

Above: The cutaway shows the waterwheel and the first-line of interconnecting cogs and shafts.

Above: In the north coastal village of Skerries is one of the greatest but least expected sights in Ireland: two working windmills and one fully equipped watermill. The size of the 5-sail white plastered-windmill is impressive and its internal machinery is in full working order. Its 4-sail companion is smaller but more rustic with its bare stone walls and thatched roof. Internally, the watermill, housed in an extensive range of stone buildings, is perhaps the most fascinating. An extremely complex series of cogs and shafts powered by the waterwheel turns or operates all the machines, wheels, grindstones, elevators and hoists. Every function is graphically explained in each of the specialist rooms including the bakery, the main engine room, the miller's office, the weigh room, the kiln room and in various grinding and storage lofts. The millers had to carefully watch the quern stones lest they got too hot with the friction and burned the corn. They used their sense of smell to spot any potential problems. This gave rise to the phrase "keeping your nose to the grindstone". The mills originated in the early 16th century and were restored by Fingal County Council in association with FÁS. The setting for the mills is a 18ha (45 acre) park which complements the buildings and the machinery. Apart from active sports areas there are meandering paths, a stream, fields in which to grow the grain for the mills, wetlands and a lake.

Above: Drimnagh Castle, situated off the Long Mile Road, was built by the Anglo-Norman de Bernival (later Barnewell) family around 1240. The stronghold later passed to the Hatch family and in the last century it was given to the Irish Christian Brothers to use as a temporary school and chapel. In 1986 a programme of detailed restoration was begun under the auspices of An Taisce (The National Trust) and FÁS (the State Training and Employment Agency). Now almost fully refurbished it presents a very authentic example of a late medieval castle that is still surrounded by a bawn and a flooded moat. The Great Hall, complete with wooden roof and galleries, contains nine effigies carved in the likenesses of people associated with the restoration.

Above: In 1873 Edward Cecil Guinness, a member of the Guinness brewing dynasty, purchased Farmleigh for his country residence from a Captain J.C.Coote. The original 12.5ha (31 acres) was increased to 31.5ha (78 acres) over a thirty-year period and Coote's house was replaced by the magnificent mansion of today. Farmleigh, situated on the western side of the Phoenix Park, is a 3716sq m (40,000sq ft) mansion which boasts a range of reception rooms of elegant proportions, with exquisite plasterwork, fireplaces and panelling. Bought by the Guinnesses for £9,000 it was sold by them to the government through estate agents Hamilton Osborne King in 1999 for £23 million, one of the most significant residential property sales for many years. It will be utilised for a wide range of uses including inter-governmental meetings and accommodation for visiting Heads of State. It is also planned to allow the public access to the grounds.

Above: The garden of Drimnagh Castle is laid out in a formal 17th century fashion with box hedges, yews, mop head laurels and hornbeam.

Above: Tallaght is an ancient part of southwest Dublin and its name is derived from the Irish word Tamhlacht meaning grave. This may allude to a plague which devastated the area in prehistoric times. St Maelruan founded a famous monastery at Tallaght in 769. The church in the photograph above stands approximately on the site of the monastery of which nothing remains except for a defensive ditch. The oldest part of the Church of Ireland's St Maelruan's is the battlemented tower and belfry which survive from the Anglo-Norman period.

Top right: St Mary's Dominican Priory, in the centre of Tallaght Village, occupies the site of a manorial castle built in 1324 by the Archbishop of Dublin, Alexander de Bicknor, as an alternative residential seat to Swords. This castle also served as a defensive bastion on the outer ring of the Pale. In 1729 Archbishop John Hoadly demolished most of the castle and built a more modern palace. The palace was levelled in 1822 when the land passed to private individuals. In 1856 the property was bought by the Dominican Order who built a church and seminary to help provide priests for Ireland and the overseas missions. Up to then Irishmen who wanted to join the order had to receive their training abroad in places such as the Dominican houses in Louvain, Rome and Lisbon. The ruin of an old tower, a survivor of the former castle, stands in the grounds of the priory.

Middle right: The ancient stone baptismal font from St Maelruan's lies in the nearby graveyard.

Bottom right: Tymon Park, a short distance east of Tallaght, is divided in two by the Western Parkway. To the east of the motorway are the playing fields while to the west lies the leisure park. The leisure facilities are built around the park's many water features which support large colonies of wildfowl. A prehistoric road, Tymon Lane, which runs along an eskar and once linked the hamlets of Greenhills and Balrothery, was incorporated into the park. Tymon Park was formerly made up of 53 separate plots of agricultural land which were assembled with some foresight by the Parks Department of the then Dublin County Council. Its successor, the South Dublin County Council, now imaginatively manages the park.

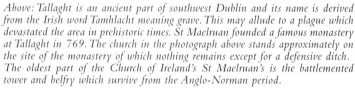

Above left: A view of the Marlay Craft Courtyard, Marlay Park, Rathfarnham.

Above right: Marlay Park is the pride and joy of Dun Laoghaire and Rathdown County Council. Its 86ha (214 acres) were bought by Dublin County Council (the predecessor of the present council) in 1972 and opened as a regional park in 1975. The land once formed the much larger estate of the La Touche family, prominent Huguenot bankers in 18th and 19th century Dublin. Their large country house is now being restored. The park leads directly into the Dublin and Wicklow Mountains, as the photograph testifies, and the famous long-distance Wicklow Way Walk (average 12 days duration) commences from Marlay Park.

Below left: Except for commercial plantings very little remains of the extensive woods and forests which once flourished on the foothills of the Dublin and Wicklow Mountains. The atmospheric woodland in the photograph is Massey Wood named after Lord Massey, one-time owner of the former estate. It lies between Tibradden Road and Kilakee Road.

Below right: A view of the surrounding countryside from the summit of Mount Pelier above the Killakee Road.

189

Above: Dun Laoghaire (named after the dún or fort of Laoghaire, a 5th century king) came into prominence when the harbour was built in the 19th century to receive the regular sailings from Holyhead. The mammoth port, enclosed by the East Pier (1817) and the West Pier (1820), was then the largest artificial harbour in the world. The Dublin to Dun Laoghaire (then called Kingstown) Railway opened in 1834 and it became the world's first suburban railroad. Today, Dun Laoghaire is a major ferryport.

Below left: Dalkey Hill quarry provided the granite for the building of Dun Laoghaire Harbour. On the crown of the hill is an old Napoleonic-era semaphore tower. The painting represents the 238 steps of the "Cat's Ladder" which connects Vico Road to Dalkey Hill and Killiney Hill.

Below right: Archbold's Castle. It and Goat's Castle (the new Heritage Centre) are all that remain of Dalkey's seven medieval castles. These fortified towers were built to store cargoes when the original Coliemore Harbour below Dalkey was the principal medieval deep-water port of Dublin.

Left: One of the best views of the Dublin coastline can be had from the top of Killiney Hill. The summit is capped with an obelisk which was commissioned by a former owner of the land, John Mapas, in 1742. His intention was to give employment to destitute families who had lost all their crops following exceptionally severe frosts.

Above: A view across Killiney Bay towards the Wicklow Mountains, an aspect often described as the Irish "Bay of Naples". Many locals must also agree with this description as a plethora of locality and house names are in Italian, such as Vico, Sorrento, Nerano, Torca, Milano, Mount Etna and so on.

Above: The thrills and spills of the Jameson Liffey Descent have been attracting hundreds of competitors every September since 1960. Stretching 27km (17 miles) over rapids and through undergrowth, from Straffan in Co. Kildare to Islandbridge in Dublin, the race is now the second biggest canoe marathon in the world.

Below left: Long a promenading resort for hardy souls, especially when the wind whips up the waves, the narrow finger of the Great South Wall juts bravely into the expanse of Dublin Bay. The approach to Dublin Port has always been plagued by sandbars obstructing the entrance and also by frequent squalls and stormy conditions. To alleviate the situation, in 1716, the Ballast Office (a predecessor of the Dublin Port Company) commenced the city's most ambitious civic construction to date. From the harbour at Ringsend to Poolbeg Lighthouse a sea wall of 5km (3 miles) in length, the world's longest at the time, was built. Initially the wall was composed of wooden piles on the outside filled in between with gravel. It soon became necessary to strengthen the walls with revetments of hewn granite taken across Dublin Bay on barges from the quarries in Dalkey. Bullock Harbour was built for this purpose. The work was more or less finished in 1786. Meanwhile at the "Head of the Piles" (i.e. the end of the wall) an island of masonry was laid down on which Poolbeg Lighthouse was built. It was ready in 1767 and initially operated on candlepower (reputedly the first in the world to do so) but innovatively changed to oil in 1786. Only when the North Bull Wall was finished in 1824 did the combined "squeeze" of the two walls force the retreating tides to satisfactorily scour a decent navigable channel into the port. The Great South Wall was strengthened and refurbished and the lighthouse was renovated in 2000 by Dublin Port Company with the support of EU grant-aid.

Below right: A large container ship heads past markers and buoys on its way into Dublin Port. All vessels have to have a local pilot on board (unless the captain is licensed for Dublin) as treacherous sandbars lie hidden under the water on both sides of the narrow entrance to the channel. This is why you will often see ships hove-to quite some distance out in the bay waiting for a pilot to guide them in.

Part Three
EBLANA TRANSMOGRIFIED

My cycle's never ending, my genesis stays the same,
but my freedom in the hills was rent and shamed downstream.

The city turned its back and snubbed a faithful friend,
only to appreciate again my healing powers of life.

And now the splendours of a bygone age are joined by wondrous halls
of glass that sparkle and dance in harmony with my rippling skin.

They call it Rediscovery, they call me Anna Livia.

Chapter Fourteen
Partnerships in Renewal

D URING THE middle years of the 20th century Dublin remained in the doldrums. When development started up again in the 1960s and '70s it was sporadic, uncoordinated and often insensitive. Individual buildings, many having highly individual characteristics or unique histories, disappeared, often overnight or by subterfuge. Demolition was sometimes on the pretext of a property's dereliction, more than once deliberately inflicted. Several Georgian and Victorian streetscapes were irrevocably scarred. Inner-city communities, at least those who still existed by then, were often compromised, sundered or engulfed. Their legitimate concerns were just simply ignored. The car was considered to be the dominant means of transport and so investment into public transport went into serious decline. Roads were widened to cater for the motorist with little or no thought for the urban environment, pollution or future gridlock. Threatened by the uncertainty of future road-widening plans, several areas around the city fell into a state of slow decay. Derelict sites, awaiting development during the regular economic downturns of that era, proliferated around the city and passed their undignified years as depressing surface car-parks. The population focus began to shift from the city centre and its immediate surrounds to the outer suburbs, thus creating a serious infrastructural imbalance. Suburban shopping centres, springing up in increasing numbers and size, imperilled the viability of the centre-city retail core. Some worthy initiatives, either involving new work or competent restoration, were certainly undertaken during this period but they were the exception rather than the rule. Those who objected to or commented on what can now only be described as institutional vandalism at worst or lack of perception or vision at best, were considered to be leftists, wasters, cranks or simply old-fashioned. To further complicate the matter it is now known from the various tribunals, still sitting at the time of publication, that a certain amount of corruption at the highest levels in the planning and political processes led to the making of some seriously defective long-term strategic decisions on the structured way the city should grow.

1| 2| 3| 4|: These four photographs amply illustrate the decrepit state into which many parts of the city had descended by the 1970s. 1| Demolition of the Capitol Theatre. 2| Gardiner Street. 3| Along the quays. 4| Parnell Street.

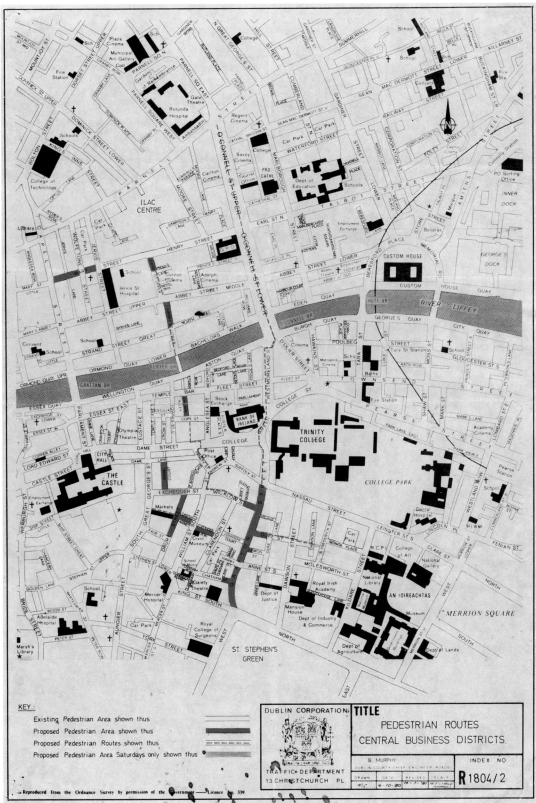

KEY:

Existing Pedestrian Area shown thus

Proposed Pedestrian Area shown thus

Proposed Pedestrian Routes shown thus

Proposed Pedestrian Area Saturdays only shown thus

DUBLIN CORPORATION	TITLE	
	PEDESTRIAN ROUTES	
	CENTRAL BUSINESS DISTRICTS.	
B. MURPHY		
TRAFFIC DEPARTMENT	DRAWN	DATE	REVISED	SCALE	INDEX NO
13 CHRISTCHURCH PL.	A.C.	6-10-80	14-7-'81		R 1804/2

Reproduced from the Ordnance Survey by permission of the Government — Licence No. 339

Map: courtesy of DCCBA.
Above: A pedestrianisation plan proposed by the Dublin City Centre Business Association (DCCBA) in the early 1980s.

Above: Henry Street today. There is a commonly held but erroneous belief that the renewal of Dublin properly started with the 1988 Dublin Millennium, a major celebration commemorating the city's Viking past. It is certainly true that the year-long festival encouraged a significant amount of renewed goodwill towards the city which was reflected by a general clean-up, by the installation of new monuments and by the restoration of many buildings. However, organisations like the Irish Georgian Society and an Taisce (the National Trust) had been campaigning for years to save and renew the city's heritage. A more strategically-based approach came in the early 1980s when the Dublin City Centre Business Association, an organisation representing city centre merchants, had the vision to lobby vigorously for an improved pedestrian environment on the streets. It succeeded after a long struggle and some opposition to have Henry Street paved as a truly pedestrianised street in 1981/2. Curiously, despite the obvious success of Henry Street, it required the intervention of the Minister of the Environment and funding from his department before other streets were similarly treated. Pedestrianisation came to Grafton Street in 1986/7, to the streets leading off Grafton Street in 1988, and to the Central Mall of O'Connell Street in 1990 and to North Earl Street in 1993. The city centre environment improved as pedestrianisation expanded, a factor which facilitated the introduction of late night and Sunday shopping to counteract the out-of-town retail centres.

Image: courtesy of DCCBA.

Above: This drawing was part of an overall street scheme drawn up by the architect Patrick Shaffrey, then president of an Taisce, on how Henry Street should look if the then tacky shop fronts were more in tune with the rich architectural character of the buildings they were set into. The plan, first published in March 1986, was sponsored by the Dublin City Centre Business Association.

When it seemed that it might be just too late, there was a gradual but palpable change of heart from the mid-1980s that would lead to the appreciation of Dublin's still-immense heritage and tackle the emerging problems of a city disintegrating at the centre and floundering at the ever-widening fringes. Positive actions to apply some corrective remedies significantly accelerated during the final decade of the last century. The private sector and Public bodies such as the Government, Dublin Corporation, the County Councils and those semi-state organisations specially set up to direct the advancement of specific tracts of the city such as Temple Bar Properties and the Dublin Docklands Development Authority, all contributed to a vast rejuvenation programme that is still ongoing.

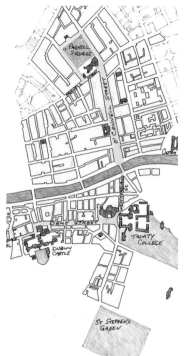

Above: The concept of a Grand Civic Thoroughfare, which divided the city into identifiable districts or villages using O'Connell Street and Dame Street as the axis, was proposed in 1997 by the city centre business community for inclusion in the 1998 Dublin City Draft Development Plan. The suggestion was considered by Dublin Corporation to be a workable model and was a factor which led to the establishment of the O'Connell Street and the North East Inner City Integrated Area Plans.

Right: An outline map of the five inner city Integrated Area Plans (IAPs). H.A.R.P., the Historic Area Rejuvenation Plan, has a genesis going back to 1993 when the Dublin City Centre Business Association submitted their "Dublin One Vision Plan" to the EU with the support of the Department of the Environment and Local Government. An enhanced and extended plan was resubmitted to the EU by Dublin Corporation and was approved to become the first IAP. N.E.I.C. stands for the North East Inner City IAP. The Dublin Docklands Development Authority has been vested with the responsibility for developing the docklands. A sixth IAP was also launched in 1998 to start a comprehensive renewal of Ballymun, a public housing suburb on Dublin's northside.

Once the Government was convinced that something had to be done to turn around the fortunes of the city it realised that neither itself nor Dublin Corporation on their own could achieve the desired results. The private sector had also to play its part. To this end a scheme of regeneration incentives, mainly involving tax concessions, was announced under the Urban Renewal Act in 1986. They mainly applied to run-down areas of the city where investment was conspicuous by its absence. The most memorable and one of the most sustained outcomes of this initiative was the establishment in November of that year of the Custom House Docks Development Authority. This body was charged with the comprehensive re-development of the large redundant docks area situated around the sheltered shipping basins immediately to the east of the Custom House. From a tentative start in 1987 the Custom House Docks project has mushroomed into the vibrant and hugely successful International Financial Services Centre. By 1991, £611 million pounds had been spent on or allocated to renewal in Dublin, £400 million of this figure was directed at the Custom House Docks.

Offices were not the only buildings to be financed through tax allowances, investment and speculation. It was realised by then that Dublin had two choices. One was to go the way of many American cities, allowing the residential population to desert the city centre and leave whole districts virtually dead by night. The other was to reverse the trend of outward migration by building apartment blocks in the central core and improving its environment. Derelict and under-developed sites along by the River Liffey were first identified as having the greatest potential and from the early 1990s, again aided by generous tax incentives, new apartment complexes began to spring up along both sides of the river from Islandbridge to O'Connell Bridge. By the late '90s, up to 20,000 new apartment units were built with as many as double that figure of additional apartments likely to rise across the city before the end of the first decade of the new millennium.

By 1998, Dublin Corporation had received approval from the Department of the Environment and Local Government for five Inner City Integrated Area Plans (IAPs). The key objectives of each plan are to ensure that a co-ordinated approach is taken in relation to the environmental, economic, social and cultural improvements in these areas, to secure an improved quality of life and achieve long-term sustainable regeneration. The areas selected were those considered in most need of renewal, and tax incentives would apply only to designated sites. Unlike previous urban regeneration initiatives, the IAPs take into account the needs of the existing communities in relation to community support programmes, employment and educational issues as well as the renewal of the physical environment. Over £300 million of public investment was pledged and in excess of £1 billion of private sector investment was expected. Both of these figures, especially the expenditures involved in public-private partnerships, are likely to be exceeded.

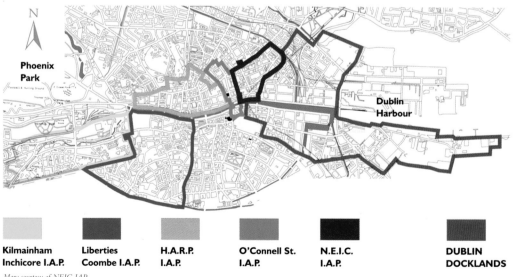

Kilmainham Inchicore I.A.P.	Liberties Coombe I.A.P.	H.A.R.P. I.A.P.	O'Connell St. I.A.P.	N.E.I.C. I.A.P.	DUBLIN DOCKLANDS

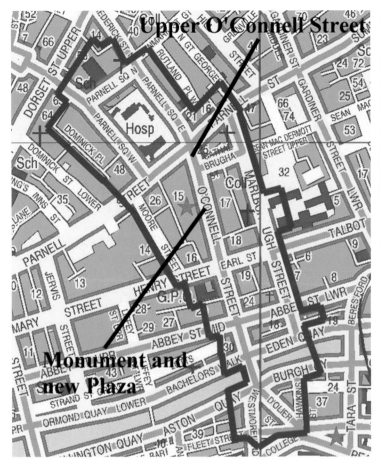

Upper O'Connell Street

Monument and new Plaza

Above: The area included in the O'Connell Street IAP.

Above: A future view up the widened centre mall of O'Connell Street.

O'Connell Street seemed to lose its way from the 1960s as the capital's main thoroughfare, the hub of the city. The imposing streetscape was depreciated by traffic congestion, some inappropriate rebuilding, poor shopfronts, several retail outlets not entirely suitable to a principal street and a perception of it being a dangerous place at night-time. The O'Connell Street Plan aims to reverse those trends and restore the street and its environs to the prominence that is their due. Over £35 million of public money and several hundred million pounds of private investment will result in a radical overhaul of the street's image. Civic improvements will include a new plaza opposite the GPO, a new street linking O'Connell Street to Moore Street, upgraded and widened pavements, enhanced street furniture and better quality building design. A sustainable mix of retail, commercial, entertainment, cultural and leisure uses is a prime objective to attract people during both the daytime and evenings. A Millennium Spire, otherwise known as the Monument of Light, is planned for the site of the former Nelson Pillar and is intended to act as a potent symbol of O'Connell Street's regeneration.

Below left: The proposed new pedestrian route linking Marlborough Street with Hawkins Street includes a new pedestrian bridge across the River Liffey.

Below middle: A photomontage of the proposed improvements to O'Connell Street, looking from the Parnell Monument.

Below: This is what the plaza in front of the GPO will look like when it is completed. O'Connell Street, no longer designated as a National Primary Route, will ultimately be restricted to two lanes of traffic on either side.

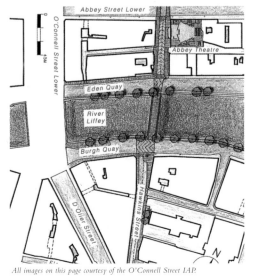

All images on this page courtesy of the O'Connell Street IAP.

Above: "Mr Screen", a sculpture by Vincent Browne (installed in 1988), shows the way to passers-by outside the Screen Cinema at the junction of Hawkins Street and D'Olier Street.

Above: Built for an insurance company, this landmark building is currently being re-developed by Treasury Holdings for retail and apartments. The Blood Transfusion Service Board will also operate a city centre donor clinic from here.

Above: The modern offices of the Educational Building Society on Westmoreland Street have retained, as their centrepiece, the quaint façade built for Lafayette Photographers in 1912. The rest of the building, designed by Sam Stephenson and Associates, dates from the late 1970s.

Image: courtesy of the National Gallery of Ireland.

Above: A mid-19th century painting of O'Connell Street executed by Michael Angelo Hayes, a brother-in-law of Peter Paul McSwiney, the founder and chairman of the Palatial Mart (later Clery's Department Store) shown on the right of the picture. Nelson Pillar, erected in 1808 and blown up in 1966, stands in the centre of the street.

Below: A photomontage of O'Connell Street showing the proposed new Monument of Light (designed by Ian Ritchie Architects) which will occupy the space once filled by Nelson Pillar. The monument, made from rolled stainless steel plate, will be a conical spire tapering from 3m (10ft) in diameter at the base to a .1m (4 inches) pointed and illuminated optical glass pinnacle. The total height will be 120m (394ft). The lighting of the lower two thirds will be by means of very narrow beams projected from buildings opposite. The top 12m (39ft) of the spire's metal skin will be perforated to allow for light diffusion from internal light sources.

Image: courtesy of ARC Digital Photo Graphic.

Note: The yellow line denotes the approximate boundary of the subject site.

Photo: courtesy of Shelbourne Developments.

Above: This photograph clearly shows the dereliction behind O'Connell Street and fronting on to Parnell Street and Moore Street. The surface car park, the group of buildings below the words "O'Connell Street" and the ILAC Centre will be re-built in a scheme costing several hundred million pounds.

Below: A computer-generated image of the new four-star, 197-bedroom hotel and retail development which is being built at the corner of Parnell Street and Moore Street. It is a joint venture by Shelbourne Developments and the Scottish property company, Morrison Developments plc. The complex, which will breathe new life into a once dismal end of Parnell Street, will directly link via the first-floor retail area into the Millennium Mall (see page 200). The architects are Burke-Kennedy Doyle and the main contractors are G & T Crampton.

Image: courtesy of the Carlton Group.

Above: This striking proposal to glaze in Moore Street will, if implemented, be part of a link between the Millennium Mall project on O'Connell Street and the re-constructed ILAC Centre. A glass roof would certainly provide welcome protection from adverse weather conditions to the street traders.

Photo: courtesy of ARC Digital Photo Graphic.

Above: A ground-level view of the Parnell Street site which has been waiting for development for over two decades.

Above: The west side of O'Connell Street as it looked in mid-2000 before the long-awaited re-development of the old Carlton Cinema (built 1938 and closed 1994) and its adjoining buildings.

Above: a view of the same stretch of street in 1850 when the street was exclusively Georgian in character.

Image: courtesy of the Carlton Group.

Above: An artist's sketch of the impressive façade of the new Millennium Mall on O'Connell Street Upper. The huge complex, promoted by the Carlton Group, will be one of the biggest shopping centres in Ireland and will have a strong focus on providing evening entertainment. Cafés, restaurants, bars, musical events, exhibitions, cinemas and other cultural attractions will reinforce the centre as an evening destination and herald a new era in developments that embrace their civic responsibilities and offer direct benefits to the local community. The Carlton Group formed a Cultural Advisory Board at a very early stage and have already offered a permanent home to the Dublin Film Festival and the Dublin Writers Festival. A new public pedestrian precinct will commence from O'Connell Street through the ground floor of the art deco façade of the old Carlton Cinema and proceed via a continental-style galleria until it reaches Moore Street and the ILAC Shopping Centre, providing a vital relief route for the sometimes overcrowded Henry Street. A similar street linkage was first mooted for here as far back as 1857. Construction of the Millennium Mall is scheduled to start in December 2000 and is a key element in the rejuvenation of O'Connell Street. The original design concept was created by Paul Clinton with Arthur Gibney and Partners appointed as Consulting Architects.

The Historic Area Rejuvenation Project (HARP) was the first IAP to be established and is partly EU funded. Since its inception in 1997 HARP as been engaged in transforming the North West Inner City, an area stretching from Henry Street to the National Museum at Collins Barracks and from around Henrietta Street south to the Liffey. The 109ha (270 acres) area already supported a thriving retail centre (Henry Street/Mary Street), wholesale markets (the Fruit and Vegetable Market) and a vast legal fraternity (based around the Four Courts). The allocation of £50 million of public money and the inward private sector investment of over £400 million have resulted, for instance, in the creation of a major civic space at Smithfield alongside a new hotel and a number of visitor centres. The new National Museum at Collins Barracks, the refurbishment of existing public housing schemes, the erection of hundreds of new apartments and the upgrading of Henry Street and Mary Street are additional achievements of the IAP. All the while, the needs of the local communities including their concerns about their own environmental issues, employment and training opportunities and their living conditions have been a core part of the plan. Other initiatives at the formative stage are the creation of an east-west pedestrian link, the North King Street road improvement scheme and the introduction of LUAS, the light rail system, which will run from the west end of HARP right through to O'Connell Street.

Above: Ormond Square, a public housing complex near the Four Courts, was completely transformed by the upgrading of the central common. Other social housing complexes in the area have also been improved by Dublin Corporation.

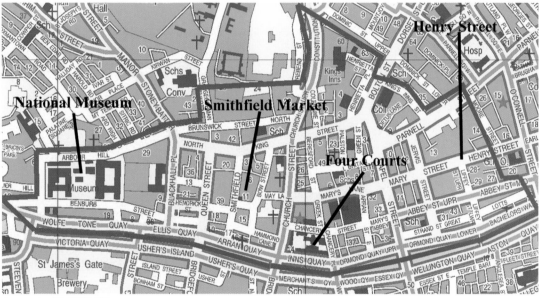

Image: courtesy of the HARP IAP.

Left: a map of the HARP area.

Below: The new North King Street Community Resource Centre is situated beside the Debtors Prison. On part of the site hundreds of human skeletons were found during an archaeological investigation, indicating that it may have been an 18th century burial ground for inmates of the various penal institutions in the immediate neighbourhood. The centre, designed by Derek Tynan and Associates and built by Rohcon, will be managed by MACRO (Markets Area Community Resource Organisation). It was funded by Dublin Corporation and grant-aided by the EU.

Photo: courtesy of the HARP IAP.

Photo: courtesy of the HARP IAP.

Above: Wolfe Tone Close is a £6 million Dublin Corporation housing scheme of 75 dwellings, attractively ranged around an enclosed courtyard reached by means of steps and lifts from Wolfe Tone Street. Designed by the City Architect's Division of Dublin Corporation, it was built by Gem Construction Ltd. and was officially opened in February 1999.

Above: The old chimney (1895) of the former Jameson Distillery.

Above & below: The same chimney transformed. The 53m (175ft) height of the stack is now crowned by a two-tier glass observation platform, served by a glass-walled lift.

Right: Smithfield Village is one of the most exciting and visually-varied new developments in Dublin. It comprises a hotel (Chief O'Neill's), an Irish traditional music centre (Ceol), a whiskey visitor centre (the Old Jameson Distillery), shops, restaurants, and a range of apartments. A & D Wejchert designed the complex on behalf of Heritage Properties.

Above: A 19th Century view of the Jameson Distillery at Bow Street.

Photo: courtesy of Barry Mason Photography.

Above left: Smithfield in the 1970s, its heyday as a hay, straw, cattle and horse market long gone.

Above right: The old cobbled market has been recreated into the magnificent civic space of Smithfield, the flagship project of HARP. The 1ha (2.5 acres), £3.5 million pedestrianised piazza (the largest open public space in the city centre) was opened on 21 December 1999 as the first part of a two-phase redevelopment of Smithfield. The project, funded by Dublin Corporation and the EU, will provide Dublin with its first dedicated venue for outdoor civic events. New granite slabs and 300,000 original cobbles were used. Twelve 26m (85ft) high gas lighting masts, each with a 2m (6.5ft) high flame, were installed along one side of the space. The whole concept was designed by Irish architects (against international competition), Michael McGarry and Siobhán Ní Éanaigh. SIAC Construction were the main contractors.

Photo: courtesy of Heritage Properties.

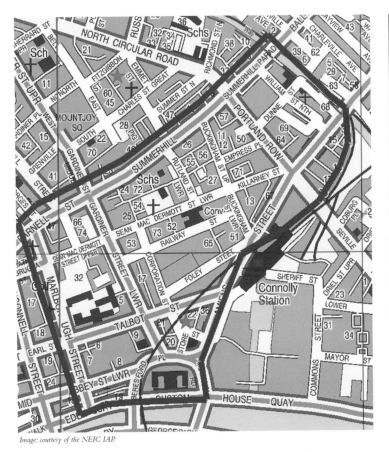

Image: courtesy of the NEIC IAP.

Above left: Map of the NEIC IAP area.

The North East Inner City (NEIC) IAP is perhaps one of the most vital of the Integrated Area initiatives, especially in how it will positively impact on most of the current population of over 3,400 residents. Embracing an area of some 45ha (111 acres), the NEIC extends broadly from Marlborough Street to Connolly Station and from the Custom House to Summerhill as far as the Royal Canal. With a public-purse budget of £100 million and, attracted by tax concessions, a further £500 million expected from the private sector, the plan will dramatically rejuvenate one of Dublin's most deprived areas. The plan's approach will be based on social as well as physical programmes with a special emphasis on skills training to unlock career opportunities for a neighbourhood traditionally beset by high unemployment. The construction of around 2,000 additional apartments will also help to infuse a greater social mix into the community. Key areas of the plan will be the refurbishment of some of the public housing complexes, the demolition of others following their replacement by a variety of more acceptable own-door homes, the provision of improved educational, leisure, cultural, social and community-based facilities, the upgrading of whole streetscapes and the stimulation of commercial and business developments. Already, the private sector has responded by commencing a number of new projects including the Linders block at the corner of Talbot Street and Corporation Street (the latter to be soon renamed James Joyce Street) and the new Bord Gáis headquarters on Foley Street and Buckingham Street.

Above right: The old fire station on Buckingham Street was made redundant in the 1970s when a new facility was built on the North Strand Road. The Buckingham Street premises were than converted into the Fire Station Artists Studios and Sculpture Workshop, one of the area's early success stories.

Far left: The building of Custom Hall on Gardiner Street in the early 1990s by the Cosgrave Property Group represented a leap of faith for any developer. The company correctly calculated that this formerly down-at-heel street deserved and, in the event, did have a better future. The architects for the apartments were Project Architects.

Left: Aldborough House, built in 1796, was the last of the city's Georgian mansions to be erected before the fateful Act of Union in 1800. Lord Aldborough never occupied the house. It became a school, a barracks, a store for the Department of Posts and Telegraphs (now Eircom) before being sold in December 1999 to IMRO, the Irish Music Rights Organisation. The proposed refurbishment at their new headquarters will include the provision of a performance hall and audio-visual facilities for the public.

Above: A view of present-day Mountain View Court, a scheme of 102 flats dating from the 1970s, which is set for demolition and re-development.

Right: This aerial view of the greater part of the NEIC area clearly illustrates the extent of the improvements necessary as well as the opportunities offered by such works to the local community. The numbers indicated on the photograph represent: 1 Our Lady of Lourdes Church, 2 School-on-Stilts, 3 Pre-School, 4 Day Care Centre, 5 Swimming Pool, 6 Parish Centre.

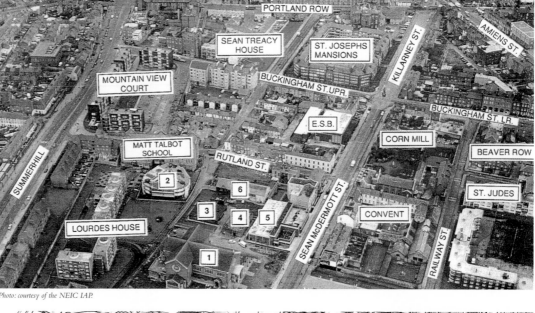

Photo: courtesy of the NEIC IAP.

Right: A sketch of Phase One of the new Mountain View Court housing where each dwelling has an own-door entrance and own private south-facing terrace. Architects for the scheme are Colette Downey Architects.

Image: courtesy of Colette Downey Architects.

Right: The design for a heroin victims' memorial at the junction of Buckingham Street and Sean Mac Dermott Street. Facilitated by the Inner City Organisations Network (ICON) and sponsored by Dublin Corporation, the memorial is intended as a support to the families of drug victims, as an acknowledgement of communal grief, as a symbol of hope and as a warning for future generations. The sculpture itself (far right), entitled "Home", was selected by the relatives themselves from a number of entries and the sculptor, Leo Higgins, chose the theme of a flame to represent hope and light for the future.

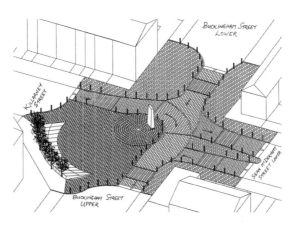

Image: courtesy of the NEIC IAP.

Image: courtesy of the NEIC IAP.

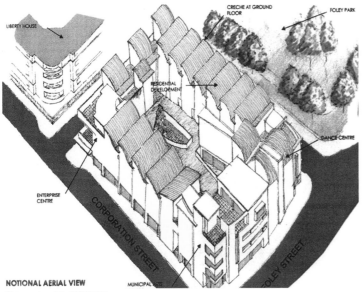

NOTIONAL AERIAL VIEW

Photo: courtesy of the NEIC IAP.

Above: Occupying a complete block between Liberty Street, Foley Park West, Foley Street and Corporation Street (James Joyce Street), the Liberty Corner Project is one of the flagships in the renewal and revitalisation of the North East Inner City. Gardiner Architects have designed a multi-purpose building of interesting and varied elevations. Accommodated here will be a large dance centre comprising six dance studios, the city's new Municipal Arts Centre, residential units (some with extra work areas or studio space) and an enterprise centre.

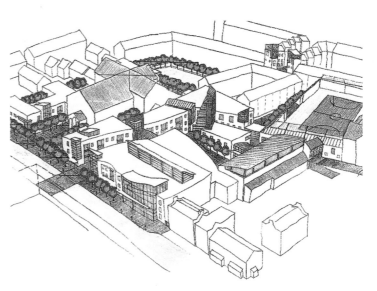

Photo: courtesy of the NEIC IAP.

Above: An artist's impression of the new Lourdes Community Centre complex which will consist of a swimming pool, sports hall, all-weather playing pitch and other community facilities as well as some retail and apartments.

Above: The former St Joseph's Convent and Home for Aged Single Ladies and the derelict sites behind it are poised for a proposed apartment and high specification office development by developer P. J. McGrath.

Photo: courtesy of the NEIC IAP.

Above: The old Macushla Ballroom at the corner of Buckingham Street and Foley Street was demolished in January 2000 to make way for the new Bórd Gáis headquarters which will house the board's 200 staff as well as containing enterprise and retail units and private apartments. The complex will infuse new confidence into Foley Street which up to now never fully recovered from its past association with Dublin's seedy red-light district of a century ago, featuring prominently as "Nighttown" in James Joyce's classic, "Ulysses". Jason Tyler of Laughton Tyler Architects was the architect of the £12 million project. The developer was Ed McGovern.

Photo: courtesy of the NEIC IAP.

Left: The site of the Convent of Our Lady of Charity which will be transformed by Dublin Corporation, in partnership with other state agencies, into a new £6 million Civic Centre and one-stop-shop for social and community services. The nuns will continue to care for 36 senior citizens in the re-vamped premises and the Salesian Fathers will maintain their drug rehabilitation projects here.

Above: Ranged around two sides of the Iveagh Market, the carved keystones of the arches are emblematic of the world's great trading nations. One face, an exception to the rest, is winking and smiling impishly and is said to represent Lord Iveagh himself.

Over £70 million of public funding will provide for a significant uplift of the area covered by the Liberties/Coombe IAP. The problems of this area really go back to the early 18th century when local industry collapsed following trade restrictions imposed by Britain. In the mid-20th century the situation was exacerbated by a lack of inward investment, by relocation or rationalisation of industries, by concentrating areas of social disadvantage and by vacancy and dereliction as a result of uncertainties regarding major road improvement plans. The rich heritage, the mixed use character and the viable social diversity in the area will form the foundations for a comprehensive revitalisation and environmental enhancement of an historic part of Dublin. Always a self-reliant and independent part of Dublin, there is a unique liveliness about Francis Street with its many antique shops and Thomas Street with its stores and street stalls. The Area Plan relates to approximately 251ha (620 acres) of the South West Inner City and serves a population of around 21,500.

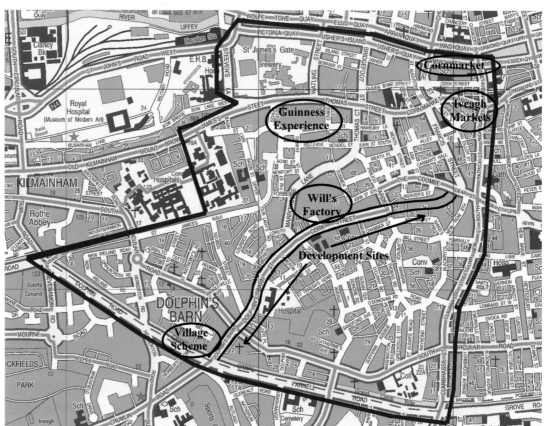

Right: Map of the Liberties/Coombe IAP.

Map: courtesy of the Liberties/Coombe IAP.

Right: The Iveagh Trust (see page 68) opened the Iveagh Market in 1907 to accommodate street traders who formerly had worked the narrow alleyways and lanes of the slums already cleared away by the Trust. By the 1990s, the only traders still operating in the Market were second-hand clothes dealers for whom business had all but dried up. The Iveagh Market and its adjoining buildings have received a new lease of life following the commencement of a thorough programme of restoration which will see it functioning again, this time as a modernised market selling such items as clothes, crafts and organic foodstuffs. A major new hotel will be imaginatively concealed within the heart of the complex. Developed by Martin Keane in conjunction with Dublin Corporation, the new Iveagh Market scheme has been designed by Henry J. Lyons & Partners.

Photo: courtesy of the Guinness Ireland Group.

Image: courtesy of the Kilmainham/Inchicore IAP.

Above left: The Guinness Enterprise Centre on Taylor's Lane is a joint venture between Dublin Corporation, the City Enterprise Board and Guinness Ireland Group. The project is managed by the Dublin Business Innovation Centre. Offering high specifications in facilities and communications, the centre provides incubator space across 77 enterprise units to new and established small businesses.

Above right: An aerial view of the proposed relief route through the Coombe. It will cut out the long-endured bottle-neck at Ardee Street.

The Kilmainham/Inchicore IAP was the last of the Integrated Areas to be established. It seeks to bring about the economic regeneration of a once prosperous and industrialised area while protecting and enhancing the built environment, the rich historical heritage, the natural green spaces and the two waterways, the Camac River and the Grand Canal. As with the other IAPs, community development in a spirit of partnership is a major priority. The area covers approximately 190ha (469 acres) and has a population of around 9,000. The area is fortunate in having several important heritage sites and these, together with walks along the river and the canal, will form a basis for a cultural and touristic trail. The LUAS light rail will serve the designated area on a west-east axis.

Above: The winding Back Lane, off High Street, looks even more intriguing since it has been enfolded by new apartment blocks.

Above: The Vicar Street music venue and bar, developed by Harry Crosbie, through its concerts and other entertainment programmes, has helped to bring life back to Thomas Street in the evenings. It was designed by Holohan Architects and opened in late 1998. The venue has been acclaimed by both audiences and performers for its advanced design features and facilities.

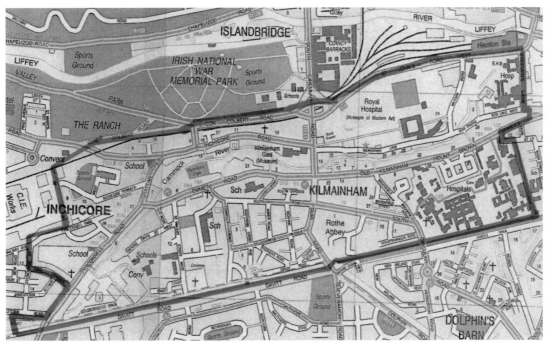

Map: courtesy of the Kilmainham/Inchicore IAP.

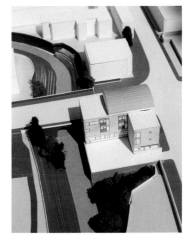

Image: courtesy of the Kilmainham/Inchicore IAP.

Above: A model of the proposed Heritage Centre destined for the corner of Emmet Road and the South Circular Road.

Left: Map of the Kilmainham/Inchicore Integrated Area Plan (IAP).

Above: The Royal Hospital at Kilmainham houses the Irish Museum of Modern Art (see page 43) and, together with Kilmainham Gaol, forms a major ingredient in the cultural and historical portfolio of the Kilmainham/Inchicore IAP.

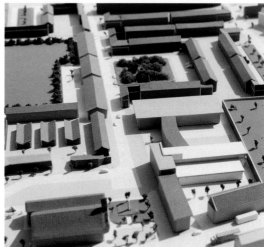

Right: St Michael's Estate from the air. It has been decided to demolish the flats and replace them with a mix of houses and apartments.

Far right: A model of the proposed new housing on St Michael's Estate.

Right: A perspective drawing of a section of the senior citizens' housing which will be built off Bulfin Road. They were designed by Cullen Payne Architects.

Photo: courtesy BRL.

Above: Ballymun was originally targeted as a new mixed-class dormitory suburb for Dublin. Instead, an acute housing shortage in the early 1960s convinced the planners of Dublin Corporation to build a scheme exclusively for social housing using the mode popular at the time in Britain and Europe: tower blocks. Some 17,000 people were moved into this housing arrangement without regard to the provision of employment or community facilities. Despite the best efforts of residents groups and Dublin Corporation, matters tended to worsen in the succeeding years and were not helped by increasing unemployment, a bleak landscape and an ever-busier dual-carriageway which effectively divided the community in two.

Ballymun Regeneration Ltd. (BRL) was established in 1997 by Dublin Corporation to oversee the complete redevelopment of Ballymun. This followed years of campaigning by local residents to seek improvements in their housing, in the surrounding environment and in community facilities. A Master Plan was agreed in March 1998, after the country's most extensive series of local consultation. The implementation of the Master Plan is expected to take around eight to ten years, although the elements dependent on generous tax incentives will have to be completed before 2002.

Above: A view of Ballymun taken across the hill known as Stonehenge, so named because of its array of standing stones which form a rather appealing sculptural group. The towers and rows of apartment blocks are destined for demolition to allow for the re-creation of a bright new town.

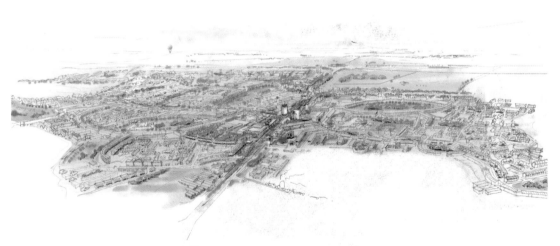

Image: courtesy BRL.

Above: Ballymun Regeneration is a £1.5 billion project to recreate a new town of 20,000 people. Dublin Corporation owns nearly all of the 350ha (865 acres) of land involved and this fact, coupled with the various packages of tax incentives on offer, allows for an integrated and rapid redevelopment to take place. Five residential neighbourhoods, with up to 5,000 newly-built houses and apartments, will surround the new Main Street. On a phased basis, existing tower blocks will be demolished and replaced with the new homes. Market-led residential units as well as affordable housing for the private sector will also be built to attract a social mix and special tax allowances will be available to occupants to refurbish existing buildings. A 40ha (99 acres) state-of-the-art Business and Technology Park, located between north Ballymun and the M50, will be jointly developed by BRL and Green Property plc. The proximity of Ballymun to Dublin City University, a world-renowned centre for software engineering and business training, is a distinct advantage. BRL is determined to offer local residents real educational and career opportunities to create a working society and remove the image of Ballymun as an unemployment blackspot.

Image: courtesy BRL.

Above: An outline sketch of the entrance to the new Main Street of Ballymun. In an international competition, the Scottish firm, ARP Lorimer and Associates, won the award to design the 172-unit housing scheme which includes two gateway or "sentinel" buildings at the Glasnevin end of the new street.

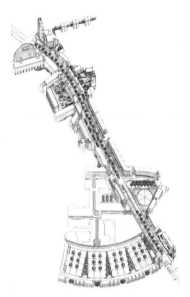

Above: An image of the new Ballymun Arts and Community Resource Centre designed by the BLR architectural team under Mick MacDonagh, Aidan O'Connor and David Byrne. Construction work by Duggan Brothers started in February 2000 and is scheduled for completion by early 2001. Facilities will include a theatre, performance spaces, recording studios, workshops, conference rooms, a large foyer/exhibition area and a café bar. A large civic plaza will front the building. The almost £6 million cost was mainly financed through ROUND (the Renewal of Urban North Dublin, a partnership organisation, which includes Dublin Corporation, the Dublin City Enterprise Board, Dublin City University, Enterprise Ireland, Government Departments and the Area Partnerships for Ballymun, Finglas and Darndale/Belcamp, set up to manage and implement EU and exchequer-funded urban initiatives). Adjoining the Ballymun Arts and Community Residents Centre will be a regional headquarters for Dublin Corporation offering a "one-stop-shop" range of community services.

Top & above: The new 1km (.6 mile) long Main Street at Ballymun will represent one of the most radical developments in the area's regeneration and will become the town's primary focus. Ballymun Road, as it is now, will be changed from a hostile and busy dual-carriageway into a pedestrian-friendly street where people can work, live and socialise. The large roundabout at the northern end will be removed. The buildings fronting the street will be designed to a scale appropriate for an urban centre and will contain shops, offices, a hotel, apartments, a Garda Station, civic amenities and leisure facilities. Public squares, meeting places, rows of trees and other landscaping will add to the street's attractiveness. The LUAS light rail system will serve Main Street where security, maintenance and cleanliness will be a top priority for a Town Centre Management Team.

Right: The Darndale Belcamp Village Centre, designed by Duffy Mitchell Architects, will bring a new focal point to a pair of public housing estates that have undergone a £25 million seven-phase renewal programme throughout the 1990s. Harvey Contracting commenced building the centre in January 2000. Apart from four retail units the centre will include an Eastern Regional Health Authority centre, a training centre, regional offices for Dublin Corporation and a Community Resource Centre. The project is supported by ROUND.

Above: An artist's impression of the houses designed for Coultry/Shangan 1 by BRL's in-house team of architects. The eventual colours will be chosen in consultation with the people who will live in these new houses which will be along the west side of Coultry Way and Shangan Park. There are thirteen Phase 1 housing schemes, each one designed by a separate architectural practice to ensure variety and individuality. The participating firms are: Coultry 1 – MacCormac Jamieson Prichard Architects; Shangan/Coultry 1 – Levitt Bernstein Associates; Shangan 2 – McGarry Ní Éanaigh Architects, McCrossan O'Rourke Architects and Derek Tynan Architects; Coultry 2 – Gilroy McMahon Architects and Peter Twamley Architects; Sillogue/Sandyhill 2 – M. V. Cullinan Architects and Gerry Cahill Architects; Poppintree 1 – Fionnuala Rogerson Architects; Poppintree 2 – Cathal Crimmins Architects and Balcurris 1 – O'Mahony Pike Architects. The tenants for the approximately 650 Phase One houses will mainly come from a group of tower blocks and other flats selected for the first round of demolitions. Additional phases of new housing will follow as Ballymun is progressively rebuilt.

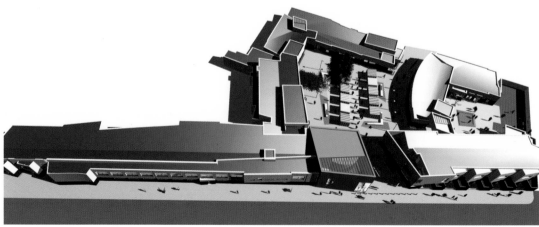

From the 1950s, the area that is now referred to as Temple Bar began to decline as businesses, shoppers and residents moved elsewhere. From 1981, CIE began to purchase and assemble property, bounded by Fownes Street, Dame Street, Eustace Street and Wellington Quay, to build a massive Transportation Centre (it was to be linked to an even larger block directly across the river). While it was dealing with the planning processes, CIE rented out its properties at low rents which attracted artists, musicians and other cultural practitioners. The area took on a bohemian atmosphere and a vibrant new life pulsated through the streets. Residents, leaseholders and other interested people began to see a new value in the place and a committee was formed in 1988 to oppose CIE's plans. Known as the Temple Bar Development Council (the name "Temple Bar", as referring to the whole area and not just to the short street which connects Fleet Street to Essex Street East, came out of a 1985 An Taisce [The National Trust for Ireland] report "The Temple Bar Area – a Policy for the Future"), the committee successfully lobbied City Councillors and the Government. The then Taoiseach, Charles J. Haughey, brought his influence to bear on the matter in favour of the Development Council. CIE was persuaded to sell its land in 1991 to Temple Bar Properties (TBP), a development company set up on behalf of the Department of an Taoiseach. The remarkable regeneration of Dublin's Left Bank had begun (see also Temple Bar Properties in Appendix D).

Above: The street sign announces that Anglesea Street (originally laid out in 1658) lies in the enclave of Temple Bar.

Above: No.18 Eustace Street, a late 18th century house, is the headquarters of Temple Bar Properties and was acquired from CIE in 1991. By then it was in a very dilapidated condition and the complete interior, including the magnificent winding and partially cantilevered timber staircase, has been restored. The outside brickwork was repointed using tuck-pointing, a traditional method employed in the 18th century. Next to it, No.17, is a house built around a hundred years earlier. It too was restored by Temple Bar Properties who reinstated the missing top floor, painstakingly recreated the interior and rediscovered the cut-stone entrance doorcase which had been encased for many years in plaster.

Photo: courtesy Temple Bar Properties.

Above: The extent of Temple Bar can be gauged from this aerial photograph. The area stretches from the river south (towards the right) to the almost parallel outline of Dame Street and from Fishamble Street (at the Civic Offices' tower) east to Westmoreland Street (in line with O'Connell Bridge, the third bridge from the bottom of this picture). The new Millennium Bridge was not yet built when this photograph was taken.

Photo: courtesy Temple Bar Properties.

Above: The Ark, housed in a 1728 Presbyterian Meeting House on Eustace Street and in a modern extension facing Temple Bar Square, is a cultural centre for children. It was designed by Shane O'Toole and Michael O'Kelly, (see also page 164).

1 2
3 4
5 6
7 8

1| The exposed base of Isolde's Tower, on Exchange Street Lower, a bastion on the north-eastern corner of Dublin's 13th century city walls. The 4m (13ft) thick walls attest to the importance of its role as it would have been the first major line of defence against an attack launched from the River Liffey. Its discovery in 1993 led to an extensive archaeological investigation and the publication of a comprehensive report by Temple Bar Properties. The site is now preserved under an apartment development and is visible from the street behind a large metal grill.

2| Meeting House Square, one of the new public open spaces created by Temple Bar Properties, is the venue for outdoor film shows during the summer months.

3| Curved Street (for that is what it is) is a new street, laid out in 1996 by Temple Bar Properties and designed by Shay Cleary Architects. It is bordered on one side by ARTHouse, a multi-media centre for the arts (Shay Cleary Architects) and on the other by the Temple Bar Music Centre which contains an auditorium, music rehearsal rooms, music information facilities and teaching areas (McCullough Mulvin Architects).

4| Designed by Murray O'Laoire Associates and built in 1994 by G & T Crampton for Temple Bar Properties, the Green Building on Temple Lane was innovative and daring in its concept. Supported under the EU Thermie Project, the building is very environmentally aware and uses natural systems whenever possible, including warm water from the underlying bedrock and electricity from solar panels and three wind-propellers on the roof. The roof itself can open in hot weather to allow excess heat to disperse.

5| St Winifred's Well (named after a 7th century Welsh saint) was rediscovered in 1991 when workmen were laying cobbles on Eustace Street. It is believed to be a late 17th century well, constructed when the street was first built, although there was a medieval well of the same name somewhat nearer Cecilia Street, the site of an Augustinian Friary of the Holy Trinity founded in 1280.

6| Temple Bar Square is a civic space created by Temple Bar Properties following their purchase of a former surface car park in 1994.

7|8 Two contrasting views, looking from Essex Street East into Parliament Street, demonstrate the improvements which have taken place in Temple Bar.

Photo: courtesy Temple Bar Properties.

Photo: courtesy Temple Bar Properties.

Míle Átha Cliath was Dublin's Millennium Partnership and involved civic, business and public bodies who came together to realise a number of significant commemorative projects which would permanently focus, in a spirit of renewal and rediscovery, on the River Liffey.

Above: A digital image of the Liffey Boardwalk, one of the projects set in motion by Míle Átha Cliath. The boardwalk, designed by McGarry Ní Éanaigh Architects, will stretch from Grattan Bridge to O'Connell Bridge and will provide a new perspective on the river. It will also serve as a venue for market stalls and special events. Construction work commenced in early 2000.

Top left: Rory O'More Bridge, resplendent in its new colour scheme, was refurbished as part of a programme to enhance all the bridges from Seán Heuston Bridge to the East Link Bridge. Clifden Court Apartments on Ellis Quay rise behind the bridge.

Photo: courtesy of Míle Átha Cliath and Dave Meehan Photography.

Above: At 1800 on New Year's Eve, 1999, thirteen bridges along the Liffey from Heuston Station to the East Link crossing were spectacularly floodlit in one single operation. The project cost £1.3 million and was jointly funded by Dublin Corporation, the National Millennium Committee and Míle Átha Cliath. National Toll Roads, Guinness Ireland Group and Dublin Port were among 21 organisations which contributed to the project. The idea for the "Liffey of Lights" came from Robbie Cahill, a resident from Dublin's Liberties, who won the Míle Átha Cliath "Dream It for 21st Century Dublin" competition in 1998. The scheme was designed by Duilio Passariello of Philips LiDAC, a company with many other prestigious international lighting projects to its credit. Dublin Corporation's Public Lighting Department implemented the project.

Above: Large and small craft in a busy Dublin Port.

Left: Dublin's newest river bridge, the Millennium Bridge, was opened on 20 December 1999 and was another successful project undertaken by Míle Átha Cliath. Built in County Carlow, the 41m (134ft) long bridge was transported to the site and lowered by crane directly onto its abutments. The designers were Howley Harrington Architects who worked in association with structural engineers, Price & Myers. The commission for the design of the bridge was the outcome of an international competition promoted by Dublin Corporation. Solely a pedestrian bridge, its purpose was to open a new route between Temple Bar and the Mary Street/Jervis Street shopping district and to relieve congestion on the nearby Halfpenny Bridge.

Above: The riverfront headquarters of the DDDA provides secure moorings for up to 25 visiting pleasure craft and the facility helps to bring life to this part of the river.

Middle right: The map shows the extent of the area under the control of the DDDA.

Bottom right: The building activity in the IFSC was lit up for the Christmas season.

Above: The campshire (that part of the quay wall between the road and the river's edge) along City Quay before improvement works were carried out by the DDDA.

Below: The same stretch of campshire in 2000. The DDDA intends to upgrade North Wall Quay and Sir John Rogerson's Quay in similar fashion with the addition of retail kiosks and quay-side restaurants.

As already has been seen in Temple Bar, Government intervention, by way of tax incentives, the provision of public capital and the establishment of a development cum regulatory organisation, was the main catalyst for the regeneration of that area. On 17 November 1986, five years before the foundation of Temple Bar Properties, the Government formally established the Custom House Docks Development Authority (CHDDA). Under the Urban Renewal Act 1986, this body was charged with the re-development of the immediate area around the semi-redundant inner docks, just east of the Custom House, which were originally built in the 18th century as a sheltered haven for shipping. While residential and cultural uses were set aside in this 11ha (27 acres) scheme, the primary objective, as provided by the Finance Bill 1987, was the successful establishment of an International Financial Services Centre (IFSC). The consortium chosen to build the Custom House Docks project comprised Hardwicke Ltd and British Land Company plc. On 1 May 1997, when this first phase was nearing completion, a new authority, the Dublin Docklands Development Authority (DDDA), replaced the CHDDA and the original area of 27 acres was extended to include a development area of 526ha (1,300 acres), spread over both sides of the River Liffey. The revised master plan then issued by the DDDA for the Dublin Docklands outlined a programme for the comprehensive social, economic and physical regeneration of the whole district. The plan provides for a 15-year development period (until 2012) and expects a total public and private investment of IR£5 billion, the creation of up to 40,000 new jobs, a population growth from 17,500 (1997) to 42,500 and the building of 11,000 new homes, 20% of which will be set aside for social and affordable housing.

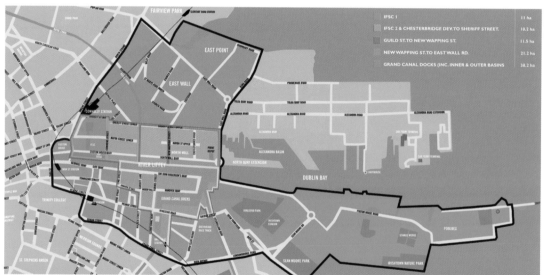

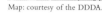

Map: courtesy of the DDDA.

Aerial photography: courtesy of Peter Barrow Photographers.

1	3
2	4
	5
	6
	7

1| A 1980s view of the north dockland area before any re-development took place.

2| The same district taken in late 1999 demonstrates the remarkable transformation which has since taken place. In all, the IFSC employs approximately 13,000 people over its 16ha (39 acres) site. Residential accommodation is spread over 1,130 apartments. Three hundred international companies located here contribute substantial revenue per annum to the Irish economy.

3| Symbolic entrance to the IFSC, this stone archway was once the Amiens Street gateway to the old Custom House Docks.

4/5| A fountain and a cascade enliven and connect the Custom House Harbour apartments to the waters of the Inner Dock.

6| A view across the River Liffey to the completed Phase One section of the IFSC.

7| The yellow and green façade of the AIB International Centre acts as a beacon to the IFSC from Memorial Road.

Above: An aerial view of the 4.8ha (12 acres) Phase Two development at the IFSC. A welcome addition to the offices and apartments is the Docklands Campus of the National College of Ireland (No.11 on the photograph). A linear park will be created along the Royal Canal (No.16).

Below: Clarion Quay Apartments on North Wall Quay are the latest generation in high specification housing and each of the nearly 200 units has floor-to-ceiling windows, two-direction aspects and unusually large balconies. In accordance with Government provisions, 36 of the apartments were made available for affordable and social housing. At street level there are shops and restaurants. The apartments are located in nine blocks, six are eight-storeys high, the other three are lower, and they all form around a private landscaped garden. The design, by architects Urban Projects, was chosen following an architectural competition organised by the DDDA. The joint developers were the DDDA and the Campshire Partnership which comprised Liberty Homes Ltd (a combination of Alanis Ltd. and the main contractor, Pierse Contracting) and Redquartz Ltd (the Kelly family, well-known Dublin developers). A new pedestrian street, Excise Walk, divides the apartment blocks from the new four-star Clarion Hotel. The 160-bedroom exclusive hotel is the second hotel, after the Jurys Custom House Inn, to be built along this stretch of waterfront. Scott Tallon Walker were the architects for the Clarion and it was developed jointly by the DDDA and the North Wall Partnership (Alanis Ltd, Pierse Contracting and Redquartz).

Above: Mayor Street, the new high street of the IFSC, was first laid down in the 1770s. Its name, like those of neighbouring Sheriff Street, Guild Street and Commons Street, mark the fact that it was the City Assembly (Dublin Corporation) which developed this whole area by reclaiming it from the sea when the North Wall was first built in the early 1700s. The Assembly later divided the land into 132 building lots for its own members. This area became known as the North Lotts.

Top & above: Still retaining part of the original structure of the former Sheriff Street Postal Sorting Office, Custom House Plaza is one of the finest buildings in the IFSC. It boasts a spectacular internal glazed atrium which is said to be the longest internal street in Ireland. Custom House Plaza forms the northern boundary of the IFSC and its remodelled façade has dramatically enlivened the formerly depressing streetscape of Sheriff Street (not shown in the photograph). It was designed by Anthony Reddy Associates and built by G & T Crampton.

Photo: courtesy of David Park 20-20 Vision Design.

Above: Grand Canal Docks, looking northwards towards Ringsend Road. This atmospheric and brooding view marks a passing era. The docks date from 1796 (see page 145).

Photo: courtesy of the DDDA.

Above: An aerial view of the south docklands area which is being prepared for a massive renewal

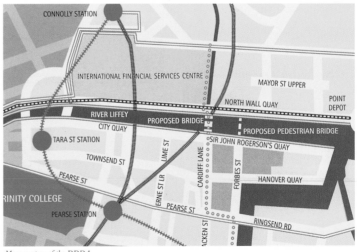

Map: courtesy of the DDDA.

Above: The DDDA's plan for the Grand Canal Docks is, if anything, more ambitious than that for the IFSC, at least in terms of the residential, cultural and leisure elements. The area comprises 29.2ha (72 acres) of land and 9ha (22 acres) of water space. The DDDA's Action Plan articulates a mixed-use redevelopment of generally 60% residential (in excess of 4,000 homes) and 40% commercial. To facilitate access to the area new pedestrian and public transport bridges across the Liffey and Dodder rivers are being proposed.

Above: In 1866 the firm of Grendon & Co of Drogheda delivered a diving bell to the port authority of Dublin to enable work to be carried out underwater to the extension and strengthening of the North Wall Quay. Once the main compartment was standing on the river bed men could work in relatively spacious surroundings unimpeded by personal diving equipment. Lying idle and rusting away for many years on Sir John Rogerson's Quay the diving bell was restored in 2000 by Fás with the financial help of the DDDA and Dublin Port Company.

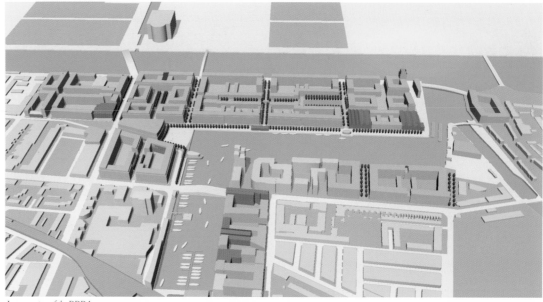

Above: The DDDA itself owns a 9.6ha (24 acres) plot to the west and north of the two canal docks called Grand Canal Harbour. Here, the DDDA intends, in partnership with the private sector, to deliver, at an estimated cost of £1.5 billion, 5,000 new jobs, 1,200 new homes, 100,000sq m (1,076,000sq ft) of offices, shops, restaurants, pubs, hotels, leisure, arts/cultural facilities and a new civic square. Formerly these lands belonged to Bord Gáis and currently £25 million is being spent to carry out remedial works to the ground which was contaminated during the decades when town gas was manufactured here. Construction work on Grand Canal Harbour is scheduled to start in Spring 2001. A government order, known as Section 25, allows the DDDA to exclusively grant full and final planning permissions in this designated area and, based on the previous experience when this order also applied to the second phase of the IFSC, this will enormously speed up the process from first design to project completion.

Right: This view of the outer dock of the Grand Canal Docks is taken from the boat yard.

Far right: The water sports and leisure potential of the Grand Canal Docks is obvious from this view.

Above: Charlotte Quay, on the south side of the outer canal dock.

Below left & right: Both of Dublin's canals are set for major environmental improvements in the docklands where they finally spill into the River Liffey. Further into the city they will also be significantly upgraded. In a pilot plan put together by Dublin Corporation and Waterways Ireland, major work is to take place on the Royal Canal from Newcomen Bridge on the North Strand to Clonliffe Bridge at Russell Street (below left). Similar enhancements are to be made to the Grand Canal from La Touche Bridge at the Institute of Education building, Portobello Bridge, to Robert Emmet Bridge at Harold's Cross.

Chapter Fifteen

More Rejuvenation

STARTING IN in the late 1960s, the wild spree of demolishing Georgian streetscapes, Victorian splendours and early 20th century building stock, from neo-classicism to art deco, in favour of bland and dour building-kit office blocks continued unabated throughout the 1970s and the legacy of this period has left shameful scars across the city. This frenzy began to run out of steam by the early 1980s but still continued here and there and no worthwhile building or terrace from past generations could be considered safe from predatory speculators. Only inadequate provisions were then in place to safeguard even the few buildings that were on official protection lists. Inventories of all the buildings that needed protection were practically non-existent and this made the work of campaigning for their preservation all the more difficult.

Partly as a result of some celebrated public protests against the destruction of historic buildings and sites the general population by the mid 1980s was beginning to question the despoiling of its heritage. In addition, property owners were slowly coming around to the view that restoration was not so old-fashioned after all and perhaps even made good commercial sense. Prestigious head offices made positive statements about their occupiers. Besides, new materials and more enlightened techniques evolved which made the task of refurbishment more economical, more enduring and less damaging to a building's fabric. The retail community in the city centre effectively lobbied the City Council arguing that unless the streets became more consumer and environmentally friendly their customers would abandon them for the suburbs. Central government and Dublin Corporation, as was seen in the last chapter, put their not inconsiderable weight behind the process of renewal. Finally, legal measures, such as fines of millions of pounds, could be applied in cases of neglect of, or unauthorised changes to historic and listed properties. A more civilised era was beginning to dawn.

Even before this seed change, individuals and single organisations often undertook exemplary restorations or conversions on their historic properties even during the early to mid-1980s when it there were few, if any, financial incentives available to cushion the costs. The economy of that period didn't help either as it was notorious for its upward and downward swings and for its high inflation rates. The designation of tax incentive areas for urban renewal, dealt with in the last chapter, clearly had a huge influence in upgrading whole tracts of the city. This chapter can look at only a small number of the conversions made to historic buildings, as well as at some district improvements and the welcome recladding and upgrading of deficient first-generation office blocks.

Above: The James Joyce Centre, 35 North Great George's Street, was built originally in 1784 by Francis Ryan for Valentine Brown, the Earl of Kenmare. When the earl sold the house following the Act of Union in 1800 the house began a slide into a decay that threatened it with demolition by the early 1980's. Senator David Norris, a well-known Joycean scholar and a resident of North Great George's Street, campaigned to save the house, not least because of its association with Joyce. Around the turn of the 20th century a colourful character, Denis J. Maginni, ran a school of dancing from a backroom of the house. He was known to Joyce who mentions him on six occasions in "Ulysses". Norris was successful in arranging the preservation and restoration of the house and it was opened as the James Joyce Centre in 1996. The house contains some important plasterwork by Michael Stapleton, leading stuccadore of the late 18th century. The library and ancillary rooms have a large collection of books and portraits dealing with every aspect of Joyce's life, work and family.

Above: No. 21 Aungier Street, a surviving late 17th century house, fell into a complete state of ruin and, because its age was not then generally known, was listed for demolition.

Above: The same building after the Dublin Civic Trust had acquired the property, stabilised the structure and in 1996 restored the brickwork and windows before selling it on. It is now a guest house.

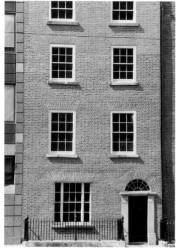

Above: Using a revolving fund (first capitalised by the Department of the Environment and Local Government), numbers 10 and 11 South Frederick Street were restored by the Dublin Civic Trust and sold on as businesses cum residences.

The Dublin Civic Trust, a company with charitable status, was founded in 1992 to promote residential renewal, cultural enhancement and maintenance of the historic fabric of the city. The Trust works in conjunction with Government, Dublin Corporation and those professional trade and voluntary organisations that share its vision for the city. Through a revolving fund, the Trust purchases endangered historic buildings, repairs them and sells them on with recommendations or stipulations for their use which usually includes a residential element. Other objectives of the Trust are to identify derelict buildings with potential for new uses, promote traditional craft skills as well as a code of practice for the repair and maintenance of historic buildings and carry out street and building inventories. From its permanent centre in Castle Street the Trust mounts exhibitions and seminars and is available to advise building owners, professional bodies and interested people about the possible solutions to particular problems associated with historic or old buildings. In 1997, funded by the European Regional Development Fund, the Historic Heart of Dublin's (HHoD) three year Urban Pilot Project was inaugurated as a partnership between the Dublin Civic Trust and Dublin Corporation. HOoD's brief included 12 specific projects ranging from preservation seminars and public information access to producing the first systematic detailed inventory of the city's built heritage. This partnership produced the most comprehensive historical and technical report on Henrietta Street to date, a vital prerequisite before the necessary restoration of the grandest Georgian street on the north side of Dublin can begin in earnest.

Above: St Kevin's Church, with its distinguishing red sandstone details and slender spire, was opened for the Church of Ireland in 1883. Its designer was Thomas Drew RHA (1838-1910), an architect who also left to posterity many other fine buildings including the former Rathmines Town Hall and two splendid bank buildings on College Green, the National Irish Bank and the Ulster Bank. Deconsecrated in 1983 the church was later acquired by Heritage Properties who (as their name might suggest) never countenanced altering the exterior let alone demolishing the building (the sad fate of several other redundant churches). Working inventively with architects (Mary) Donohoe & (Desmond) Fitzgerald, Heritage completed a major restoration of the building and created 31 individual apartments within the existing structure. Many of the apartments have stunning interiors which feature such exotica as stained-glass windows, Gothic architectural details and pitch pine floors and panelling. St Kevin's is located at the corner of Bloomfield Avenue and the South Circular Road.

Below: The new Trinity Capital Hotel occupies the partly reconstructed, partly restored former Tara Street Fire Station and was opened in 2000. The hotel has 86 bedrooms and a bar aptly called 'Fireworks'. The bar section has been preserved as close to the original interior as possible, retaining much of the brickwork and steelwork. Tara Street Fire Station, which has been relocated around the corner to Townsend Street (see page 87), was first built in 1907. The 38m (125ft) high watchtower, based on the architecture of Renaissance Florence, is, like the façade of the corner building, on the city's Preservation List. The limestone-faced ground floor of the old fire station was copied around the new sections of the scheme. Dublin Corporation developed the site in association with Rohcon Ltd. Architects were Henry J. Lyons and Partners. The hotel and bar are owned by Capital Bars plc.

Below: The Café en Seine, 40 Dawson Street, opened in 1994, was one of the first, if not the first, café style bar to open in Dublin. It broke away from the traditional type bar and focused on the food and coffee culture that has now become the norm. It was converted from offices originally occupied by Caledonian Insurances. Before that again there were shops and a church hall on the site. It is owned by Capital Bars plc.

Photo: courtesy of Capitol Bars Ltd.

Above: A view of part of the campus of the National College of Art and Design off Thomas Street.

Above: A couple of pot stills stand in the grounds of the NCAD, a reminder of when the distillery of John Power & Son operated from here.

Above: Starting life as an 18th century Georgian town house, No.18 Parnell Square has been home to lords, Members of Parliament, the Jameson distilling family and, in later years, the City of Dublin Technical School. In 1991, in celebration of Dublin becoming that year's European City of Culture, the property was converted by Dublin Tourism into the Writer's Museum. It features a display of books, manuscripts, portraits, letters and other memorabilia relating to Irish writers such as Swift, Shaw, Behan, O'Casey, Wilde, Yeats, Joyce and Beckett.

Image: courtesy of John Power.

Above: Highly ornate pages extracted from advertising leaflets produced by the John's Lane Distillery of John Power & Son. Established in 1791 by James Power, it grew over the next century into one of the country's largest distilleries. The plant closed in the mid 1970s and was subsequently purchased by the National College of Art and Design (NCAD). Founded in 1750 by the Dublin Society as the School of Figure Drawing, thence becoming the Dublin Metropolitan School of Art (1877) and the National College of Art (1936). The current institution came under the control of the Higher Education Authority in 1971 and received its present name. From 1980 the NCAD gradually began to move its student body to its newly acquired premises along John's Lane and Thomas Street. An inspired conversion of the old distillery retained as much as possible of the Victorian industrial architecture. Architects for the project were Burke-Kennedy Doyle.

Below: In 1891 the Dublin Working Boys' Home and Harding Technical School, designed by Albert E. Murray, was opened on Lord Edward Street to accommodate boys as young as thirteen or fourteen years of age who came from rural counties to take up poorly paid apprenticeships in Dublin. The home had sleeping accommodation for 75 boys and operated Ireland's first technical school in an effort to improve the boys' opportunities for gaining better employment. Developer P. J. McGrath purchased the by then closed down home in the mid-1980's and prepared the building for its eventual purchaser, USIT, a youth and student travel organisation who turned it into a quality hostel.

Below: A copy of the Gaiety Theatre's opening night programme, 27 November 1871. The evening opened with Oliver Goldsmith's comedy "She Stoops to Conquer" followed by a burlesque, "La Belle Sauvage", both performed by the St James' Theatre Company from London.

Above: Designed by C. J. Phipps, an architect renowned for his London theatres, Michael Gunn opened his Gaiety Theatre on South King Street in 1871. Except for the demolition in 1955 of "The Gods", an acutely steep gallery served by 86 steps, the horseshoe-shaped auditorium, with its Victorian boxes and tiered circles resplendently decorated with rococo embellishments, is still very much as Phipps would have seen it. Drama, opera, dance, pantomime, children's theatre and late night weekend clubs for young people are the standard bill-of-fare at the Gaiety. Under the present owners, Denis and Caroline Desmond (they bought the theatre in April 1999), the interior of the Gaiety will be restored and upgraded in 2000 and it will become the first fully air conditioned theatre in Dublin. A large proportion of this work was aided by a grant of £500,000 from the National Millennium Committee.

Below: In 1906, the Iveagh Trust engaged Frederick G. Hicks to design the Iveagh Baths on Bride Road. Essentially designed as a swimming pool for the local community, many of whom were tenants in the Iveagh Flats, another philanthropic endeavour of the trust, the baths were sometimes pressed into public health uses. For instance, they were once utilised as a de-lousing centre for large areas of the inner city affected by a wide-spread skin lice infestation during the Second World War. The baths, by now under the control of Dublin Corporation, closed down in 1985. They were subsequently refurbished and enlarged and re-opened in 1995 as the exclusive Iveagh Fitness Centre.

Above: The exterior of the Gaiety Theatre, designed by Charles Ashworth and dating from 1913, was restored to its original glory in 2000 including the replacement of the previous plain canopy with a more ornate version. Dublin Corporation will be providing a small plaza in front of the building.

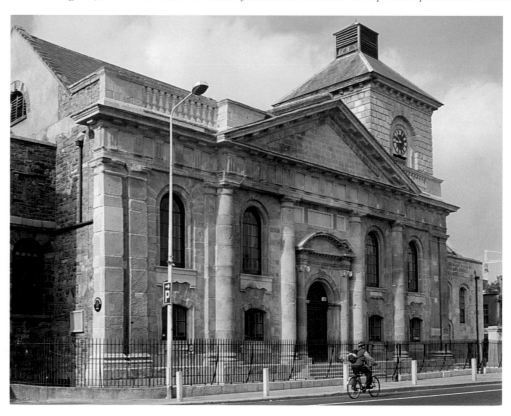

Top: A view of O'Connell Bridge House, a landmark but visually outdated building, at the corner of Burgh Quay and D'Olier Street before it was reclad in 2000.

Above: A redundant cut-stone distillery and malthouse along Beresford Street was superbly converted in the mid-1990s into apartments by Dunloe Ewart plc.

Above: Whatever one might think of the architectural honesty and appropriateness of building mock Georgian houses the completion by Zoe Developments of such a scheme around two sides of Mountjoy Square has fortified the 18th century setting for the genuine survivors on the north and east terraces. The appalling neglect of this square over the years, with the gaunt ruins of buildings on the west and south sides threatening to spread their decay, was thus finally arrested in the mid 1990s.

Above: When the Midland and Great Western Railway Company built their Point Depot, an extensive rail terminus, in 1878, at the eastern end of the North Wall, they could not have possibly envisaged its eventual future when the trains no longer ran from here. Entrepreneur and road transport haulier Harry Crosbie had his clear vision in the 1980s for the massive and, by then, redundant building. He saw it as the city's premier dedicated concert venue and he spent several million pounds on its conversion. He later signed on Apollo Leisure as a partner to facilitate the completion of the work. The 6,500-seat venue opened in 1989 and has been very successful since then. Architects for the project were Stephen Tierney and Shay Cleary.

Below: The money ran out before a tower and spire could be added to St Catherine's Church on Thomas Street which was completed in 1769. The most famous event associated with the church, or rather with the street outside, was the hanging in September 1803 of failed revolutionary, Robert Emmet. Fellow insurrectionists, who also paid the price of treason, are commemorated on an outside-wall tablet. It is interesting to note their stations in life. A preponderance, seven in all, were carpenters; a trade which undoubtedly supervised the reliable construction of their scaffold. Lying empty for many years, with the fabric deteriorating at an alarming rate the building was finally restored in 1999 by CORE (City Outreach through Renewal and Evangelism), a movement within the Church of Ireland. The restoration was supervised by Paul Arnold Architects.

Below: In 1985 the Ronan Group (led by developer John Ronan) purchased the redundant Boland's Bakery on Lower Grand Canal Street. Ronan's initiative was not only an expression of supreme self-confidence at a time of economic downturn but its outcome was to have a direct influence on regenerating a part of Dublin that had become run-down and depressed. By January 1991 the building had been transformed out of all recognition. This had been the first time, outside of the fledgling International Financial Services Centre, that a speculative office block had been outfitted to such a high specification. The five original floors, with higher than normal floor to ceiling heights, were augmented by a sixth storey, giving a total of 12,077sq m (130,000sq ft) of rentable space. The outside walls were stupendously reclad with handmade wire-cut clay bricks, polyester powder-coated aluminium window frames and pink tinted double glazed windows. The new atrium building was clad in polished granite. From the canal bridge the finished building seemed almost to represent an impressive gateway to a newly bullish inner city. It is now known as the Treasury Building (the National Treasury Management Agency is one of the main tenants). Designers for the Treasury Building were Henry J. Lyons & Partners in conjunction with Mahler Architectural Consultants of New York (for the façade). The main contractor was John Sisk & Son.

Above left & right: Two views of Bolands Bakery, Lower Grand Canal Street, designed by S. Stephenson & Sons of Belfast and built by G & T Crampton in 1948. This building replaced an earlier one which featured prominently in the Easter Rising of 1916 as an outpost commanded by Eamon de Valera.

Above: An interior photograph of a section of the new atrium block built onto the original bakery building. The 36.5m (120ft) high octagonal-shaped atrium was the first of its kind in Dublin. Bronze, mahogany, marbles and polished granites of varying hues, tinted glass and a cascading waterfall blend together to exude a self-assured, luxury. Even the atrium toilets and the four huge lifts were given the ornate treatment.

Above: Situated at the intersection of the Royal Canal and the Phibsborough Road, at Cross Guns Bridge, this old stone mill had stood empty since 1980 when the Ranks Flour Milling Company had ceased operating from there. Before Ranks the mill was owned by the Dublin North City Milling Company. The building was first erected in 1846 for the Robert Mallet Iron Works (this company built the railings for Trinity College on the stretch from College Green to and along Nassau Street). In 1860 Murtagh Brothers bought the premises to conduct their milling business. The mill was once served by its own railway siding and a quayside for loading barges.

Above: Of special interest to this author was the conversion of the former Ranks Flour Mills in Phibsborough into an apartment block. He had lived the first thirty-two years of his life in Leinster Street with the mills as his rear garden backdrop. Once the 24 apartments in a new block to the east of the mill were built in 1991 work commenced to entirely demolish the core of the old stone giant while continuing to preserve the four outside walls. A completely self-supporting new building was erected within the interior which was then tied to the original external walls. Curiously, a culverted mill race was found during construction work under the ground floor. It was apparently used until 1947 to provide electrical power to the mill. There are 50 apartments in the six storied mill building now called Cross Guns Quay. Architects for the project were Campbell Conroy Hickey Partnership. The developers were Woodsim Ltd and the main contractors were Woodgreen Builders Ltd.

Photo: courtesy of Woodgreen Builders Ltd.

Above: During the mill's conversion to apartments it was completely gutted on the inside and a temporary steel framework was inserted at roof-top level to stabilise the limestone walls. In order to cut away the wall at ground floor level on the canal side (for the car park), jacks were inserted and then permanently encased in reinforced concrete to hold up the rest of the north-facing façade.

Above: The Labour Historical Society Museum occupies the front square of Beggar's Bush Barracks while, around to its side, the National Print Museum is located in the former Garrison Church.

Above: The courtyard in front of a couple of terraces of former army houses on the Shelbourne Road side of Beggar's Bush Barracks. These houses and their surroundings were magnificently restored in 1997 by Dublin Corporation for use as senior citizen flats. Beggar's Bush Barracks was built in 1827 as a recruiting depot for the British Army's other major installations in Dublin. It earned some notoriety during the War of Independence (1919-1921) when it became a base for the infamous Auxiliaries, a para-military police force recruited mostly from demobilised army officers who had endured the barbarities of the First World War. It was the first Dublin Barracks to be taken over after the Treaty from the British Army when Commander Paddy Daly occupied it on 31 January 1922. It became a recruiting post again, this time for the National Army during the Civil War (1922-1923). One of the post's most shameful records was that several executions were carried out here including that of Erskine Childers (1870-1922), father of the later and very popular President of Ireland, also named Erskine, who sadly died in office in 1974. Erskine Childers Senior was famous both as a writer (his pre-World War One spy novel "Riddle of the Sands" won him international fame) and as a patriot. His most famous exploit was the Howth gun-running, the landing of arms from his yacht 'Asgard' for the Irish Volunteers in 1914. His prominent anti-Treaty role in the Civil War led to his capture and subsequent death sentence. Long since demilitarised, the original buildings in the barracks were abandoned and a new six-storey office block was built in the 1980s for the Department of Labour. Because of its size and red-brick construction, the location of this building is incongruous in the extreme. Amends have since been handsomely made with the restoration, in the 1990s, of the rest of the barracks. In 1994 Gem Construction bought the Haddington Road side of the barracks compound and sensitively converted the cut stone and brick buildings surrounding the front square (the architect was Shay Cleary). Heritage Properties followed suit to the rear of the complex and installed 47 townhouses and apartments by restoring the original stone buildings and constructing some new ones in the same style. The design here was handled by O'Mahony Pike Architects.

Above & below: Two aspects of High Street and Cornmarket, the first taken in the late 1980s, the second in 2000, demonstrate the improvements brought about in the intervening period. The blight which arose from the lack of investment and uncertain road widening plans, affected this whole district until various incentives and market demand began to transform the area from the mid 1990s.

Below: The Rt. Hon. Sidney Herbert, second son of the 11th Earl of Pembroke, instigated the building of St Stephen's Parochial School which opened in 1861 on Northumberland Road. Many of the pupils came from the married quarters of the nearby Beggar's Bush Barracks. Another military involvement, of a more serious nature, took place when the school desks were used as barricades at the Battle of Mount Street during The Easter Rising of 1916. The school finally closed in 1969. It was miraculous, in an area overflowing with office blocks, that it was not demolished. It somehow survived and in the 1990s it was splendidly refurbished, adapted and cleverly extended to accommodate Terry Sweeny's Schoolhouse Hotel. Spain Courtney Doyle were the project architects for the hotel, building on the original design of Deane and Woodward. The building itself is owned by Treasury Holdings.

Above: An array of mock Georgian façades, with their uneven widths, heights and building lines create a pleasing aspect to Zoe's development on Bachelor's Walk. Number seven, a fine panelled house, was restored but little else remains of the rest of the original 18th century houses. Unfortunately, the art deco CIE building, which would have stood in the middle of the scheme, was also demolished.

Above: Bachelors Walk in the 1980s after it had reached its nadir as a result of property speculation by a company called Arlington Securities who had assembled the .81 ha (2 acres) site to build a shopping centre. This scheme was dependant on the government authorising the building of a new central bus station on neighbouring Ormond Quay. When the transportation centre idea was abandoned Arlington sold its site in late 1992 to Zoe Developments, one of Dublin's biggest apartment builders.

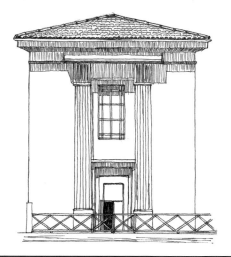

Left: In 1898 the Dublin United Tramway Company built an electricity gererating station at their Ringsend Depot to supply power to their fleet of trams. With the advent of a national electricity grid this building was demolished to make way for a new tramsformer station which became operational in 1931. When the last tram was withdrawn in 1949 the transformer station was closed and it became offices for the Bovril Company. Now a listed building, it is currently occupied by the famous Windmill Lane Recording Studios whose clients include U2, Clannad, Metallica, Riverdance, Rod Stewart, The Cheiftains, The Corrs, The Cranberries, Van Morrison, Sinéad O'Connor, Kate Bush and many more. Film scores, such as those for "Mission Impossible", "Michael Collins", "The Mask" and many others were also recorded here.

Above: Goat Castle, built in 1498, was one of the seven tower houses of medieval Dalkey which were used as defensive store houses for the cargoes coming in and going out through the nearby harbour, Dublin's main deep-water port of that time. More recently, the Castle served as the local Town Hall cum rates office and as a public theatre. It was skilfully converted and upgraded in 1998, with the assistance of the South Dublin County Council, into the Dalkey Castle & Heritage Centre. The 19th century hall and other rooms behind the tower are extensively used by various local community groups.

31st March-4th April 1741. **𝔇𝔲𝔟𝔩𝔦𝔫 𝔑𝔢𝔴𝔰 𝔏𝔢𝔱𝔱𝔢𝔯** Issue No. 2687.

This is to give Notice, that the BOWLING GREEN in Great Marlborough-Street, is now open'd in compleat Order, with several new Additions and Improvements. The Musick will perform in the Green and Musick Room (for the first time) on Friday the 10th of April, and will continue every Tuesday and Friday during the Summer Season, if the Evening proves fair, if not the Musick will attend the next fair Evening following.

The Prices are as usual, viz. a British Shilling on Musick Evenings, and a British Sixpence every other Evening; the Ladies Gratis.

Subscriptions will be taken in the said Green for the Summer Season at one Guinea for the Green and Musick Room, and a half a Guinea for the Green only.

Chapter Sixteen

Dublin Nouveau

U NLESS A city grows, evolves and constantly reinvents itself it will stifle, stagnate and, in extreme cases, die. Cities with a rich heritage in authentic and intact period buildings can count themselves fortunate but they too have to be on guard lest they simply become museums or mausoleums of the past, trapped in their own history. At the other extreme, too much of Dublin's built legacy was sacrificed for third-rate development in previous decades but the mistakes of earlier generations have since provided opportunities for injecting new life and fresh visions. Derelict sites, surface car parks, demolished buildings, infill gaps, redundant factory lots, empty docklands, outdated facilities and the "air space" over certain low rise premises are all providing scope to make new statements and create a vibrant synergy between the old and the new. Many of these modern creations have been visited in preceding chapters but the next few pages allow a further exploration. The reader will not find anything too avant-garde here as progress in this direction has been tentative and cautious. Besides, the planning laws endeavour to protect the ambience and integrity of what is still essentially an 18th century to early 20th century city by imposing certain restrictions, for example, on maximum heights. A revised interpretation on building height regulations is due soon, especially in reference to developing dockland areas and to other areas beyond the core city.

Above: The archway over the goods entrance to the former Kennans Ironworks, on Fishamble Street, is one of Dublin's most revered cultural landmarks. It was here, behind the arch, that stood the Music Hall wherein George Frederick Handel conducted the world premiere of his oratorio "Messiah". Every year, since 1991, on the anniversary of that performance, 13 April, at midday, Our Lady's Choral Society performs extracts from the "Messiah" in front of the arch. Unfortunately, in March 2000 the arch became unstable during construction work on apartments behind it and had to be dismantled. It has since been faithfully reinstated by TBP and will again be a backdrop to the yearly performance of Handel's masterpiece. The composer himself is commemorated by a sculpture, commissioned by TBP, in a courtyard setting behind the arch. The sculptor was Laurent Mellet.

Left: Dublin's newest street, Cow's Lane, was opened in mid-2000 and runs through the Old City, the last residential development to be undertaken by Temple Bar Properties. Five different schemes, each designed by a different firm of architects, make up the complex.

Above: The new Citibank Headquarters building in the International Financial Services Centre (IFSC) is situated along the North Wall Quay directly overlooking the River Liffey. Citibank, part of the Citigroup Corporation, set up its first Dublin office at No.1 Dawson Street in 1965 before moving two years later to St Stephen's Green. A strong advocate of the IFSC from the beginning, Citibank opened a presence there, with 89 staff, in 1993. Competing successfully with other cities abroad, Dublin was subsequently chosen as Citibank's second main Processing and Servicing Centre for Europe. A search for a suitable site began. Eventually, in what was a major boost to the Phase II extension of the IFSC, Citibank purchased a .9ha (2.25 acres) waterfront site and commenced building in April 1998. At approximately 34,600sq m (372,570sq ft) gross floor area and six storeys high, it was the largest single project to date in the IFSC and allowed the bank to centralise its widely dispersed staff and to provide ample room for further growth. With a potential for almost 2,000 staff, the landmark building was ready for full occupation in mid-2000.

Right: An interior view of the impressive West Atrium of Citibank's new office building in the IFSC. The building's open-plan floors are arranged between two full-height landscaped atria which permit natural daylight to flood through from the structural glass walls and the glazed prismatic roofs. The angled main entrance, which leads into the West Atrium, has the effect of creating a large civic space at the corner of the North Wall Quay and Commons Street and gives the building a focus on the river frontage. The external finishes of Ballyknockan (Co. Wicklow) granite and white aluminium were selected and designed having regard to the surrounding office blocks. Citibank's Corporate Realty Services undertook the project management and real estate management of the project. Architects for the scheme were Scott Tallon Walker. Construction was handled by Pierse Contracting Ltd. and Arup Consulting Engineers.

Photo: courtesy of Citibank

230

Above: The drab exterior of the old ESB stores and workshops facing Erne Street before their remodelling.

Above: The Winter Garden on Erne Street/Pearse Street was one of Dublin's first successful conversions from a large warehouse to an apartment block. The former Electricity Supply Board (ESB) stores and workshops, standing on a 1.1ha (2.5 acres) site were converted into offices (for WorldCom) at the corner of Erne Street and Hanover Street, 183 apartments and a hotel (on Pierce Street for the Holiday Inn Group). The building of this scheme in the mid-1990s provided a major stimulus to the renewal of Pearse Street which had been gradually descending into a run-down condition. The Holiday Inn opened in 1998 with the complete development finishing a year later. The architects were O'Dwyer & Associates, consulting engineers were Carew Associates and the main contractor was Ellen Construction. The site was developed by a consortium which included the Flynn Property Partnership and developer Tony Tyrell.

Below: An internal view of the central area of the ESB engineering workshops and stores just prior to their conversion. The roofing was subsequently stripped from over the retained metal trusses and replaced throughout with glazing. Dating from the 1930s, the reinforced concrete building lent itself ideally for adaptation to large loft-style apartments with much higher than average floor-to-ceiling heights-from 3.3m (11ft) to 4m (13ft).

Below: The entrances to the Winter Garden apartments lead off from the spacious glazed central atrium. The apartments also have access to eight landscaped open courtyards.

Above: Malahide Marina Village as seen from the original Malahide Village. Over 14km (9 miles) north of Dublin, Malahide has been settled since ancient times and was given in 1176 by King Henry II to one of his knights, Sir Richard Talbot, whose descendants remained at Malahide Castle until 1976.

Image: courtesy of Alcove Properties

Above: A view of the east side of Charlemont Street during the initial stages of redevelopment by Alcove Properties. Long derelict, the street received its first uplift when the Cosgrave Property Group recently completed a range of new apartments.

Photo: courtesy Peter Barrow Photography

Above: Malahide Marina Village, developed between 1992 and 1999, was Ireland's first major residential marina scheme. Seán Reilly, of developers McGarrell Reilly, showed extraordinary foresight in acquiring the 4ha (10 acres) site, much of which had to be reclaimed from the sea. This was a time of high inflation and economic belt-tightening and most pundits doubted the viability of an apartment scheme so far outside the city centre. In the event, Malahide Marina Village has gone from strength to strength and the 404-apartment development is a much-sought-after location. Architects for the residential element were Conroy Crowe Kelly and the main contractors were Fajon Construction Ltd. The actual marina, with around 400 berths, was a separate development. The site was originally occupied by the Malahide Boatyard, which closed in 1972.

Above left: An image of the refurbished and extended Iveagh Court, an office block off Harcourt Road. The original block's façade was re-clad in GRC (Glassfibre Reinforced Concrete), a lightweight and attractive panel made from alkali-resistant glassfibre, a cement and sand mix and faced with an integrally bonded reconstructed stone finish. Materials such as GRC allow older out-of-date façades to be given better insulation and a more modern appearance. Iveagh Court is owned by Alcove Properties, a development company controlled by Seán Reilly.

Left: A view of the original Iveagh Court office block before refurbishment commenced in 1999.

Below: Alcove Properties' new project on Harcourt Road and Charlemont Street includes the preservation and intergration of a listed Georgian house which will become a focal point of the office scheme, offering period-featured reception rooms. The new buildings, designed by Arthur Gibney and Partners, will be linked to Iveagh Court (see above) and will comprise 23,225sq m (250,000sq ft) of office and residential accommodation.

Image: courtesy of Alcove Properties

232

Above: Developed and built by Capel Developments, Riverpark enjoys a view to the River Liffey on its south side and to the Wellington Monument and the Phoenix Park on its north-facing side. Work commenced in 1999 and the third and final phase is due to be completed by December 2000. Aided by sloping ground, the apartment blocks will range in height from four storeys along Conyngham Road to eight storeys fronting on to the river. Paul Brazil & Associates were the architects. The railway line to the left of the photograph, linking Heuston and Connolly Stations by a circuitous route, is shown entering a tunnel under the Phoenix Park.

Left: Constrained by the elevated railway and Spring Garden Lane, the resulting triangular site acquired for the Service Centre of the Educational Building Society was brilliantly utilised by the architects, Turlough O'Donnell Associates. The angle at Townsend Street, shown in the photograph, is particularly acute. A landscaped courtyard, partially used for car parking, also features the restored bricked arches of the railway viaduct. When the EBS had this site developed in 1987 there was nothing but dereliction all around. By contrast the unique building now stands with distinction among a host of modern developments. The main contractor was John Sisk & Son.

Top: Once hailed as the largest office block in the world (as regards the ground floor area), the Irish Hospital Sweepstakes' buildings, built in the 1930s, occupied a large site in Ballsbridge opposite to the Royal Dublin Society Showgrounds.

Above: Following the demise of the Irish Hospitals Sweepstakes in the 1980s the site was redeveloped from 1990 into the Sweepstakes Apartments (developer-the Cosgrave Property Group, architect-Frank Elmes) and into offices, The Sweepstakes Centre (developer-Ryde Developments, architects-Gilroy McMahon)

Below: The Bar Council Headquarters on Church Street was completed in 1998. As this is a very historic site, an archaeological survey was carried out before building commenced. Some of the earlier finds included an 11th or 12th century boundary ditch, possibly belonging to St Michan's Church. The ditch contained eight bodies dating from the same period.

Above: This site on Lower Mount Street was a derelict gap for many years and was acquired in the late 1980s by Aranas, a Swedish company. It engaged architects A & D Wejchert to design a prestigious building which would not only repair the gap in the street but would also blend in with the Georgian composition of the houses towards Merrion Square while reflecting the modern character of the adjoining Grattan House. Granite and brick form the main constituents of the façade while white-coloured steel forms the projecting curtain wall as well as the balconies and balustrades. The building contractor was P. J. Walls.

Below: An interior view of the main atrium of the Bar Council Headquarters on Church Street. The new building was strikingly married to the rubble stone walls of the former grain store of Jameson's whiskey distillery. Private rooms for nearly 180 barristers are included in the scheme as well as accommodation for an international arbitration centre and a legal library. The project team included architects, Brian O'Halloran & Associates and main contractor, C. Bennett & Sons.

Dublin City University (DCU) started life as the National Institute for Higher Education (NIHE) when it opened in the Glasnevin premises of the former Albert College in 1980. Dr Daniel O'Hare was appointed as first Director. The NIHE was formally inaugurated as Dublin City University when it was elevated to full university status on 29 September 1989. Student numbers have risen from 200 in 1980 to over 7,000 by 2000 and they are continuing to rise with the ongoing introduction of new and extended facilities. Known principally for its science, technological and business courses and for its links with industry through a vast array of research and development projects, DCU entered a new phase when it became, in 1999, the headquarters and main centre for the state-funded National Academy for the Performing Arts.

Image: courtesy of A & D Wejchert Architects

Above: The interior of the main concert hall in DCU's new Performing Arts Centre and Aula Maxima. The concert hall, with a capacity for 1,250 people, has retractable seating so that it may be adapted for a variety of uses including graduation ceremonies, examinations, banquets, trade exhibitions and other events. The stage is designed to accommodate a large orchestra. To facilitate patrons arriving for public performances the neighbouring five-storey car park is directly linked to the Arts Centre by an underground passage.

Photo: courtesy of A & D Wejchert Architects

Above: The new Performing Arts Centre currently being built at DCU will be a multi-use performance centre incorporating a concert hall venue (the RTE Concert Orchestra will be based here) and two theatres and will also couple with its university function as an Aula Maxima and Examination Hall. The building, acting as a link between DCU and the wider community, stands as a visual gateway to the university in its prominent location near the entrance to the campus. The use of granite cladding sets it apart as a public venue from the other brick-faced academic buildings. The Performing Arts Centre/Aula Maxima was designed by A & D Wejchert Architects.

Above: The School of Biological, Mathematical and Chemical Sciences completed in 1998.

Below: The masterplan of DCU, prepared by Anthony Reddy Associates, shows the extent of the building programme. In 1980 the college consisted solely of the original Albert College buildings. The first major addition, the Henry Grattan Building, was opened in 1982. It would seem quite likely in the future that more land in the neighbourhood will have to be purchased to accommodate the burgeoning campus.

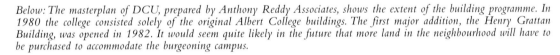

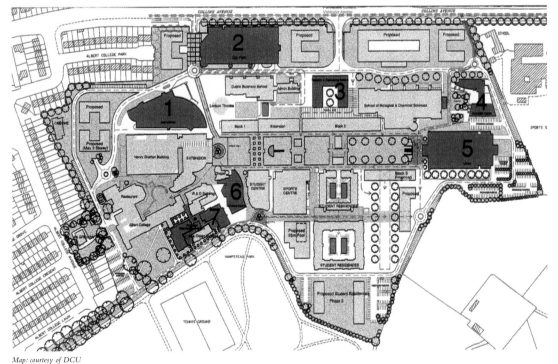

Map: courtesy of DCU

Above: DCU is built on the grounds of the former Albert College, a 19th century institution which commenced in 1838 as an agricultural college and from 1926 served as the Faculty of Agricultural Science of University College Dublin. The college, was named in honour of Prince Albert when he paid a visit there in 1853.

Photo: courtesy of Ray McManus, Sportsfile

Above: The completed new stand on the site of the former Cusack Stand. It was officially opened in June 1996 and represented the completion of Phase One of the redevelopment of Croke Park. Phase Two (the Canal End) is due for completion in 2000 and Phase Three (the Hogan Stand site) is expected to be fully operational in 2002 when Croke Park will then have seating for around 80,000 spectators. It was remarkable that no playing season was lost during any stage of the construction which was the single largest building and financial project ever undertaken by an Irish sporting organisation. The main contractor is John Sisk & Son.

Top: A 1999 perspective of Croke Park. On the left is the Hogan Stand (named after Michael Hogan who was shot dead, while playing for Tipperary, along with twelve other people, in November 1920 in a reprisal attack by British forces) before it too fell to the demolition squads in autumn of the same year.

Above: The new stand curving around from the Canal End (that part of the stadium closest to the Royal Canal) and beginning to reach the site of the old Hogan Stand. The photograph was taken in late summer 2000.

Founded in 1884, the Gaelic Athletic Association (GAA or, in Irish, Cumann Lúthchleas Gael) is Ireland's largest sporting and cultural organisation (see appendix D). Croke Park, the headquarters of the GAA, has been a sportsground since the 1870s when it was known as the City and Suburban Racecourse. The GAA frequently used the grounds and in 1895 two All-Ireland finals were played here. In 1908 this 5.6ha (14 acres) Jones Road site was bought for £3,250 by Frank Dineen, a GAA supporter, who hoped that the grounds would one day become a major venue for the Association's games. His foresight was validated when, in 1913, the GAA purchased the property from him for £3,500. (1.6ha [4 acres] had already been sold to the Jesuit Fathers of Belvedere College to help service Dineen's loan). At that time the grounds possessed just two small stands and over the next 45 years Croke Park (named after Archbishop Croke, first patron of the GAA) was developed and re-developed in an ad hoc manner as finances permitted. Hill 16 was constructed in 1917 from the rubble of buildings destroyed in Sackville (O'Connell) Street as a result of the 1916 Rebellion. The first Hogan Stand was built in 1924 followed by the Cusack Stand in 1937. The Hogan Stand was subsequently rebuilt between 1957 and 1959.

Above: The Cusack Stand (named after Michael Cusack, a founder of the GAA) shortly before its demolition. By 1987 Croke Park was in a seriously deteriorating condition and recent legislation was making new demands to improve public safety. A decision was then made to comprehensively reconstruct the stadium. The obsolete and by now dangerous Hill 16 was rebuilt and opened in 1988. A design team, which included Gilroy McMahon Architects and structural engineers, Horgan & Lynch, produced plans for an impressive new horseshoe-shaped stand which would replace the Cusack Stand, the Canal End terracing and the Hogan Stand. It was then estimated that the venture would cost in the region of £110 million and a substantial portion of this revenue has since been raised by leasing out corporate hospitality suites and pre-selling premier seating for periods of five to ten years. Grant-aid was also received from the Government.

Photo: courtesy of ARC Digital Photo Graphic

Left: In 1998 Green Property purchased the former ACC Bank headquarters building on Upper Hatch Street (built 1972) and immediately set about refurbishing it to the highest modern specifications. Architects Gilroy McMahon remodelled the previously gloomy and outdated façade and thus created an imposing and bright city centre landmark. The frontage of mostly green-tinted glass is deliberately transparent to allow the public to see in as much as for the staff to see out. The stone used is composed of warm Spanish granite. The curve at the corner softly joins modern Upper Hatch Street with (mostly) Georgian Harcourt Street. The building was renamed Styne House in memory of the river of the same name which used to flow nearby but is now absorbed into the public drainage system. John Sisk & Son was the main contractor.

Photo: courtesy of Green Property

Left: The striking atrium of one of the twin six-storey office buildings, designed by Horan Keogan Ryan, currently being developed by Green Property at Sandyford. Designed to provide an airy and light-infused interior, the atria will also serve as a social amenity for staff and visitors. The development is appropriately called The Atrium.

Image: courtesy of A & D Wejchert Architects

Above: This interior view of Beresford Court shows the spacious first floor atrium which is dramatically approached by a staircase from the street level. In a winter garden setting the atrium provides a central hub to the two main wings of the building and also houses a coffee area for staff and visitors, an exhibition hall and a waiting area for the adjoining conference rooms. A continuous band of reflecting mirrors, running as a frieze just below roof level, projects the illusion of the roof floating in space without visible supports.

Above: Beresford Court seen from Beresford Place. Both places are named after John Beresford (1738-1805), Chief Commissioner of Revenue and the inspiration behind the building of the Custom House. The original building on this site was demolished after the 1916 Easter Rising. It was followed by a warehouse for the Clery's department store which in turn was levelled to make way for Beresford Court. Completed in 1991 for Irish Life Assurance, Beresford Court makes a noble statement at the pivotal corner of Beresford Place and Abbey Street. A & D Wejchert were the architects and P.J. Walls Ltd carried out the construction.

Below: The Irish Life Centre on Lower Abbey Street, a mixture of retail, offices, apartments and an underground public car park, was begun in 1973 and was built in several phases before being completed in the late 1980s. It was the first such integrated scheme in Dublin and represented a bold move for its developers, Irish Life Assurance. It also represented a commitment by the company to the city centre, especially to the northside, when many others refused to invest there and prefered to move out to Ballsbridge and other near-suburban, mostly southside, locations.

Image: courtesy of A & D Wejchert Architects

Above: The ILAC Shopping Centre was built in 1981 over an existing warren of narrow streets and back lanes. Due in part to a then difficult economic climate the original ambitious plans for the centre were never realised and it essentially remained as a single-storey building more appropriate to a suburban location than to a city centre street. ILAC's owners, Irish Life Assurance plc, decided, in 1997, to refurbish and enlarge the centre. A & D Wejchert Architects won an invitation architectural design competition and following their plans all the malls will be raised to increase volume and to add another retail floor. The external elevations will be refurbished or rebuilt and new entrance pavilions will improve the image and identity of the complex (the photomontage shows the new Mary Street entrance). As part of the scheme around 250 apartments and a new Dublin Corporation Central Library will be built over the centre at the corner of Moore Street and Parnell Street (see page 245).

Photo: courtesy of GE Capital Woodchester

Above: A view towards Golden Lane (and the present site of GE Capital Woodchester) in the 1950s. The street, which has a history dating back to at least the 14th century, was named after the Guild of Goldsmiths, although the Goldsmiths' Hall did not locate to the street itself until 1815 and then only remained there until 1839. John Field, (1782-1837) composer and originator of the Nocturne style of piano composition, was born in Golden Lane.

Above: The management of GE Capital Woodchester were both courageous and far-seeing when they moved their headquarters in the early 1980s to Golden Lane. Although only a short distance from St Stephen's Green the area was then considered to be out of fashion, to say the least. But that has all turned around and real estate values have since soared in the neighbourhood. Built in four different phases between 1981 and 1998 by G & T Crampton, Woodchester House forms an interesting and varied streetscape on Golden Lane. The interior is very environmentally-friendly. Rather than employing straight-forward air conditioning, the heating, cooling and air circulation systems are efficiently and economically enhanced by the interior design of the building, by the fabrics used in its construction, by the automatic or manual-override opening and closing of vents and windows and by the beneficial effects of a large and lush internal garden. The architects were W. Kenneth Hunt & Associates, for the phases during 1981-1996, and Scott Tallon Walker for the more recent additions.

Below: The north docklands had initially been blighted by poverty originating from the notoriously unfair system of employing casual labour for the docks and the railways in the early 20th century. The organisation of trade unions offered some protection and stability from the 1920s but the introduction of containerisation and bulk-handling of cargoes from the 1960s and the lack of alternative local industry brought back the spectre of unemployment on a wide scale to the dockland suburbs. Additionally, the massing of social housing in the area further disadvantaged the district. The DDDA policy of social integration is beginning to bring significant benefits in improved housing, environment upgrading and enhanced personal career and educational opportunities to the local population. Bordered by Commons Street, Manor Street, Guild Street and Sheriff Street, Custom House Square, a major apartment development in Phase 2 of the IFSC, represents part of a major turnaround for an area previously rather depressed and run-down. Project architects for Custom House Square were Anthony Reddy & Associates and John Paul Construction built the complex on behalf of Chesterfield Developments Ltd.

Image: courtesy of Archimedia Studios Ltd

Above: Grand Canal Plaza took full advantage of its position on the canal as the waterway makes a curve on its way to the Grand Canal Docks. Developed by Rohan Holdings Ltd., the office block complex was designed by Burke-Kennedy Doyle and completed in early 2000.

Below right: East Point, the first high-tech development of its type in Ireland, is unique in a number of ways, not least for its splendid location. Only 2.5km (1.5 miles) from O'Connell Street, it is surrounded on two sides by the River Tolka Estuary and the waters of Dublin Bay. This estuary used to lie much nearer to the River Liffey until the building of the North Wall and land reclamation in the 18th century forced the Tolka to bend northwards. Comprising a site area of circa 13.75ha (34 acres), the first phase of East Point (8.5ha/20.5 acres) was completed in 1999, whereupon the second phase was immediately started. Part of the heavily landscaped site has been reserved for the portals of the Dublin Port Tunnel. The developers were Dermot Pierce & Associates and Scott Tallon Walker Architects provided the designs.

A characteristic of Dublin's suburbanisation is the rapid growth of industrial and business parks on the city's outskirts. From the 1960s, the increased level of industrialisation and commercial activity could no longer be accommodated in traditional back-lane premises or in cramped or outdated factories and warehouses. Green-field sites were selected to build, at first, rather functional and tacky industrial estates of poor visual quality. As traffic congestion increased these developments moved ever further away from the city to gain easier access to an expanding roadway and motorway network. By the 1990s a new generation of industrial estate emerged which paid as much attention to high-specification architecture and creative landscaping as to mere floor area capacity. More grandly titled as industrial parks, business campuses or science and technology parks, these new complexes began to attract not just manufacturing or distribution firms but also corporate headquarters, call centres, service centres, research establishments, electronic enterprises, telecommunication and financial services. Altogether, there are approximately 180 of these business centres, old and new, scattered around the city with several new ones in the building or planning stage, especially on sites near the airport and the M50 motorway.

Image: courtesy of Park West

Above: A 24m (79ft) high structure, which glows internally at night, is the signature tower sculpture for the campus at the Park West Business Park. It was designed by Michelle Fagan following an international competition organised by Esat Digifone and Park West.

Right: Park West, the 91ha (225 acres) site on the M50/Naas Road Interchange is currently Ireland's largest business campus and is mainly aimed at the IT industry. It features a wide range of sculptures and landscape designs. Developed by Harcourt Developments, Park West expects to employ up to 25,000 people. The first company opened in the park in April 1999.

Image: courtesy of Park West

Chapter Seventeen

The Shape of Things to Come

IT WOULD be impossible to predict what Dublin will look like in ten years time, just as ten years ago nobody could possibly have imagined the unprecedented building and restoration programmes now presently in full swing. The economy, which is fueling the boom, is likely to still forge ahead but, as has happened before, some world crisis could throw it off course. The city is becoming truly cosmopolitan and this welcome trend has built up its own momentum and seems irreversible. Easier access into and out of Dublin, both physically and through communications technology, has removed forever the notion of island isolation. Dublin is a world capital. The population of the Greater Dublin Area (Dublin city and county and the surrounding counties of Meath, Kildare and Wicklow) is set to nearly double to around 2 million by at least 2015. Most of the extra people will live within the present limits of the so-called Metropolitan Area, a fact that will concentrate minds to provide an adequate public transport system. The Government recently unveiled plans for several metro lines which will operate in conjunction with a new light rail network already at the preliminary construction stage (the upgrading of public transport throughout the state is a core ingredient in the £40 billion National Development Plan). City centre apartments, unknown a decade ago, have become fashionable for single people and couples but future designs will have to address the accommodation, social and leisure needs of families if the latter group is to be attracted into this style of living. Always a touchy point in Dublin, the question of high-rise, as to the limits of how high and where tall buildings can be located, is due to be shortly decided upon by Dublin Corporation.

Image: courtesy of Martyn Turner and The Irish Times
Above: A cartoon by Martyn Turner which appeared in The Irish Times in July 2000 when the Government announced plans for a metro system in Dublin.

Left: This map traces the growth of Dublin over the centuries. From relatively small beginnings the city has grown dramatically, particularly in the last thirty years. Over the next 10 years the increase in households will be even more dramatic than the increase in population (in 1991 an average of 3.4 people shared the same household, by 2011 it is anticipated that the figure will fall to 2.5). The hundreds of thousands of new homes that will be needed will not be allowed to sprawl ad infinitum into neighbouring counties. The so-called "footprint" or extent of Dublin's growth will be more or less kept to its present limits and development will be consolidated. This will mean greater densities and some high-rise where appropriate.

Above: An articulated bus, a common sight in many European cities, on trial on Dublin's streets in 2000. It is one of several measures regarding buses currently being examined to encourage commuters to leave their cars at home. A number of Quality Bus Corridors (QBCs) have already been introduced and more are planned. QBCs are dedicated lanes allocated exclusively to buses and taxis along continuous stretches of road during certain times of the day.

Above: Two trams on the Hill of Howth line which was regrettably closed (as seen with hindsight) in 1959. One of these venerable vehicles has been lovingly restored and is now on view in the National Transport Museum based at Howth Castle.

Right: The sleek lines of a modern tram. This type, made by the Spanish company, Alstom S.A., was ordered for the LUAS light rail system in August 2000. Each tram unit can carry 235 persons and will operate at 5-minute intervals during peak hours. The lines will be run by a Public Private Partnership operator.

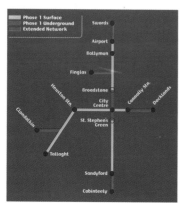

Image: courtesy of the Light Rail Project Office

Image: courtesy of ARC Digital Photo Graphic

Above: An artist's impression of the entrances to the proposed Port Tunnel. The scheme will provide a dual-carriageway tunnel, 4.5km (2.8 miles) long, from the M1 (at a point between the Coolock Lane Interchange and Whitehall) to Dublin Port (the exit will be adjacent to the East Point Business Park). When fully operational the tunnel will bring many benefits including the removal of the majority of heavy trucks from inner-city streets by conducting this traffic directly from the port to the M1 and the M50 motorways.

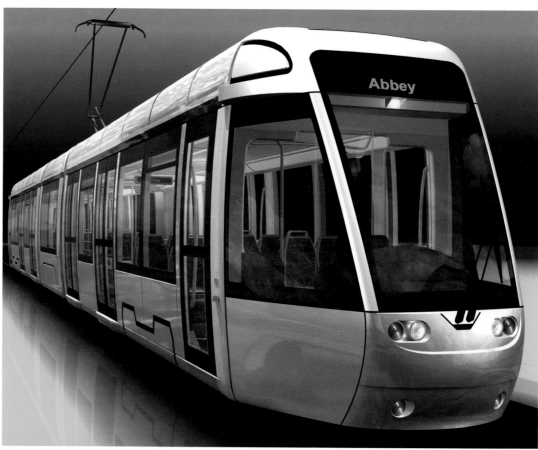

Image: courtesy of the Light Rail Project Office

Left: A diagram of the proposed LUAS (the Irish for "Speed") Light Rail network. By 1990 somewhat of a stalemate had arisen regarding the transport issue in Dublin. In May of that year the Department of Engineering at Trinity College, under Dr Simon Perry, organised a symposium on the feasibility for light rail transit in Dublin. Consequent to this, the Dublin City Centre Business Association set up a working group "People First – Dublin Initiative" to provide an authoritative voice on behalf of the city centre business community and other interested parties on matters relating to transport and the promotion of a living city. By 1991 the group had successfully placed the introduction of a light rail system firmly on the political agenda. In April 1994 the Government-sponsored Dublin Transport Initiative proposed a three-branch system linking Tallaght, Ballymun and Cabinteely to the city centre. Various delays then ensued, some revolving around the later decision to put the St Stephen's Green to Broadstone section of the line underground. The end of 2002 should see LUAS running on at least one of the lines.

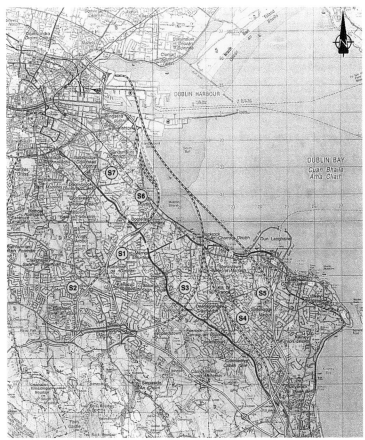

Above: A map of seven possible alternative routes for the proposed Eastern bypass. One of the objectives of such a bypass is to connect both ends of the C-ring (M50) of Dublin to provide an orbital motorway around the city.

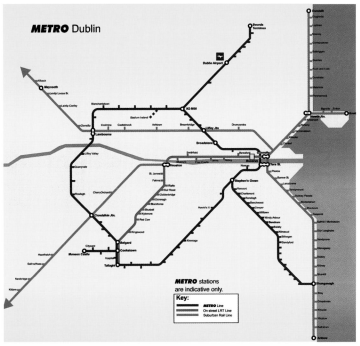

Above: In July 2000 the Government approved in principle the development of a £4.3 billion metro system for Dublin. To be developed on a Public Private Partnership basis, the metro will be different to light rail (LUAS) in that it will operate on a fully segregated (from road traffic) alignment and will include tunnelling where required. Metro trains, running at one-minute frequencies, can carry up to 56,000 passengers per hour in one direction compared to 6,500 passengers for LUAS (at 3-minute intervals). A Quality Bus Corridor can transport an average of 5,000 passengers per hour. The metro, due for completion in the next 10 to 15 years, will integrate with DART, Suburban Rail, Main Rail, LUAS and the Quality Bus Corridors.

Above: Liberty Hall, opened in 1965 as the head office of the Irish Transport and General Workers Union (now SIPTU), has not borne its age well. Still the city's tallest office building, at seventeen storeys, it will likely lose this distinction before too long. Some fairly major refurbishment to the adjoining annexe on Eden Quay is shortly due to commence but the union will ultimately have to consider a recladding to the tower itself. As the service well (lifts, stairwell etc.) takes up an inordinate amount of room compared to available floor space, some outward extension seems to be called for. The union would prefer to do this rather than move elsewhere as they have been here since 1912 and feel historically bound to the site.

Above: This proposed redevelopment at Mespil Road and Burlington Road will see the demolition of the former headquarters of the Blood Transfusion Service Board on Mespil Road, a building erected in the 1970s. Many such blocks, dating from the 1960s and 70s, will be demolished or redesigned in the future to make way for more up-to-date and better finished buildings. This particular example was designed by Henry J. Lyons for Treasury Holdings.

Image: courtesy of The National College of Ireland

Above: A computer-generated image of the new National College of Ireland (NCI) building currently being constructed in the centre of the Phase Two development of the International Financial Services Centre on Dublin's North Docklands. The presence of a third-level college campus in the IFSC will not only greatly enhance NCI's own mission to increase access, opportunity and excellence in education to people of all ages and backgrounds but will also add a welcome extra dimension to the life and activity of a mainly commercial and residential district. The NCI, established at Ranelagh in 1951 as a non-profit institution and known then as the National College of Industrial Relations, offers a wide range of full-time and part-time courses to over 5,000 students (12% of students are full time and 80% are part-time, many of whom are working adults ranging in age from 17 to 70). Around half of its student body attend 40 off-campus centres and a growing number study on-line. The courses are arranged through NCI's two constituent schools, the School of Business and Humanities and The School of Informatics. Designed by Burke-Kennedy Doyle, the new Docklands' campus is expected to be open in 2002.

Below left: Grangegorman Mental Hospital, now known as St Brendan's Hospital, was established in 1816. The large buildings (the earliest were designed by Francis Johnston) and the expansive tracts of land surrounding the hospital are no longer needed as the treatment of mental illness is now more community-based. The Dublin Institute of Technology (DIT), the country's largest third-level institution, on the other hand, is grievously short of space. Its 22,000 students are scattered around the city in 23 different locations, often in cramped or unsuitable accommodation. Judging the 26.3ha (65 acres) site of St Brendan's to be the perfect location for a central DIT college campus, negotiations have opened for its purchase from the Eastern Regional Health Authority (the ERHA will retain some of the lands to develop modern special care facilities). When the property is, as expected, sold to the DIT, the institution will relocate several faculties to Grangegorman in addition to the transfer of its central administration and support services. The proposed new campus will be very conveniently located next to the planned LUAS station at Broadstone. The student population would also bring new life to the north-west inner city and to the nearby Smithfield area.

Below right: Hundreds of apartments as well as offices, shops, restaurants, hotels and a multi-storey car park will form around Millennium Square, the new premier public space for Tallaght. The square will act as the hub for the town centre and will also function as a major area for outdoor events. One side of the square is already partly in place, the north line is enclosed by the South Dublin County Council Headquarters and the Civic Theatre. The west entrance into the square will be the terminus for the LUAS line, already in the preliminary stages of construction. Millennium Square will be jointly developed by the South Dublin County Council and the owners of The Square Shopping Centre.

Image: courtesy of the DIT

Image: courtesy of the South Dublin County Council

Above: As part of the North East Inner City Integrated Area Plan (NEIC IAP) there is a proposal to open a new street between Talbot Street (near the railway bridge) and Foley Street.

Above: This proposed new scheme at Smithfield, if it goes ahead in this or similar form, would wonderfully reinstate the west side of the civic space and it will also complement the Heritage Properties' development on the opposite side. It is intended to build around 400 apartments in a range of six and seven-storey buildings and in the 23-storey tower, the latter being specially floodlit at night. Offices, retail outlets and cultural venues (including a children's museum) are also planned for the complex. A new curved street between this scheme and a neighbouring development will link Smithfield to Queen Street. Developers for the Smithfield project are Fusano Properties, a consortium composed of Linders (car dealers based at Smithfield), the Flynn Property Partnership and Paddy Kelly. The architects are Horan Keogan Ryan.

Below: Although the planning application is currently on hold, at least until Dublin Corporation completes its high buildings study and publishes its recommendations, this artist's impression gives an idea of the kind of designs that are now being promoted for large sites. This particular scheme is being mooted by developer Bernard McNamara, CIE and Trinity College and would, if built, provide extra space for the college, a completely revamped Pearse Station for CIE as well as offices, apartments and a hotel. It was designed by international architects Pei Cobb Freed. To the left of Westland Row, Trinity College is already building an underground sports centre and a group of lecture halls. The intention here is to open a new courtyard style entrance to the college campus from Westland Row. The underground concourse will be daylit through a glazed cone-shaped pavilion which was also designed by Pei Cobb Freed, the same designers of the Louvre Pyramid in Paris.

Above: An outline view of the proposed ILAC retail and apartment development at the corner of Moore Street and Parnell Street. The scheme will include prestigious new premises for Dublin Corporation's Central Library and its entrance will have the effect of creating an urban corner of some civic importance.

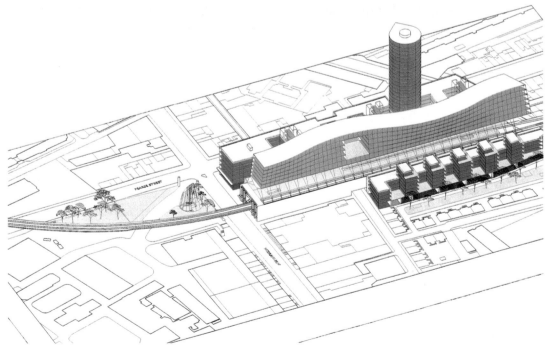

Above: An intended mixed-use development at the top end of Gardiner Street Lower.

Right: The Marine School, quaintly named the Hibernian Nursery for the Support and Education of the Orphans and Children of Mariners, was opened on Sir John Rogerson's Quay in 1773. The institution prepared boys for service with the Merchant Marine or the Royal Navy. Following a fire in 1872, the Marine School moved out and the building fulfilled a variety of uses, mostly as a warehouse. The present owner, James E. Carroll Ltd. Haulage Contractors, in association with developers John Flynn and Paddy Kelly, are planning to build offices and apartments on the 1.1ha (2.7 acres) site. The scheme will include the preservation of the last remaining archway of the old Marine School. The design was handled by Burke-Kennedy Doyle.

Above: An image of the National Conference and Exhibition Centre, the celebrated centrepiece of the 20.2ha (50 acres) Spencer Dock scheme. The Conference Centre itself, designed by Irish-born, US-based architect, Kevin Roche, had received planning permission but an Bord Pleanála turned down the planning application in mid-2000 for most of the rest of the scheme. As Spencer Dock is so pivotal to the overall development of the north docks a revised plan is expected from the developers, a consortium led by Treasury Holdings and CIE.

Above: This proposed additional bridge across the River Liffey will link Blackhall Place with Usher's Island. Spanish architect and engineer, Santiago Calatrava, was commissioned by Dublin Corporation to carry out the design.

Above right: Santiago Calatrava was also invited to design this graceful bridge which is intended to connect Guild Street and Macken Street. Still awaiting Ministerial approval, the structure, if and when built, will be a cable-stayed construction with a span of 120m (394 ft) between the north and south quay walls. It will swing open on a rotation mechanism to allow the passage of ships.

PROPOSED DEVELOPMENT AT SIR JOHN ROGERSONS QUAY

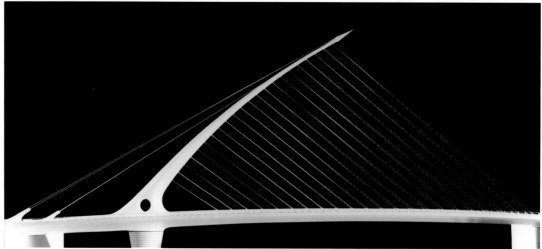

Often, while living through a momentous event or period its significance or consequence will be unheeded or unobserved. It may only be after due reflection or through the distance of elapsed time that the enormity of a given circumstance can be digested and evaluated. The tremendous changes that are currently happening in and to Dublin cannot fail to be noticed but may indeed be difficult to take in. Rejuvenation and renewal, new construction and expansion are materialising on so vast a scale that no other period in the city's long and noble history can begin to compare with the present. The flurries of growth and adornment in the past have, of course, left us enormous legacies but were often followed by decades of depression and melancholy. Perhaps this was due in part to the colonial status of Dublin and to the city's susceptibility to the whims of the Empire. After almost eighty years of independent nationhood Ireland's capital is at last reaping the rewards of a booming economy. The finances are now available to provide the level of infrastructure necessary to enable Dublin to function efficiently as a modern, thriving metropolis and, at the same time, to enhance the heritage of the past while creating the environment and structures that will enrich the lives of people now and into the future. That Dublin will worthily rise to this challenge can only be judged by future generations.

Appendix A
Residents of Note

DUBLIN IS famous the world over for its coterie of renowned writers. Not so celebrated, perhaps, are the legions of scientists, doctors, church people, innovators, sports people, explorers, actors, business people, entertainers, soldiers and others who have made enormous contributions in their own chosen fields and have achieved international acclaim. Some will have been mentioned already in the preceding chapters but this appendix is an opportunity to salute a few more, both living and dead, who have imprinted an indelible mark on history or have, in one way or another, enriched the lives of "ordinary" mortals.

Above, below & left: A year after Oscar Fingal O'Flahertie Wills Wilde (1854-1900) was born at 21 Westland Row (above) the family moved to No.1 Merrion Square (below). The statue to Oscar Wilde in Merrion Square Park (left) stands opposite his childhood home (for information on the statue see page 257).

Above: Number 15, Marino Crescent was the birthplace in 1847 of Abraham (Bram) Stoker, the author of one of the world's most chilling novels, "Dracula". Although loosely based on the macabre and cruel character of Vlad Tepes or Vlad the Impaler, a 15th century prince of Wallachia in Transylvania, a region also renowned for stories of vampires and werewolves, Stoker had plenty of material to draw on from early and contemporary Irish history. The Great Famine (1845-47) and subsequent cholera outbreaks fuelled many stories of horror and of people being buried alive. In Celtic times storytellers passed on dreadful tales of the "undead", those who were destined to wander the earth forever seeking the blood of others. These ghouls were known to have had bad blood or, in Gaelic, droch fhola (pronounced as druc ula!).

Above: James Gandon (1743-1823), Dublin's best known architect, was, in fact, born in London. After a long, fruitful and noble life he was buried, by his own request, in the simple grave of his life-long friend, Francis Grose, in Drumcondra Cemetery. The inscription reads: "Such was the respect in which Gandon was held by his neighbours and friends from around his home at Lucan that they refused carriages and walked the 25kms (16 miles) to and from Drumcondra on the day of his funeral. Gandon, who left supreme magnificence in the city, is now somewhat neglected in death and deserves a more fitting tribute at his final resting place than a simple weather-worn gravestone.

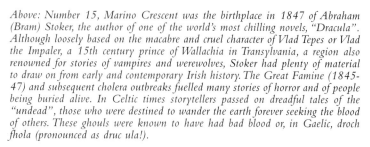

Above: On 2 February 1882, James Joyce was born in No. 41 Brighton Square to Corkman, John Stanislaus Joyce and his Longford wife, Mary Jane Murray. The family fortunes soon dipped considerably due to the regular inebriation of John Stanislaus and young James was to know nine more addresses in Dublin before he struck out on his own. All this wandering helped to steep Joyce in the geography of Dublin, a necessary prerequisite for the topographical descriptions that were to follow in his great novels including "Ulysses" and "Finnegans Wake".

Above: For many, despite considerable fame in their day, there is now little to remember them by. They have left no great legacy in literature, art or science, no institution bears their name, no statue commemorates their achievements. They might have been totally forgotten except for one thing - a city street named in their honour. One such person is John Fane, the 10th Earl of Westmoreland. He was Lord Lieutenant to Ireland 1790-94. In 1801, the Wide Streets Commissioners decided to name their new street leading off Carlisle (O'Connell) Bridge after the good earl, i.e. Westmoreland Street.

Above: Stephen Roche (born 1959) from Dundrum, Co Dublin became a professional racing cyclist in 1981 and quickly showed his mettle. He was the first cyclist ever to win the Grand Slam—the Tour de France, Tour d'Italia and the World Championship—in the same season, i.e. in 1987. He was awarded the Freedom of Dublin on his triumphant return to his native city.

Above: A plaque on No. 67 Upper Stephen Street bears the following inscription: "The first pneumatic tyre factory in the world was started here in 1889 to make tyres under John Boyd Dunlop's patent of 7 December 1888". Dunlop (1840-1921) was born in Ayrshire, Scotland and trained as a veterinary surgeon, commencing practice in Belfast. Always inventing things, he developed the world's first practical pneumatic tyre to help reduce the terrible jolting felt on solid-wheel bicycles. Shortly after the founding of the Stephen Street factory Dunlop sold his share in the company, thus unfortunately denying himself and his heirs the vast wealth which might have been theirs.

Above: Mount Temple Comprehensive School, off the Malahide Road on Dublin's northside, was the birthplace in 1976 of the world-famous band, U2. Drummer Larry Mullen founded the band by advertising on the school notice board for potential band members. The poster attracted Adam Clayton (bass guitar), Paul Hewson (vocals), and Dave Evans (guitar). Paul adopted the nickname Bono Vox (after a hearing aid), later shortened to Bono and Dave was called "The Edge", a reference to his guitar playing style. The band's first performance was under the name "Feedback" at a talent contest run by the school, which, incidentally, they failed to win but it was a popular entry. Changing their name to "Hype" the band struggled for attention and in an effort to get a more marketable name they settled on "U2" in 1978. The early years were difficult and major success was elusive. Their main coups were the hiring of Paul McGuinness as their manager and their association with Steve Lilywhite of the Island record company. Immensely successful hit singles and albums and world tours followed in the 1980s and '90s. Their position as one of the world's most popular and talented bands was confirmed in 1987 when "The Joshua Tree" became the fastest-selling album in British musical history. Their unique brand of music often reflects on issues such as human rights, the environment and world peace and they have actively supported famine relief and the peace process in Northern Ireland. The members of the band and Paul McGuinness were awarded the Freedom of Dublin in 2000.

Right: The Chieftains playing on the Great Wall of China in 1983. Formed in the early 1970s out of Ceoltóirí Chualann, a traditional music ensemble founded by Seán Ó Riada (1931-1971), the Chieftains went on to gain vast and enthusiastic audiences all over the world for Irish traditional music and are still going strong. Their collaboration with renowned international singers and musicians as well as writing and playing scores for several successful feature films has maintained their popularity and reputation at a high level. The current members are Paddy Moloney, Martin Fay, Seán Keane, Kevin Conneff, Derek Bell and Matt Molloy.

Above: The first Irish team owner to enter the high-octane world of Formula One motor racing was Eddie Jordan. The Jordan Grand Prix team was formed in 1991 and impressively finished in fifth position in the Constructor's Championship for its debut year. In 1999 the team convincingly won third place in the championship. Jordan, born in Dublin in 1948, gave up a career in banking when he was twenty-two years of age to take up kart racing, then successfully progressed through the various motor sport categories including Formula Ford, Formula 3 and Formula 2 before forming his own team, Eddie Jordan Racing, later to become Jordan Grand Prix.

Above: George Bernard Shaw (1856-1950) was born in No.22 Synge Street. He hadn't the happiest of childhoods with his less than abstemious father becoming estranged from his much younger wife. The young Shaw adored his mother and from her he cultivated a life-long interest in music. His first love in his adolescent years was art and he spent many happy hours in the National Gallery of Ireland. He generously repaid a debt of gratitude to the gallery by granting the institution a share in the royalties of one of his most successful plays "Pygmalion" and its spawn, the musical and film "My Fair Lady".

Above: Sandycove-born Captain J. C. Kelly-Rogers (1905-1981) graduated as a pilot in the Royal Air Force in 1927 and eight years later joined Imperial Airways (a forerunner of British Airways). He was put in charge of the flying boat division. To help establish non-stop transatlantic flights from the UK to America, Kelly-Rogers carried out the world's first in-flight refuelling tests in 1938. During the Second World War he was in command of the aircraft used to ferry Winston Churchill to and from the USA. In 1946 he inaugurated the first land-based scheduled services between London and New York. He received the Freedom of London for his services. In 1947 he joined Aer Lingus as technical manager, eventually becoming deputy general manager.

Above: The heart of St Laurence O'Toole, contained in a tiny casket, is venerated at a side chapel in Christ Church Cathedral. The saint was elected as Dublin's first archbishop in 1162. Closely allied to the Viking rulers of Dublin, O'Toole tried to parlay with the attacking Anglo-Normans in 1170 but to no avail. At first hostile towards them, he soon learned to accommodate himself to his new masters. He persuaded Strongbow, the Anglo-Norman leader in Dublin, to rebuild Christ Church Cathedral, which still stands today as a testimony to both men. O'Toole later fell out with Henry II and was banned from re-entering Ireland. He followed the king to Normandy to seek the lifting of the prohibition but died in Eu in 1180. The archbishop was canonised in 1226.

Above: Ayesha Castle, built in 1840 near Killiney, Co. Dublin, is the home of Eithne Ní Bhraonáin (Brennan), better known as Enya. She was a member of Clannad (Family), a Co. Donegal based Irish folk-rock band (composed of her sister, two brothers and two uncles) that achieved international fame for their haunting brand of music. Enya left the band in 1982 to pursue her solo career. Her own very distinctive mystical sound entered the UK singles chart's number one position with "Orinoco Flow" in 1988. Further successful albums have placed her firmly and deservedly in the category of world super-star.

Above: Four of the Dubliners, a hard-hitting folk cum contemporary ballad group formed in the 1960s, which was still capturing world-wide hearts and audiences into the '90s. From left to right in the drawing are Barney McKenna, Ronnie Drew, the late and much-missed Luke Kelly and John Sheahan. O'Donoghue's Pub on Baggot Street was the cradle of the group.

Above: Author Cornelius Ryan (1920-1974) was born at 33 Heytesbury Street and went on to become a war correspondent during the Second World War. He is best remembered for his epic books on the conflict, all made into films: "The Longest Day", "The Last Battle" and "A Bridge Too Far".

Above: Born in Edinburgh, James Connolly (1868-1916) served in the Royal Scots Regiment before joining the socialist movement. He arrived in Dublin in 1896 to help organise the Dublin Socialist Club. Penury forced him to take his family to live in New York in 1903 but he again returned to Ireland in 1910. The family moved to Belfast but Connolly himself often operated from Dublin in his work for the Irish Transport and General Workers' Union (ITGWU). The poverty of the Irish worker, labour disturbances, the Great Lockout of 1913 and the resultant violence all turned Connolly to a militant socialism. He helped to form the Irish Citizen Army to protect workers against the brutality of their bosses and the authorities. He led this small but disciplined force from the ITGWU headquarters at Liberty Hall to participate in the Rising of 1916. Wounded in the ensuing engagement with the British Army, he was executed, seated on a chair, by firing squad at Kilmainham Gaol on 12 May 1916. The sculpture by Eamonn O'Doherty, commissioned by the successor to the ITGWU, SIPTU (the Services, Industrial, Professional and Technical Union), was unveiled in 1996.

Above: The statue by Oisín Kelly of James Larkin, with arms dramatically outstretched, was unveiled on O'Connell Street in 1979. Larkin (1876-1947) was an almost larger-than-life character in the Irish labour movement during the early part of the last century. He was appointed in 1909 as the first general secretary of the Irish Transport and General Workers' Union and in 1913 he organised the General Strike which led to lock-outs and violent baton charges by police on striking workers. In the mid 1920's he founded his own union, the Workers' Union of Ireland, now absorbed into SIPTU.

Above: No. 422 North Circular Road was the last Dublin home of playwright Sean O'Casey (1880-1964) before he left for London in 1926. In this house he wrote, among other works, two of his most famous plays, "Juno and the Paycock" and "The Plough and the Stars".

A FURTHER GALLERY OF DUBLIN NOTABLES, NATIVE BORN OR RESIDENT.

Above: Countess Constance Markievicz (1868-1927), née Gore-Booth, revolutionary and member of the first Dáil Eireann, was elected as a Sinn Féin candidate in 1918 to the British Parliament and became the first woman Member of Parliament. She never took her seat.

Erwin Schroedinger (1887-1961) developed wave mechanics, a mathematical theory which explains the structure and properties of atoms. Austrian by birth, he lived in Dublin during the Second World War.

Michael William Balfe (1808-1870) was born in Pitt Street, now renamed Balfe Street in his honour. As a composer he is best remembered for the opera "The Bohemian Girl".

Thomas John Barnardo (1845-1905), Dublin-born philanthropist, founded a chain of homes for destitute children, starting in London in 1870 and now known as Barnardos.

Gabriel Byrne (1950-), film actor, was born in Walkinstown, Dublin. His movies include "Defence of the Realm", "Millers Crossing", "The Man in the Iron Mask", "End of Days" and "The Usual Suspects".

Thomas Romney Robinson (1792-1882) developed at Trinity College, Dublin, in 1843, the cup anemometer for measuring wind speed.

George Francis Fitzgerald (1851-1901), Professor of Physics, set out the theory that moving objects contract in the direction of motion. This helped pave the way for Albert Einstein's Theory of Relativity.

William Robert Wilde (1815-1876), the father of Oscar Wilde, invented the ophthalmoscope, an instrument for measuring eyes.

Dr. Francis Rynd (1801-1861) invented the hypodermic syringe.

Lucien Bull (1876-1972) invented the electrocardiograph (ECG) in 1908 for monitoring heart illnesses.

31st/30th May 1786.   **Freeman's Journal**   *Issue No. 16362.*

Aerial Voyage
NO. 31, College Green

As Mr Crosbie, since his late Experiment in Limerick, has been preparing for his Aerial Voyage across the Irish Channel – His favourite and original object, he thinks it incumbent on him to give information of it to the public; if supported by his Countrymen, (as he has little reason to doubt) he will make his second attempt at the first favourable opportunity. – North Cumberland-street, May 29th.

Appendix B

Statuesque

IN TERMS of public statues, street art, monuments and memorials Dublin is singularly fortunate both in their quality and in their dissemination. In some respects the city was a late starter in the provision of sculptural pieces either as stand-alones or as part of a building's decoration. Apart from ecclesiastical representations there are virtually no extant sculptures predating the 18th century. Some notable exceptions include the 17th century statues of Kings Charles I and Charles II which once stood on top of the City Tholsel and are now displayed in the crypt of Christ Church Cathedral. The carvings over the entrances to the Royal Hospital at Kilmainham date from the 1680s. Previous paucities were certainly compensated for in the 18th and more especially in the 19th century. The achievements of noteworthy politicians, soldiers, patriots, churchmen, businessmen, scientists and adventurers inspired a virtual industry in statue production. A lull occurred in the 20th century at least until the 1980s, when there was an upsurge in commemorative and decorative sculpture. Now corporate bodies and the municipal councils generously provide opportunities to raise the awareness of the value of public art and financially support the creation of new pieces.

This appendix supplements the many examples of sculpture already distributed throughout the main body of the book but it can still only embrace a tiny proportion of what is now available for all to enjoy.

Above: Soaring to the skies like the planes that take-off at the adjacent Dublin Airport, this fine granite-clad 17m (56ft) high piece is entitled "Spirit of the Air". This work was commissioned from Richard Enda King in 1991 by the Department of the Environment in conjunction with Aer Rianta and Dublin County Council.

Above: A detail from the Famine Group bronze sculpture by Edward Delaney RHA, unveiled by President Eamon de Valera in 1967.

Above: A companion piece to the Famine Group is that of United Irishman leader, Wolfe Tone (1763-1798), also crafted by Delaney, which stands on the opposite side of the screen wall at the north-east corner of St Stephen's Green.

Above: The Liberty Bell stands in St Patrick's Park, appropriately with the cathedral as a backdrop. The artist was Vivienne Roche and the work was commissioned as part of the 1988 Millennium Sculpture Symposium. AIB and Dublin Corporation were the main sponsors.

Above: One of the most pleasing arrays of sculpture in the city is the Literary Parade in St Patrick's Park. Crafted by Colm Brennan and John Coll in 1988 and set into the arched alcoves on the red-bricked east wall, the 12 bronze oval plaques feature portraits and short biographies of Dublin's most famous writers.

Above: "The Children of Lir" is an impressive focal point in the Garden of Remembrance on Parnell Square. It was designed by Oisín Kelly, cast in the Marinelli Foundry in Florence and unveiled in 1966. It symbolises that people are often changed utterly by significant events (in this case the Easter Rising of 1916). The design is obviously based on the ancient legend of King Lir's children who were changed into swans.

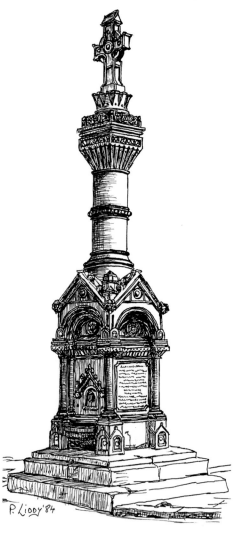

Above: In 1995 Treasury Holdings commissioned Rowan Gillespie to produce the dramatic sculpture which appears to be climbing the impossibly sheer walls of the Treasury Building on Grand Canal Street. It is suitably entitled "Aspiration".

Above: The Constable Patrick Sheahan Memorial on Burgh Quay commemorates an officer of the Dublin Metropolitan Police who gave his life to save others in a sewer gas tragedy in 1905. The sewers in question lie close to the monument.

Above: Thomas Heazle Parke was a Co. Leitrim man who distinguished himself as a doctor in the service of the British Army in Africa. He served on the relief expedition to Khartoum to relieve the doomed General Gordon in 1885 and accompanied Sir Henry Stanley on his famous Nile Expedition of 1887. The statue, by Percy Wood, was unveiled in 1896 and stands in front of the Natural History Museum on Merrion Street.

Above: This statue to Matt Talbot (1856-1925), an ascetic whose case for canonisation is currently before Rome, was presented to the city by the Dublin Matt Talbot Committee in 1988. It stands on the south side of the Liffey bridge opened in 1978 and named in his honour. The sculptor was James Bower.

Above: Commissioned by the North Earl Street and the Dublin City Centre Business Associations, this life-size bronze of James Joyce by Marjorie Fitzgibbon was installed in North Earl Street in 1990.

Above & below: Inserted at intervals along the façades of the Dublin Corporation flats on Bride Street and Golden Lane are a series of terracotta roundels upon which are depicted scenes taken from an 1899 edition of Jonathan Swift's "Gulliver's Travels". Weighing half a ton each, the roundels were designed and moulded by Terry Cartin before being fired at Cartin Ceramics.

Above: One of seven panels crafted by Grace Weir and fixed to the façade of the Chief State Solicitor's Office on Little Ship Street. The panels are extracted from Richard Stanyhurst's drawing of the 1534 abortive attack on Dublin by Silken Thomas Fitzgerald (see page 26).

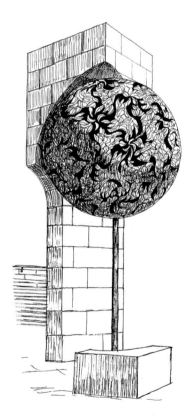

Above: Crann an Óir (the Golden Tree) was commissioned by the Central Bank to mark Dublin's year as European City of Culture in 1991. The work, executed in golden bronze and surrounded by stone features in Wicklow granite, is intended to symbolise the wealth of Ireland, shared out among the public and not hidden away in bank vaults. The sculptor was Eamonn O'Doherty and the monument stands on the public plaza in front of the Central Bank on Dame Street.

Above: The Linesman, an appealing bronze from the hands of Dony MacManus, located on the Campshire along City Quay. The sculpture, unveiled in February 2000, was commissioned by the Dublin Docklands Development Authority.

Above: The Carrara marble group entitled "La Pieta" was a gift from the Italian Government for the relief supplies sent from Ireland to Italy immediately after the Second World War. Executed by Ermegildo Luppi, the statue group was unveiled in 1948 and is located in the grounds of the Department of Education in Marlborough Street.

Above: "Reclining Connected Forms" by Henry Moore on Liberty Square, Trinity College. The bronze, dating from 1969, was donated by the artist, with special support from the college, in 1971.

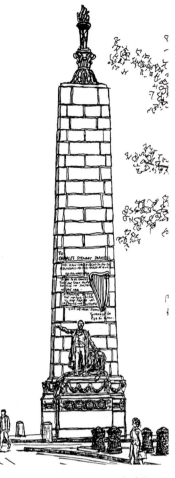

Above: Over 200,000 people followed the funeral of Charles Stewart Parnell in 1891 and such was the sustained popularity of the founder of the Home Rule Movement that tens of thousands of pounds were collected by public subscription towards a suitable monument in his memory. The resultant memorial, unveiled in 1911, stands proudly at the top of O'Connell Street. The sculptor was Augustus Saint Gaudens.

Photo: courtesy of the Radisson SAS St Helen's Hotel.

Above: "Continuum" by Linda Brunker. Placed on the forecourt of the Radisson SAS St Helen's Hotel on Stillorgan Road, the sculpture reflects the lavish interior of the period house (which forms the central part of the hotel), especially the garlands of motifs in the carvings and plasterwork. The sculptor was inspired by three basic elements of life—nature, space and the passing of time. The piece was commissioned by the hotel which was developed by the Cosgrave Property Group.

Right: In a little hide-away rooftop garden at the Irish Life Centre in Abbey Street is a striking and highly colourful mosaic by Desmond Kinney. The inspiration for the piece came from Seamus Heaney's poem "Sweeney Astray".

Above: This plaque displays the shamrock and the thistle, recording a marriage between the children of two great whiskey distilling families, the Jamesons of Dublin and the Haigs of Scotland. King Edward VII unveiled the plaque in 1907 at the Jamesons' Portmarnock mansion, now the Country Club Hotel.

Above: "Memories of Mount Street" was unveiled at Mount Street Crescent in 1988. Ivor Fitzpatrick & Company commissioned the work from Derek A. Fitzsimons and it is a nostalgic reminder of the street games of a bygone age.

Above: One of the most enjoyable sculptures to be installed in recent years is, in this author's view, the Oscar Wilde Memorial in Merrion Square Park. A full view of Wilde himself is featured on page 247. The female figure, one of two torsos forming the group, is Wilde's pregnant wife, Constance, and represents Life. Around the plinths supporting the torsos are many marvellous witticisms taken from the works of Wilde. On a site provided by Dublin Corporation, Guinness Ireland Group commissioned Danny Osborne to produce his eloquent and colourful arrangement. The materials used included jade, granite, quartz, thulite, porcelain, glass and bronze.

Above: Some street furniture started life in a more utilitarian mode before the passage of time rendered them redundant, such as this example of a dockside winch in the International Financial Services Centre.

Above: Cast-off carvings can turn up in unusual places. "Anna Livia" is one of a couple of keystones from the first O'Connell (then Carlisle) Bridge, designed by James Gandon, now fixed to a former warehouse on Sir John Rogerson's Quay.

Above: Many commercial premises around the city have splendid timepieces affixed to their frontages. "We'll meet under the clock at Clerys" (see page 137) became a standard rendezvous arrangement for generations of young couples. The example above is attached to the Irish Times building on D'Olier Street.

Above: The Trophy of Arms on top of the Bank of Ireland Arts Centre in Foster Place is a reminder of the origins of the building when it served as an armoury for the militia who guarded the bank in the 19th century. The sculptor was Joseph R. Kirk.

Above: Remco De Fouw used copper cylinders, recycled piping, old taps, bits of cogs and discarded gauges to create his montage on the doors of the Green Building on Temple Bar's Crow Street in 1994. Murray O'Leary Architects commissioned the work.

Above: "The Kiss" by Rowan Gillespie dates from 1989. It was commissioned through Burke-Kennedy Doyle Architects and funded by the Earlsfort Centre. The sculpture stands at the corner of Earlsfort Terrace and Hatch Street Lower.

Above: The Death of Cú Chulainn, one of the heroes of ancient Irish mythology. The bronze statue, by Oliver Sheppard, stands in the public concourse of the General Post Office.

Above: Commissioned by Amnesty International, Tony O'Malley created this sphere of interlinked chains and bars to represent the jails holding prisoners of conscience all over the world. A permanent gas-powered flame rises from the centre. The memorial, known as "Universal Links on Human Rights", was erected in 1995 on a traffic island at the junction of Memorial Road and Amiens Street.

Above: The pitiful group of bedraggled souls dragging themselves down Custom House Quay are a heart-rending reminder of the thousands of famine victims who struggled down to the docksides to take the emigrant ships to Britain in the 1840s. Commissioned through businesswoman Norma Smurfit, Rowan Gillespie completed this work in 1997.

23rd/26th January 1790.

Freeman's Journal

Issue No. 16362.

Aerial Voyage

NO. 31, College Green

Mr Sylvester having completed his collection of Wax-work Figures, modelled by him, from Nature, has the honour to present them to the Public, dressed in the newest and most brilliant Taste of their respective countries. The likenesses of the following august Personages are so striking, that each spectator feels an awe, at finding himself in company with our most beloved Sovereign and his Royal Consort; the Prince of Wales, the Duke of York, and the Princess Royal; Lords Rodney and Hood; Right Honourables William Pitt and Charles Fox; the King, Queen, and Dauphin of France; the Emperor of Germany; Empress of Russia; Queen of Naples, and Archduchess of Tuscany; with numerous other Figures; also two Venusses of Beauty, exquisite beyond description. The Figures appear so animated, that they seem engaged in conversation, and to command silent attention from the admiring visitors.

Appendix C
Miscellany

THIS APPENDIX provides an ideal opportunity to include, in a random fashion, many images which did not easily find accommodation in the preceding chapters. Some are everyday scenes, others are representative of those oddities which Dublin seems to possess in abundance while yet more are pictures that a home simply had to be found for.

Right: The ubiquitous crane, as much the symbol of Dublin's regeneration and expansion as are the new glass palaces or the restored classical edifices. It never ceases to amaze how such a slender piece of obviously precise engineering can lift heavy weights and not crumple or fall over in the attempt.

Captions are unnecessary in this montage which shows Dubliners of all ages going about their business or simply relaxing.

Above: An aerial view across the River Liffey to that part of Dublin approximating to the site of the walled medieval city. In the foreground are the Civic Offices, behind which is Christ Church Cathedral.

Below: In the centre foreground are the institutions of state including Government Buildings, Leinster House, the National Museum, the National Library and the National Gallery.

Above: St Patrick's Cathedral and its adjoining park dominate this view. New apartment blocks complement the well-built flats erected by the Iveagh Trust at the beginning of the 20th century.

Below: The tree-lined Grand Canal encloses this section of the south inner city. Near the top of the picture (below St Stephen's Green) is the secluded Iveagh Gardens Park situated behind the National Concert Hall.

Above: The River Liffey threads its way towards Dublin Bay. In Celtic times the river broadened into its estuary at the lower end of the photograph.

Below: The world's second tallest obelisk, the Wellington Testimonial, stands in the Phoenix Park, directly across from the railway shunting yards of Heuston Station. A rail line enters a tunnel under the Phoenix Park at this point.

Above: Colloquially called the Bottle Towers, these curious structures off Whitehall Road in Churchtown were built by Major Hall, the local landowner, in 1742. Their exact use is uncertain but living accommodation was provided in the various rooms of the larger tower. They were served by the external spiral staircase. The towers were probably built to give employment to neighbouring small farmers made destitute following the devastating frosts of the previous winter.

Above: Lord Fitzgibbon, the Lord Chancellor, had his resplendently gilded new coach paraded before the people of Dublin in 1791. The large and heavy vehicle needed six horses to draw it efficiently. Built in London at a cost of £7,000, it was restored in 1982 and is now housed at Newbridge House, Donabate.

Above: Once a redoubtable bastion for men-only bathing, the "Forty Foot", a rocky outcrop at Sandycove, now also echoes to the splashes of the fairer sex, at least the dauntless few who, like their male counterparts, swim here the whole year round, even in minus degree temperatures. The cove is claimed to be named after the Forty Foot Light Infantry Regiment, a unit of which was once based in the locality, most probably as a garrison to the adjacent Martello Tower, now the James Joyce Museum. However, the name most likely refers to the depth of the water here at its deepest point.

Above: The monument to the Four Masters commemorates four 17th century chroniclers who gathered ancient histories of Ireland into a masterly tome commonly referred to as the Annals of the Four Masters. It stands in a small park beside St Joseph's Church on Berkeley Road.

Above: All that remains today of the gateway to the former Pigeon House Fort, a heavily armed and garrisoned redoubt occupied from 1798 by the British Army to protect Pigeon House Harbour. It was relinquished by the War Department in 1897 and sold on to Dublin Corporation to fulfill a less glamorous role as a waste-water treatment works.

Above: The formidable keep is basically all that remains of Dunsoghly Castle at Finglas in north Co. Dublin. Built in the early 15th century by Sir Robert Plunkett, Chief Justice of the King's Bench, the castle still retains many of its original oak roof trusses.

Above: The original St Doulagh's Church was a Celtic foundation in early Christian Dublin and was situated near present-day Fishamble Street. It was renamed St Olaf's by the Vikings. Circa 1160 the church (at least its name) was transferred to Kinsealy where it stands today just off the Malahide Road.

Above: Bullock Castle is a medieval fortress which overlooks tiny Bullock Harbour. It was built by the Cistercian monks from St Mary's Abbey on Dublin's northside to control their local fishing rights. They operated their own small fishing fleet from here and were also empowered to impose taxes on other fishing craft using their fisheries. The castle keep is today attached to a home for the elderly run by the Carmelite nuns.

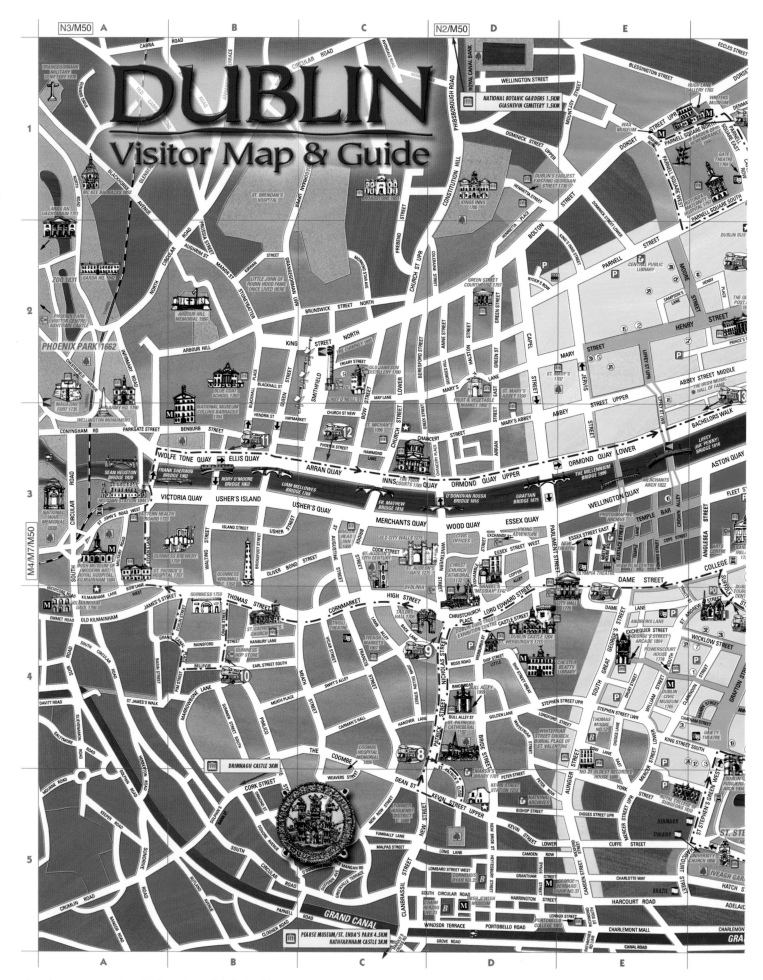

A modern tourist map drawn by the author on behalf of Dublin MCR Services Ltd. and the subscribing members of the Dublin City Centre Business Association. The city is shown split into colour-coded districts to enable visitors to select a particular area of interest on a given itinerary. In 2000 over one million maps were distributed free of charge to visitors.

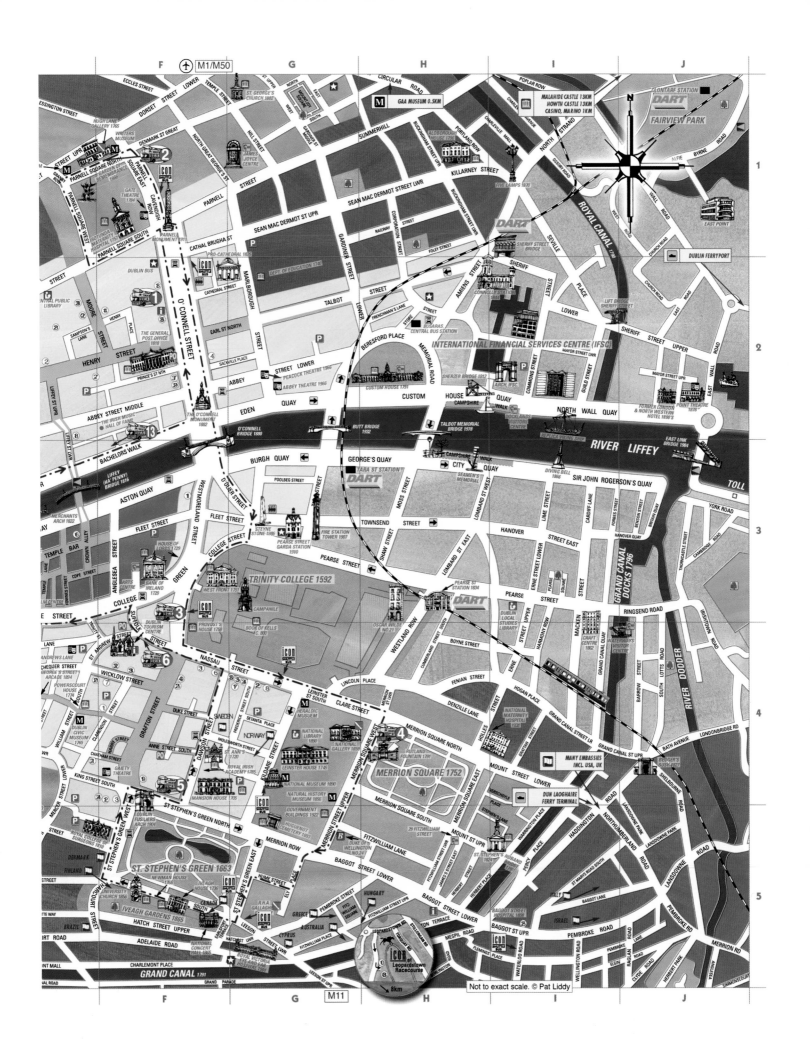

Above: Six rooftop views of Dublin show the variety of architectural styles that are such a distinguishing feature of Dublin's skyline. Reading left to right from the top: D'Olier Chambers, D'Olier Street; a selection of Dame Street buildings; looking across the Bank of Ireland towards College Green; Connolly Station, Amiens Street; the towers of Dublin Castle, Dvblinia, Christ Church and John's Lane Church (i.e. the Church of St Augustine and St John) and Westmoreland Street. This last example is typical of the Victorian fondness for copying older European styles. Here you have an Italian palazzo, a Dutch gable and a French baroque sitting cosily side by side.

Above: Dunsink Observatory in north County Dublin has been operating as an astronomical and meteorological observatory since it was founded by Trinity College in 1785. It is now part of the Institute for Advanced Studies. An early student of Dunsink was Francis Beaufort, the inventor of the wind scale. Arguably its most famous director, from 1827-1865, was the mathematician, physicist and astronomer, William Rowan Hamilton (see page 153)

Above: A montage of the monument and tomb to Daniel O'Connell at Glasnevin Cemetery. It was erected in 1869 in the style of an ancient Irish monastic round tower.

Above: The "Rare Oul Times". A view of the now closed clothes market at the Iveagh Markets. The building is currently being redeveloped (see page 206).

Above: The entrance gates to the Cabbage Garden Park off Cathedral Lane near St Patrick's Cathedral. It is said that Oliver Cromwell's soldiers grew cabbages here, the first time the vegetable was introduced into Ireland. It became a graveyard in 1666 and included a section for Huguenots.

1 | The Stone-Breakers Yard at Kilmainham Gaol where the leaders of the 1916 Rising were executed by firing squad.

2 | Grangegorman Military Cemetery, off Blackhorse Avenue, was opened in 1878. It is the last resting place for hundreds of British Army soldiers, many of whom were Irish-born, and members of their families.

3 | The Easter Military Parade was an annual event in Dublin and commemorated the Rising of 1916. It was discontinued in the 1970s owing to the unfolding tragedies in Northern Ireland. This picture was taken in O'Connell Street in April 1965.

4 | An Avro Anson, being admired by a pair of enthusiasts, constitutes part of the outdoor museum of retired aircraft at Baldonnel Military Aerodrome.

5 | The Anna Livia (River Liffey) fountain in O'Connell Street. The bronze figure is by sculptor and architect, Eamonn O'Doherty. The feature was sponsored by the Jefferson Smurfit Group as a Millennium (1988) gift to the people of Dublin.

6 | What's the poor motorist to do? A sign seen in a Dublin car park.

7 | A quaint thatched period cottage in Malahide, North Co. Dublin.

Appendix D

Introduction

THE PAGES of this appendix have been set aside to show the author's and the publisher's appreciation for the substantial help received from the following sponsors towards the publication of this book. Many of these companies have themselves already made or are still in the process of making significant contributions to the built heritage of Dublin.

Aer Rianta

Aer Rianta was set up by the Irish Government under the Air Navigation and Transport Act 1936 and began in 1937 to "operate lines of aerial conveyances directly or by means of Aer Lingus". Ownership of all airport assets at Dublin, Shannon and Cork Airports was transferred by the Minister for Public Enterprise to Aer Rianta on 1 January 1999. The total turnover for the Group in 1999 was £293 million, an increase of 10% on the previous year despite the ending of intra-EU duty-free shopping in June 1999. Total traffic for the same year was 16.5 million with the Dublin/London route maintaining its position as the busiest international scheduled route in Europe with 4.3 million passengers. Aer Rianta embarked on a £520 million five-year capital expenditure programme in 1999, a year in which £95 million was spent on capital works at its three Irish airports. In July 2000 the first phase of Dublin Airport's new terminal extension came on line. When fully completed this terminal, together with the newly opened Pier C, will bring the airport's passenger handling capacity to at least 20 million passengers per annum. Aer Rianta (through its international division) has large stakeholdings in Birmingham (UK), Hamburg and Dusseldorf Airports. In Ireland the company owns the Great Southern Hotels, a group of hotels situated around the country including one at each of the three airports. The expertise gained in the area of duty-free shopping has served Aer Rianta well and in addition to managing shops in Canada, the Commonwealth of Independent States and the Middle East, it has recently been awarded a contract to manage Hellenic Duty Free, a company comprising 37 duty-free shops in Greece. Aer Rianta has also secured a contract for a management assistance programme for Sofia International Airport in Bulgaria.

Alanis

Alanis Ltd has been heavily involved in the development of the International Financial Services Centre (IFSC) and has interests in a number of other ongoing projects in the city and county area. In addition to jointly developing the Clarion Quay Apartments and the Clarion Hotel, Alanis is also a partner in the redevelopment of the former National Children's Hospital on Harcourt Street.

Right: A view of the Clarion Quay Apartments taken from Excise Walk, a new pedestrian street.

Allied Irish Bank

AIB Group is Ireland's leading banking and financial services organisation. It operates principally in Ireland, Britain, the USA, Poland and Asia. It employs more than 31,000 people worldwide in more than 1,000 offices. Over 10,000 people, in over 400 outlets, work for AIB Bank (the group's retail and commercial division in the Republic of Ireland), First Trust Bank (Northern Ireland) and Allied Irish Banks [GB] (Britain). AIB Capital Markets comprises the Treasury, International Banking, Investment Banking and Corporate Banking activities of the Group and are based in the Financial Services Centre. Between AIB's own outlets and its subsidiary, Allfirst, there are over 300 branches in the USA. In Poland AIB has a 60% shareholding of the leading regional bank Wielkopolski Bank Kredytowy and an 80% stake in Bank Zachodni. Combined they total 332 outlets and rank together as the sixth largest bank in Poland. Based on the performance for the first half of 2000, AIB is likely to be the first bank in Irish history to report an annual profit of more than £1 billion.

Right: The modern AIB branch in Dublin City University.

Peter Barrow Photography

Peter Barrow is Ireland's leading aerial photographer and works for major architects, civil engineers, auctioneers, county councils and municipal corporations. He also carries out assignments in London and travels there about six times a year.

Right: This photograph show Peter Barrow hanging out of a helicopter over London's Wembley Stadium.

Image: courtesy of Peter Barrow Photography.

Capel Developments

Capel Developments is a development and building company founded and controlled by Liam Kelly, Eddie Keegan and John O'Connor. From the mid-1990s it has created several very successful and high specification apartment complexes. Some of the sites developed and built by Capel include (architect and year of completion in parenthesis): The Riverpark Apartments (Brazil & Associates, 2000), Goldstone Court, Clogher Road (O'Mahony Pike, 1998), apartments on the site of the former British Embassy on Merrion Road (Horan Keogan Ryan 1999), Dunstaffinage, Stillorgan (Brazil & Associates, 2000), Chandlers Guild, James's Street (Breffni McGrain 1998), Capel Court (Reddy & Associates 1996) and College Court (Brazil & Associates 1997). Capel is planning to build an apartment scheme on the grounds of the National College of Ireland at Sandyford Road, Ranelagh when the college moves to its new home at the IFSC in Dublin's docklands.

Right: The Linden house and apartment scheme at Blackrock, Co. Dublin, was built on the grounds of the former Linden Nursing Home by John Paul Construction and designed by Brazil & Associates. Phase One was completed in September 2000. An historic feature of the area was an 18th century plantation of linden (lime) trees and this has been echoed by the planting of the same species along the main avenue to the development.

Image: courtesy of Capel Developments.

The Carlton Group

The Carlton Group takes its name from the former Carlton Cinema, from 1938 until 1994 one of the principal places of entertainment on O'Connell Street. Now, as part of the proposed Millennium Mall, the old cinema is to become a central feature of the massive new retail, leisure and cultural development that will help to re-instate O'Connell Street as the true heart of the capital (see page 200). The consortium that makes up the Carlton Group comprises leisure operator Richard Quirke, tourist retailer Colm Carroll, hotelier Jim McGettigan and architect and Chief Executive of the Group, Paul Clinton. The first three individuals are already committed property owners with ongoing businesses on O'Connell Street.

Right: The proposed glazed linkage between the Millennium Mall and the ILAC Centre across Moore Street.

Image: courtesy of Carlton Group.

CIE Group Property Division

The overall property asset owned by CIE amounts to approximately 1,620ha (4,003 acres) of land and 2,810km (1756 miles) of railway track, occupied by Iarnród Éireann, Bus Éireann and Bus Átha Cliath in 550 separate urban and rural locations around Ireland. The management of this asset falls to the Group Property Department of CIÉ. The department's policy is to exploit the maximum commercial gain from property while at the same time improving facilities for customers. This involves joint venture developments with the private sector (including realising the "air space" assets over certain properties) and creating modern commercial lettings at the various railway stations and bus stations. This policy has allowed the major refurbishment of stations such as Connolly and Heuston and there are plans to carry out significant developments at Tara Street and Pearse Station. CIE also has a principal stake in the company seeking to develop Spencer Dock on Dublin's north docklands.

CIE Group of Companies

Citibank

Citibank is a member of Citigroup, the largest and most diverse financial services company in the world with total assets of USD717 billion at the end of 1999. Citibank is one of the oldest US banking institutions and was founded on June 16, 1812. Today, as part of Citigroup, the company has 3,500 offices in more than 100 countries and serves over 100 million customers worldwide. As part of the global expansion of Citibank in the1960s, the bank opened a branch in Dublin on 3rd June 1965 at No.1 Dawson Street. The bank was called the First National City Bank at the time (later renamed Citibank in the 1970s). The bank was one of the first foreign banks to open an office in Ireland. In 1966, the bank moved to offices at No.71 St Stephen's Green.

CITIBANK
A member of citigroup.

The bank's target market in Ireland is large Irish corporates, foreign multinational subsidiaries, public sector utilities and financial institutions. The bank re-located to the IFSC in 1993 with a staff of 90 people. In 1996, the bank decided to locate a European services centre in Dublin, which initially created over 600 new jobs. By 1998, this figure had risen to 1,300. The bank commenced construction in May 1998 on a new 374,000 sq. ft building to co-locate the European services centre and the corporate and treasury offices. This new building is one of the largest single office blocks to be constructed in Dublin. By the end of September 2000, the building will be accommodating in excess of 1,500 staff. As part of Citigroup, the bank has made significant contributions to the rejuvenation of the Docklands area where the bank is now located. Donations were made in 2000 to the Community Training Workshop in Seville Place, Dublin 1 and the National College of Ireland. Citibank has been voted best foreign bank in Ireland consecutively for the past 7 years by *Euromoney* magazine. The bank is celebrating 35 years in Ireland in 2000.

Right: A view of Citibank's new headquarters on North Wall Quay (see page 230).

Cosgrave Property Group

In August 1979, brothers Joe, Peter and Michael Cosgrave turned the first sod on their Farmleigh development in Stillorgan, This was the inception of Cosgrave Brothers which later became Cosgrave Homes and is now Cosgrave Developments, part of the Cosgrave Property Group. Since then the group has built up a fine reputation as one of Dublin's premier house and apartment builders in Dublin. More recently the Cosgrave Property Group has developed houses in Celbridge in Co. Kildare and is now commencing building in Co. Wicklow. Some of its best-known sites in Dublin include (architect and date of completion in parenthesis): Clearwater Cove (Frank Elmes & Co., 1996), Custom Hall (Project Architects, 1993), Morehampton Square (Frank Elmes & Co., 1989), the Northumberlands (Projects Architects, 1995), St Helen's Hotel (Project Architects, 1999), Rathmines Town Centre (Project Architects, 1996), Salthill (Frank Elmes & Co., 1991), Sweepstakes (Frank Elmes & Co., 1993), West Pier (Scott Tallon Walker, 2000), Westend Office Park (Burke-Kennedy Doyle, 2000), Shrewsbury (Frank Elmes & Co., 1990) and West End Village (Burke-Kennedy Doyle, 1999). The above list represents less than half of Cosgrave's total portfolio.

Right: Pembroke Square, on Grand Canal Street, designed by Project Architects and completed in 1997, is one of the Cosgrave Property Group's flagship apartment developments.

Crampton

Established in 1879, G & T Crampton has become one of the largest construction companies in Ireland. It was founded by George J. Crampton in Pearse Street. The "T" in the company name comes from George's nephew T. A. Crampton, who joined 26 years later and contributed to the name it has had ever since. The firm was incorporated in 1924. A few of the more recent projects completed by G & T Crampton in Dublin include: the Eagle Star Headquarters, Ballsbridge; many of the buildings in the International Financial Services Centre; The Towers Hotel, Ballsbridge; Curved Street, Temple Bar; Mater Private Hospital; Marks & Spencer store, Grafton Street; the restoration of the Dining Room, Trinity College after the disastrous fire in 1984; the Green Building, Temple Bar; Four Seasons Hotel, Ballsbridge; the remodelling of UCD's former Aula Maxima, Earlsfort Terrace for the National Concert Hall and the headquarters buildings for Allied Irish Bank and the Bank of Ireland.

Right: Part of a scheme of 700 houses built by G & T Crampton in Oxmantown for the Dublin Artisans' Dwellings Company between 1903 and 1906.

Image: courtesy of G & T Crampton.

Dublin Port Company

The origins of Dublin Port Company can be traced back to the 9th century longphort (fortified harbour) which the Vikings founded near the site of today's Dublin Castle. Dublin's development from that point onwards was inextricably tied to its harbour. The Norse traders and their Anglo-Norman successors gradually enhanced the limited port facilities by narrowing and deepening the river channel at Wood and Merchant's Quays. However, by the 16th century shipping had to be moved further downriver in the quest for more landing space and deeper water, thus commencing a movement ever more eastwards that would continue right up to the present day. Continuous silting and shoaling across the estuary of the River Liffey made entry into the harbour extremely hazardous, especially in the case of the larger ships of the 16th and 17th centuries. In an effort to improve the navigation of the channel and to encourage the construction of more adequate berthages the City Corporation was vested by an Act of Parliament in 1708 with responsibility for the establishment of a Ballast Office. To this end the Corporation formed a committee popularly known as the "Ballast Committee". The control of ballast operations at the port was necessitated by the practice of unscrupulous ship's masters who, having discharged their cargoes, required ballast for the outward voyage and dug away part of the river bank for this purpose. Conversely, these captains, when arriving in port with ballast, tossed the now unwanted ballast overboard when proceeding up the estuary. In 1786, management of the port was transferred to a new body officially termed "The Corporation for Preserving and Improving the Port of Dublin" but generally called the "Ballast Board". Under its aegis the Great South Wall was completed and the North Bull Wall was constructed. Hemmed in by these two great walls the receding tides scoured out much deeper channels for shipping.

In 1867 the Ballast Board was reconstituted as the Dublin Port and Docks Board and it soon set about reconstructing the North and South Quays, a project which took until 1913 to more or less complete. Alexandra Quay was finished in 1935 followed by the North Wall Extension in 1937, the latter after 66 years of labour. The 1950s saw further extensions and the building of jetties, basins, a second graving dock followed by a dry bulk jetty at Alexandra Basin and a car ferry terminal, the last two in 1968. Containerisation in the 1960s saw the building of three new container terminals between 1969 and 1972. By the 1990s several new ro-ro (roll on-roll off) and passenger ferry terminals had been constructed, huge tracts of dockland were modernised, rail extensions were laid and more land was reclaimed from the estuary. Close on £100 million has been invested in port facilities since 1993. Under the Harbours Act 1996, Dublin Port Company Ltd was formed (Vesting Day was 3 Mar 1997). The shareholder is the Minister of the Marine and Natural Resources who appoints the chairman. The directors comprise the chief executive of the company, three members from Dublin Corporation, two worker directors and five others nominated by the shareholder. Today, Dublin is the busiest port in the country with a total throughput per annum (1999) of 7,424 ship arrivals, 1.35 million passengers, 37 cruise liners, 274,000 tourist cars and 451,000 ro-ro units. Current developments include the strengthening of the Great South Wall, additional terminal ramps, extra facilities to service the introduction of ever-larger ferries including the world's biggest car ferry (for Irish Ferries) due in Spring 2001 and the controversial application to the Minister for the Marine & Natural Resources to reclaim 21ha (52 acres) of land at the east end of the north port.

Dublin Docklands Development Authority

Due to the location and considerable development potential of the Dublin Docklands Area (DDA), the Government decided in January 1996 that a strategic approach should be adopted to the renewal and redevelopment of the DDA. The Dublin Docklands Development Authority Act, 1997, was enacted by the Oireachtas on 27 March 1997. The Dublin Docklands Development Authority (DDDA) was set up by Ministerial Order on 1 May 1997. The DDDA's general duty is to secure: the social and economic regeneration of the DDA on a sustainable basis, the improvement of the physical environment of the DDA and the continued development in the Custom House Docks Area of services of, for, in support of, or ancillary to the financial sector of the economy (see also pages 214 to 218).

Dúchas The Heritage Service

A constituent part of the Department of Arts, Heritage, Gaeltacht and the Islands, Dúchas The Heritage Service cares for many of Ireland's national monuments, inland waterways, parks, gardens and nature reserves. Every year in September, Dúchas (meaning "Heritage") promotes National Heritage Week in which over 350 events take place nationwide, including walks, lectures, displays, pageants, music recitals and free entrance to sites. The Dublin Heritage sites include: The Casino, Lusk Heritage Centre, Kilmainham Gaol, Pearse Museum and St. Enda's Park, Phoenix Park Visitor Centre, National Botanic Gardens, the Iveagh Gardens, St. Stephen's Green, Garden of Remembrance and the War Memorial Gardens.

Right: President Eamon de Valera opened the Garden of Remembrance on Easter Monday 1966, the golden jubilee of the 1916 Rising. The Garden, designed by Daithí P. Hanly, honours the memory of all those who gave their lives for Irish Freedom. The floor of the sunken pool displays a mosaic pattern of blue-green waves interspersed with ancient weaponry. The spears are shown broken, following the Celtic custom of throwing weapons into rivers and lakes as offerings to the gods when hostilities ended (see also page 254).

Dunloe Ewart

Dunloe Ewart plc is Ireland's only all-Ireland publicly quoted property development company. Headed by solicitor, Mr Noel Smyth, and a small management team, the company has grown rapidly in the last 3 years. Major developments currently underway or in the pipeline include Cherrywood Science and Technology Park in South County Dublin, North Park in Finglas, Harristown near Dublin Airport and, in the heart of Dublin, Sir John Rogerson's Quay and Barrow Street. Dunloe Ewart plc are also heavily involved in Northern Ireland. Projects include the prestigious Lanyon Place development adjacent to Belfast's Waterfront Hall, the Howden Sirocco (a riverside development), Bedford Street offices and Fitzwilliam Terrace apartments in Belfast City Centre. Plans are also well advanced for a major city centre retail scheme on Royal Avenue following site assembly. Dunloe Ewart plc also has a number of developments underway in Limerick, Tralee, Wexford and Dundalk.

Right: A Dunloe Ewart development at Cherrywood Science and Technology Park.

Image: courtesy of Dunloe Ewart.

Eastern Regional Health Authority (ERHA)

The Eastern Regional Health Authority was established in March 2000 to replace the former Eastern Health Board and is responsible for health and personal social services for over 1.3 million people who live in Dublin, Kildare and Wicklow. It plans, commissions, funds and monitors the three new health boards which will actually deliver the health services. These are: the South Western Area Health Board (based at Leinster Mills near Naas, Co. Kildare), the Northern Area Health Board (based at the Swords Business Campus) and the East Coast Area Health Board (based at Boghall Road, Bray, Co. Wicklow). The ERHA also has similar service agreements with voluntary hospitals and other voluntary agencies in the region. The new structures were introduced to cope with the vastly increased population of the eastern region of the country, the scale and complexities of the health and social service issues and the historic fragmentation of services between statutory and voluntary providers.

Right: The modern health centre at Swords, Co. Dublin.

Educational Building Society

Since it was founded in 1935 by a group of primary school teachers, the EBS has helped over 100,000 people to buy or build their own homes. The society was established to assist teachers and others to purchase homes, hence the name "Educational". Under the leadership of Mr Alec McCabe, a former T.D. of the First and the Second Dáil, the society opened its first office at No.5 Lower Abbey Street. The core ethos of the organisation is that it operates as a Mutual Society, which simply means that it is owned by the members themselves with the objective of ensuring the best value in loans and the best returns on investments for members. The EBS employs nearly 600 people in 137 offices nation-wide. Its Head Office is based in Westmoreland Street (see page 198).

Euroscreen

What is now the Euroscreen Group was founded in the mid-1970s as a display company. It has since become one of Ireland's largest and most versatile print resources (after all, it did print this book which, it has to be said, was not one of the easiest jobs in the world). Using a range of printing presses from the small to the gargantuan, the company, operating 24 hours a day, offers repro, litho, screen and bindery services.

Right: The Euroscreen plant at Ballymount Industrial Estate.

FLS Aerospace

FLS Aerospace is part of a Danish international company that was first set up in Copenhagen by Fredereck Laessoe Smidth in 1882. Engaged at the outset in building cement plants the firm, then known as F. L. Smidth, was commissioned by the Irish Government to construct two cement plants at Drogheda and Limerick between 1936 and 1938. The Danish company went on to manage Cement Ltd. until Roadstone became financially involved in 1971 and changed the name to Irish Cement Ltd. In 1997 Sean Quinn ordered his new cement plant from F. L. Smidth. The parent company of F. L. Smidth, FLS Industries A/S, is now involved in five main sectors: engineering, environmental plants/boilers, shipping/logistics, building materials and aircraft maintenance and employs nearly 19,000 people Europe-wide. Currently the aircraft maintenance, division, FLS Aerospace, is Europe's largest independent aircraft maintenance provider. The TEAM Aer Lingus operation at Dublin Airport, once the maintenance and engineering arm of the Irish airline, was acquired by FLS Aerospace in December 1998 and is known as FLS Aerospace (Irl). See also page 160.

Flynn Property Partnership and Paddy Kelly

The objective of John Flynn and Paddy Kelly is to invest both capital and expertise in commercial projects in Ireland and the UK, both on their own behalf and in participation with others. Flynn and Kelly, friends and business partners for over 30 years, have been or are currently involved in the following joint developments in Dublin: 35,000sq m of office accommodation at Belfield Office Park in Clonskeagh (architect: Horan Keogan Ryan), 6,000sq m of offices at Arena Road in Sandyford (architect: Horan Keogan Ryan), construction of 9,000 sq m of offices at Blackrock Business Park (architect: Horan Keogan Ryan), plans to construct 20,240sq m of commercial, office and retail space, housing, a children's museum and leisure facilities at Smithfield (in partnership with Linders, architect: Horan Keogan Ryan), construction of 20,000sq m of offices on the Carroll Transport site on Sir John Rogerson's Quay (in partnership with James Carroll, architect: Burke-Kennedy Doyle) and the redevelopment of sites at Sandyford, the old Harcourt Street Children's Hospital (in partnership with Alanis Ltd) and various developments in the IFSC.

John Flynn was also responsible for: the reconstruction of the ESB Central Stores at Erne Street/Pearse Street to accommodate the new 90-bed Holiday Inn as well as almost 200 apartments in the Winter Garden scheme and 4,000sq m of offices for WorldCom (in partnership with Tony Tyrell. Architect: Paul O'Dwyer & Associates), the building of 2,000 sq m of offices for the OPW at Clonmel Place (architect: Arthur Gibney & Partners), the conversion of 25,000sq m Motorola factory at Swords Business Park to a computer and software facility (in partnership with Tony Tyrell, architect: Paul O'Dwyer & Associates), the refurbishment of the Hitachi factory at Clonshaugh to accommodate Web hosting facilities (engineer: Carew Associates) and developments at Tara Street and Belgard Road for offices and retail warehousing. Paddy Kelly's other projects include: Monkstown Valley and Tallaght Retail Centres. He is also involved in the hospitality industry through PremGroup and Choice Hotels Ireland.

Above right: Flynn Property Partnership (in association with Paddy Kelly, Alanis and Pat Ryan) are constructing 7,000 sq m of offices at the former National Children's Hospital on Harcourt Street. First occupied in 1845 by the hospital, the building was sold to the developers in 1998 after the hospital relocated to Tallaght. The architects for the project are Arthur Gibney & Associates.

Right: Belfield Office Park, a joint development between John Flynn and Paddy Kelly.

Gaelic Athletic Association

The modern Cumann Lúthchleas Gael (Gaelic Athletic Association or GAA), now Ireland's largest sporting and cultural organisation, was officially founded in a billiards room in Hayes' Hotel in Thurles on 1 November 1884. The history of Gaelic Games goes back much further. A 9th century text, taken from the legendary story "Táin Bó Cuailgne" refers to the hero Cú Chulainn taking "his hurley stick of bronze and his silver ball and he would shorten his journey with them". That first meeting in Thurles was called by Michael Cusack who had previously demonstrated an interest in reviving ancient Gaelic Games. The other attendees at the meeting were John Wyse Power, John McKay, John K. Bracken, P. J. Ryan, John McCarthy and Maurice Davin. Ten days after the Thurles meeting, the first GAA fixtures were held at Macroom, near Cork. Throughout 1885, hurling and football games were held in towns and villages throughout Munster and Leinster. The GAA had nationalistic undertones from the beginning and this factor alone ensured that, in the words of Cusack, "the Association swept the country like a prairie fire" (see also page 236). The GAA Museum, under the New Stand at Croke Park, deals with the history and the development of the GAA and is one of the most facinating museums of any kind in the country.

GE Capital Woodchester

Founded in 1977 by Mr Graig McKinney, Woodchester Finance established its head office on Golden Lane in the early 1980s. Since then, the company has grown considerably and now employs over 600 people at the Golden Lane site. In December 1997 Woodchester became part of General Electric, one of the world's largest companies, and now trades under the name of GE Capital Woodchester. The company is a provider of financial solutions for businesses and private customers and the product range includes everything from car hire purchase and business equipment leasing to consumer loans and credit insurance. Golden Lane is also headquarters for a pan-European business division which operates in 20 countries and employs as many as 15,000 people.

Right: An internal view of the Golden Lane headquarters of GE Capital Woodchester. The building was innovative in several ways and had the country's first genuine green and naturally-conditioned interior. The fabric and form of the various structural elements of the building have been carefully designed to ensure a comfortable environment throughout the year (see also page 239).

Image: courtesy GE Capital Woodchester.

Green Property

Green Property plc is a property investment, development and trading group. Its principal investment properties in Dublin (the company also has an extensive property portfolio in the UK), many of which it developed itself, are: the Blanchardstown Centre and Retail Park, Blanchardstown; the Ardilaun Centre, St Stephen's Green; the Irish Express Cargo Building, Rosemount Business Park; The Atrium, Sandyford; No.2 Harbourmaster Place, IFSC; Northside Shopping Centre, Coolock; Styne House, Upper Hatch Street; Fonthill Business Park; Setanta Centre, Nassau Street. In 1999, Green Property purchased Microsoft's entire office portfolio in Dublin in an almost £60 million deal, said at the time to have been the largest single property transaction in the history of the state. Green was recently chosen to develop the new business and technology park at Ballymun jointly with Ballymun Regeneration Ltd., a subsidiary company of Dublin Corporation. The park is expected to be the biggest development of its kind in the country.

Right: The Atrium, an office development at Sandyford, designed by Horan Keogan Ryan.

Image: courtesy of Green Property.

Guinness Ireland Group

Guinness Ireland Group, the controlling company for Guinness in the Republic of Ireland, is the original and most significant of six regional operations within Guinness, the brewing arm of Diageo plc. In Ireland Guinness presently owns five breweries which brew over one billion pints each year. More than one million pints per day (actually 400 million pints per year) are exported by the Irish operation of Guinness. Since the 1980s, Guinness Ireland Group has invested over £650 million in its operations. St James's Gate in Dublin is now one of the most technologically advanced breweries in the world (see also pages 171-2).

Hamilton Osborne King

The firm's foundations reach back to 1935 when the firm of Hamilton & Hamilton (Estates) Ltd. was founded by Hugh Hamilton and his father. From its premises at No.17 Dawson Street (the site of the present Royal and Sun Alliance building) it became one of the leading agencies in Dublin in the country houses, residential and fine art sectors of the market. Its auction rooms were at the opposite corner of Dawson Street and Molesworth Street on what is now the site of the European Union building. Osborne King & Megran was established at 64 Dawson Street in 1961, under the directorship of John McFarlane, when it took over Smith Griffin and Co. The firm became a market leader after rapid growth throughout the 1960s and 1970s, particularly in the property development and investment sectors. A Cork office was opened in 1974. The two companies merged in 1987 to form Hamilton Osborne King, based at No.32 Molesworth Street creating one of the largest and most broadly based property companies in the country. Further offices were opened in Blackrock, Clontarf, Swords, Rathgar and Phibsboro. The firm created a seperate identity for its residential business in June 2000, HOK Residential, and opened a new headquarters for that section at No.20 Dawson Street, thus returning the firm to the street of its roots.

Some of Hamilton Osborne King's most memorable sales in recent times have been: "Pitcairn", a family home on Shrewsbury Road, the first Dublin house to break the one million pound barrier at auction when it sold within ninety seconds for £1.55 million in 1996; "Glencairn", the British Ambassador's residence in Sandyford; the Loreto School in Rathfarnham; the Guinness home at Farmleigh, Castleknock (see page 187); the former Masonic Girls School now Bewley's Hotel, Ballsbridge; the former Church of St Michael and St John, now the Viking Adventure and the huge conversion of the redundant Jameson Distillery at Smithfield into Smithfield Village.

Above right: Hamilton Osborne King's Head Office at No.32 Molesworth Street.

Right: The offices of HOK Residential at No.20 Dawson Street, newly opened in 2000, specialising in the residential market.

Hollybrook Construction

Hollybrook Construction is owned by Austin Kelly, a Cavan-born developer. Its flagship development is the Ripley Court Hotel and Ripley Inn on Talbot Street. As well as developing green field sites the company has a long record in reinstating derelict sites and restoring old houses. The company was responsible for building the Glasnevin Downs housing estate and also Chapel View Apartments at Chapelizod. No.5 Parnell Square, the one-time home of surgeon and politician, poet and wit, Oliver St John Gogarty, was combined with No.6 by Hollybrook Construction to form the premises of the Charles Stewart Hotel where some fine 18th century decoratively plastered ceilings were preserved. Other projects include 16 apartments at No.61 Mountjoy Square and the refurbishment of North Strand Cottages, a row of 10 single-storey houses that had lain virtually derelict for years.

Right: No.61 Mountjoy Square.

Institute of Education/Portobello College

The Institute of Education, one of the country's largest private second-level colleges, was founded in 1969 by Mr Raymond Kearns who also owns the third-level business institute, Portobello College (opened in 1989). The Institute operates from some Georgian buildings in Leeson Street including a rebuilt "Dutch Billy" (see page 163). Portobello College is spread among some modern buildings centred around the 18th century Portobello House (see image on page 218), a one-time hotel opened in 1807 to serve the passenger boats on the Grand Canal. It closed as a hotel in 1860 and from 1898 it was used as a private nursing home. The painter Jack B. Yeats spent his last years here. The nursing home closed in 1971 whereupon the building was extensively restored and was acquired by the Institute of Education in 1989.

Right: Harbour House, one of the college buildings attached to Portobello College.

Irish Life Assurance

Irish Life Assurance now forms part of Irish Life & Permanent plc, one of Ireland's leading companies and the country's third largest financial services institution. The company has £18 billion of funds under management including £1 billion of property assets. Irish Life were pioneers in investing in the re-development of Dublin city centre and its extensive track record includes the development of the Irish Life Centre (1973), the ILAC Shopping Centre (1983), Abbey Court (1987), Beresford Court (1991) and George's Quay (1993).

John Paul Construction

John Paul Construction is the building and civil engineering subsidiary of John Paul & Co. which was founded in 1949. A small selection of the more recent buildings erected or restored by John Paul Construction includes the following (the architectural practice and the date of completion is in parenthesis): Original phase of the Civic Offices (Sam Stephenson, 1986), Faculty of Engineering, UCD (Scott Tallon Walker, 1989), Riverview Fitness Club (Horan Cotter & Associates, 1990), Westland Square (Arthur Gibney & Associates, 1991), South Dublin County Council Headquarters (Gilroy McMahon, 1994), restoration of Curvilinear Glasshouse, Botanic Gardens (OPW, 1995), extension to The Square, Tallaght (Spain Courtney Doyle, 1996), Tallaght Hospital (Robinson Keefe Devane, 1997), Ferryport (Traynor O'Toole, 1997), Great Southern Hotel, Dublin Airport (Aer Rianta Technical, 1998) and the Women's Prison (OPW, 1999). Other examples will be found throughout the book.

Right: The new glazed-in atrium to the rear of the ESB offices on Fitzwilliam Street (Architect: Sam Stephenson, 1990).

Image: courtesy of John Paul Construction.

McGarrell Reilly/Alcove Properties

Sean Reilly, a native of Co. Cavan, has lived in the Dublin area for the last twenty years. His companies, McGarrell Reilly and Alcove Properties, have been involved in a number of residential and commercial projects. The most notable of these were the residential schemes at Malahide Marina Village (see page 232), Stepaside Park, Woodside in Rathfarnham and Grosvenor Lodge in Rathmines, all under the McGarrell Reilly umbrella. The company's first scheme was two semi-detached houses in Kilcoole in 1981. Commercial developments at Hogan Place (currently occupied by the Health & Safety Authority) and Holles Street were completed by Alcove Properties. This company is currently developing a significant office and residential scheme bordered by Harcourt Road (see page 232) and Charlemont Street, its largest project since the development of Malahide Marina.

P. J. McGrath & Company

P. J. McGrath & Company, property developers, managers and consultants, has been operating, mostly in the Dublin city centre, since 1983. Starting in a small way by upgrading old houses, the company soon moved on to refurbishing and converting more prominent city centre buildings for residential use and constructing large-scale apartment developments. In the mid-1990s P. J. McGrath completed Clifden Court, a much-praised apartment complex on Ellis Quay, and more recently built an office and retail development at Le Fanu Road in Ballyfermot. One of its most ambitious projects to date will be an office and residential scheme planned for the site of the former St Joseph's Convent in Summerhill (see page 205).

Master Photo

Master Photo, in business for more than 25 years, is well-known for its blend of traditional craft skills and the latest technological advances, all of which were applied in the final assembly of this volume prior to platemaking. The facilities at Master Photo include design and typesetting, scanning, file and film assembly, proofing, platemaking and digital printing.

National Gallery of Ireland

The National Gallery of Ireland was founded by an Act of Parliament in 1854 and opened to the public in 1864. The architect was Francis Fowke. The Gallery has been extended twice; in 1903 (architect: Thomas Newenham Deane, and in 1968 (architect: Frank du Berry). The refurbished 1968 wing was reopened in 1996 (architect: OPW). A new extension to the Gallery, known as the Millennium Wing, is scheduled to be completed by 2001 (architect: Benson & Forsyth). The Gallery collection comprises 13,000 works of art, 2,500 of which are oil paintings. The National Gallery is one of Ireland's top cultural attractions with an average attendance of one million people. See also pages 105 and 106.

National Millennium Committee

The 14-member National Millennium Committee, chaired by Minister Séamus Brennan TD, was established by the Government in 1998 to select projects with which to mark the Millennium in a lasting, memorable and dignified way while at the same time reflecting the excitement and the anticipation of the new millennium. The National Millennium Committee has committed £33 million to supporting five flagship projects, another 32 at national level, 175 in the regions, 200 at county level and 2,000 events at local level. It has striven to make this the "People's Millennium" and to put into place lasting legacies for this and future generations to enjoy. Flagship projects included the planting of a native tree in the name of each of the 1.2 million households in the country, the raising of £4 million to help more than 100 children's causes and the rescue and restoration of redundant lighthouse properties.

O'Callaghan Hotels

The O'Callaghan Hotels group comprises the Davenport (designed by Arthur Gibney & Partners), the Alexander (architect: Henry J. Lyons) and the Stephen's Green (architect: Arthur Gibney & Partners). The Mont Clare Hotel in Dublin and the Eliott Hotel in Gibraltar are two more properties owned by the group. O'Callaghan Hotels is controlled by hotelier and property developer, Mr Noel O'Callaghan.

Right: The Davenport Hotel started life as the Merrion Hall, a church meeting hall for the Plymouth Brethren. It was originally designed by Alfred G. Jones (1822-1915) and opened in 1863 under the Reverend Joseph Denham Smith. Between seats and standing room the building could accommodate a congregation of up to 5,000. It ceased its role as a church building in the 1980s and was sold in 1988. Several owners followed until the exterior was restored and the inside rebuilt before reopening in 1993 for O'Callaghan Hotels.

Thomas Read Holdings

Initially set up by Hugh O'Regan and still controlled by him, Thomas Read Holdings has assembled an impressive muster of pubs and hotels including the Budabor at the Blanchardstown Centre, the Morrison Hotel on Ormond Quay, the Bailey in Duke Street, Searsons in Baggot Street, the Dawson Lounge (reputedly Dublin's smallest lounge bar) in Dawson Street, the Harbourmaster in the IFSC, the Pravda in Liffey Street, Life at the Irish Life Centre off Lower Abbey Street, Hogans in South Great George's Street, Thomas Read's on Parliament Street, the Ambassador on Parnell Square facing the top of O'Connell Street and the Pavilion in Dun Laoghaire. The company is named after Thomas Read & Co., who once owned a cutlers business on Parliament Street.

Right: Thomas Read's at No. 1 Parliament Street, a Parisian-style café and bar.

Royal College of Surgeons in Ireland

Founded in 1784 by Royal Charter of King George III, the College is governed by the President and a 21-member Council who are elected by the fellows. The College is a registered charity for the promotion of the practice of surgery, anaesthesia, dentistry, radiology and nursing as well as the provision of medical education, training and research. While the College is rich in history and tradition it is also an extremely progressive institution. It has a cojoint board in Ireland with the Royal College of Physicians of Ireland and is a recognised college of the National University of Ireland. The principal teaching hospital for the college is Beaumont Hospital where a major education and research centre is being established. International connections include managing the North-West Armed Forces Hospital in Tabuk, Saudi Arabia, conducting training courses and examinations throughout the Middle East, a shared academic venture with Malaysia's Penang Medical College and a special relationship with three other "Royal" Colleges in the U.K. As it receives no state subsidies it has to successfully market itself and apply the latest teaching techniques and medical and surgical technologies to stay relevant. The RCSI continues to invest heavily in research into cancer, molecular biology, new surgical techniques, mental illness, cardiovascular disease, ageing and Third World medicine. It also specialises in CME or Continuing Medical Education, a programme for qualified practitioners to help them keep pace with their constantly changing environment.

Image: courtesy of the RCSI.

Right: an interior view of the Royal College of Surgeons on St Stephen's Green.

Shelbourne Development

Shelbourne Development Ltd. is a property development company and is the Irish operation for the US company Shelbourne Development L.L.C., a real estate development company based in Chicago. The latter firm, started in 1986, has an exstensive background in condominium and rental loft projects, commercial real estate development and hotel renovation. With the growth of the Irish economy Shelbourne Development Ltd. was formed to explore the many opportunities in Ireland and at present it is pursuing developments in Dublin, Limerick, Northern Ireland, the UK and Chicago. In November 2000 the company will commence to build a 197-bedroom hotel, which will also have three floors of retail and leisure accommadation, on a site bounded by Parnell and Moore Streets.

Right: In summer 2000, Shelbourne Development purchased the former Irish Press building on Burgh Quay from The Irish Times Newspaper Group who had intended to occupy the premises for their own purposes. Based on the planning permission already received by The Irish Times, Shelbourne will commence in October 2000 to reclad and refurbish the building to third-generation office standards. The architects for the project are Henry J. Lyons.

Image: courtesy of Henry J. Lyons.

John Sisk & Son

The family building firm of John Sisk & Son was founded in 1859 and remained essentially a Cork-based operation until the depression years of the 1930s forced the "emigration" of a direct descendant of the founder, John G. Sisk, to Dublin in the pursuit of elusive business. His only two employees at that point were his new bride and his cousin Herbert Dennis, secretary and foreman, respectively. He is reputed to have been the first builder to use a tower crane in Ireland; now they sprout like natural landscape features all over the country! The new Dublin company was an off-shoot of the original Cork company and they remained closely linked until they were merged in 1974. In the same year John G. Sisk retired and handed over ownership and management of the business to his three sons and his nephew. The long list of Dublin buildings constructed by Sisks (the firm also builds extensively in Ireland generally, in the UK and Zimbabwe) includes: the Department of Industry and Commerce (now Enterprise, Trade & Employment), Kildare Street; the Irish Life development on George's Quay; the Treasury Building, Grand Canal Street; the TEAM (now FLS Aerospace) hangar at Dublin Airport; Civic Offices for Dun Laoghaire Rathdown County Council; the current redevelopment of Croke Park; the Liffey Valley Shopping Centre, Steyn House, Upper Hatch Street; the new Guinness Visitor Centre and Swords Town Centre and Shopping Centre. The firm also carried out the prestigious restorations of the Royal Hospital, Kilmainham and the Custom House.

David Slattery

David Slattery is one of Ireland's leading conservation architects. A senior architect with the Office of Public Works (OPW) for most of his professional life, he has worked on such prestigious projects as the re-facing and restoration of the Custom House. Slattery left the OPW in 1991 to become a conservation consultant and has since been involved in a diverse number of restorations ranging from cathedrals to pubs. The portfolio in Dublin includes St Patrick's Cathedral, Doheny and Nesbitts pub, Marks and Spencer on Grafton Street, the Merrion Hotel, the Corporation Rates Office, the Fruit and Vegetable Market, Sunlight Chambers, Leinster House, the Westin Hotel, Collins Barracks, the Liberties College on Bull Alley, City Hall, the Four Courts and bridges and other historic monuments along the new LUAS lines.

Right: The Liberties College, Bull Alley (see page 68).

Temple Bar Properties

Through community pressure, a plan to turn the Temple Bar area into a central bus terminal was defeated and the government launched the Temple Bar Initiative as a flagship project to mark Dublin's year as European City of Culture in 1991. Temple Bar Properties (TBP) was set up under the Temple Bar Area Renewal and Development Act, 1991. It is a limited company whose shareholder is the Minister of the Environment and Local Government. The company is not a planning authority for the area and is subject to the usual planning permission process. In addition, the company's developments are subject to approval by Temple Bar Renewal, a company also established by the Government under the 1991 Act to sanction tax incentives for projects. TBP's mandate was to develop Temple Bar as Dublin's cultural quarter in a given time frame, to specific objectives and within particular financial parameters. Building on the existing historical, architectural and archaeological features in the area, TBP's aim was to develop a bustling, cultural, residential and small business precinct that would attract visitors in significant numbers. On the whole, these aims have been eminently fulfilled. A two-phase programme for the area was launched by TBP. Phase One (1991-1996) saw the realisation of many objectives: cultural (14 new or refurbished cultural centres), commercial (approximately 140 new businesses established including 63 retail units and 7 new hotels) and residential (155 new apartments). Some of the cultural organisations now operating from Temple Bar include the Irish Film Centre, Design Yard, Temple Bar Gallery and Studios, Blackchurch Print Studios, the Ark, the Gallery of Photography, ARTHouse, the Temple Bar Music Centre, the Dublin Institute of Technology School of Photography and the Viking Adventure. Phase Two (1996-2000) was mainly concerned with developing the west-end of Temple Bar into a residential and cultural quarter. Into this area have come the Viking Adventure and a newcomer, the Contemporary Music Centre. The Project Arts Centre, in Temple Bar since 1966, reopened its newly designed premises in June 2000 (architect; Shay Cleary). TBP also opened new streets in Temple Bar, enhanced the east-west axis and commissioned many permanent works of art in new buildings or along public spaces. The resident population grew from 200 in 1991 to almost 2,000 by the end of Phase Two. The total state investment was over £40 million, TBP borrowed £60 million to fund retail and residential development (repaid through sales and lettings) and the private sector invested around another £100 million.

Treasury Holdings

The Treasury Holdings Group, well-known for its development of the Treasury Building on Grand Canal Street, is one of Ireland's largest property companies. It was established in 1989 by former barrister Richard Barrett and chartered accountant John Ronan. Some of the current development projects controlled by the group in Dublin include: the Spencer Dock site on the North Quays; the M1 Business Park, north of Dublin Airport; Central Park Office Scheme in Leopardstown; the Allegro site in the Sandyford Industrial Estate; the Stillorgan Shopping Centre and the Westin Hotel on College Street. The company's investment portfolio includes: Russell Court, St Stephen's Green; AIB Investment House, Percy Place; The Schoolhouse Hotel, Northumberland Road; St James House, Adelaide Road; the Lafayette (former ICS) Building (the new Manchester United store) at the corner of D'Olier and Westmoreland Streets; Bewleys Building, Grafton Street; Charlemont House, Charlemont Place; College Gate, Townsend Street (built in partnership with Dublin Corporation who gave Treasury the air space over the public swimming pool provided the developers rebuilt the pool and upgraded the leisure facilities); the Temple Bar Hotel and many more. Treasury Holdings has recently diversified into the area of wind-generated electricity and already has an operating windfarm at Arigna in Co. Roscommon. See the main text for more details on properties developed by Treasury Holdings.

Right: Connaught House, Herbert Street, in the neo-classical style, is one of Treasury Holdings' developments from the mid-1990s. It was designed by Jimmy O'Connor in Arthur Gibney Architects.

Trinity College

Trinity College was founded in 1592 on the site of the suppressed Augustinian monastery of All Hallows. Today the college stands on a 17ha (42 acres) site, enclosed on all four sides by the city centre of Dublin. The continuing rapid expansion of the college has meant that new sites close to but outside the central campus have had to be acquired. These include property on Foster Place and along Pearse Street including an office block at Westland Square and the former IDA Craft Centre. For a fuller account of Trinity College (see pages 32-35).

Right: A detail from the Examination Hall, Trinity College.

Image: courtesy of The Board of Trustees, Trinity College Dublin

20-20 VisionDesign

20-20 VisionDesign was established in 1986 and specialises in the design of effective graphic design projects. Our services include design of corporate identities, corporate communications, annual reports, marketing literature and through our web division, 20-20 WebWorld.com, the design, production and maintenance of websites. Our company has worked with many leading companies and are proud sponsors and designers of this book.

P. J. Walls

The founder, P. J. Walls, originally came to Dublin from Belfast in the late 1940s. His firm, incorporated in 1950, has since become one of the major construction companies in the country. During the 1950s and '60s its main activity was in the civil engineering sector. In the 1970s expansion into building construction evolved and by the end of that decade major construction works such as Tralee General Hospital and the Institute of Industrial Research and Standards in Glasnevin had been completed. In 1986 a rationalisation was undertaken which saw P. J. Walls (Civil) Ltd established to operate in the civil engineering sector leaving P. J. Walls (Dublin) Ltd. (changed in 1995 to simply P. J. Walls Ltd.) to concentrate on the building market. In recent years the company expanded operations into Canada and England. Due to move to larger premises at the junction of the Northern Cross and the Malahide Road, P. J. Walls recently sold its Rosemount Office Park headquarters on Glandore Road for an apartment development. A selection of the company's projects in Dublin include: the extension to the College of Catering, Cathal Brugha Street; the O'Reilly Hall, UCD; No.3 Harbourmaster Place, IFSC; Fleet Street Car Park; Organon Pharmaceutical Plant, Swords; Irish Life's Beresford Court; multi-storey car park at Dublin Airport; rebuilding an old railway depot into the Point Theatre; Blackrock Clinic; the Merrion Centre; the Westin Hotel; RTE television studios at Montrose and the Dublin Port Centre.

Woodgreen Builders

Cross Guns Quay (see page 226) was a very successful conversion from an old flour mill into modern apartments by Woodgreen Builders (this company's development arm is Woodsim Ltd. and both are controlled by Mr Joe Kenny). Another acclaimed development, uniquely a housing scheme for an inner city site instead of the more usual apartments, was Palatine Square (named after a parade square in Collins Barracks, behind which the Woodgreen site lies). The architects for the scheme were Campbell Conroy Hickey

Right: The Palatine Square site as seen from Arbour Hill before the conversion. The buildings on the left were once stables for army horses.
Far right: The same street after the conversion.

Bibliography

Bennett, D., *Encyclopaedia of Dublin*, Dublin, Gill and Macmillan, 1991.
Bowers, M., *Dublin City Parks and Gardens*, Dublin, Lilliput Press, 1999.
Cowell, J., *Where they Lived in Dublin*, Dublin, O'Brien Press, 1980.
DeBreffny, B., *Ireland: A Cultural Encyclopaedia*, London, Thames and Hudson, 1983.
Deane, C., *Irish Facts and Feats*, Enfield, Middlesex, Guinness Publishing, 1994.
DeCourcy, J.W., *The Liffey in Dublin*, Dublin, Gill and Macmillan.1996.
Gilligan, H.A., *The History of the Port of Dublin*, Dublin, Gill and Macmillan, 1989.
Grimes, B., *Irish Carnegie Libraries*, Dublin, Irish Academic Press, 1998.
McCready, C.T., *Dublin Street Names*, Dublin, Carrig Books, 1994.
Mulligan, F., *One Hundred and Fifty Years of Irish Railways*, Belfast, Appletree Press, 1983.
O'Donnell, E.E., *The Annals of Dublin*, Dublin, Wolfhound Press, 1987.
Pearson, P., *Between the Mountains and the Sea*, Dublin, O'Brien Press, 1998.
Ó Riain. M., *On the Move, CIE 1945-95*, Dublin, Gill and Macmillan, 1995.
Quinn, P. (Editor), *The Power of an Idea, Temple Bar*, Dublin, Temple Bar Properties, 1996.
Share, B. (Editor), *Root and Branch*, Dublin, Allied Irish Banks, 1979.
Share, B., *The Flight of the Iolar, Dublin*, Gill and Macmillan, 1986.
St. John Joyce, W., *The Neighbourhood of Dublin*, Dublin, The Skellig Press, 1988
Summerville-Large, P., *Dublin, The Fair City*, London, Hamish Hamilton, 1979.
Sweeney, C., *The Rivers of Dublin, Dublin*, Dublin Corporation, 1991.
Williams, J., *Architecture in Ireland 1837-1921*, Dublin, Irish Academic Press, 1994.

Index

Page numbers in bold indicate illustrations.